MEDIA AND THE SEXUALIZATION OF CHILDHOOD

Media and the Sexualization of Childhood examines the ongoing debates surrounding the prominence of sexual themes in children's lives, from clothes and accessories, toys and games, to music, entertainment media, advertising, and new media platforms.

Parents, educators and politicians around the developed world have raised concerns about the effects that all these experiences can have on the socialization and psychological development of children, and the extent to which the premature introduction of sexuality into their lives can place them at risk of unwanted attention. This book explores these issues using an evidence-based approach that draws on research findings from around the world, representing the most comprehensive single account of the field.

The book will be invaluable to students studying topics surrounding children and the media and childhood studies, as well as students of communication, media, cultural studies, sociology, psychology and health science.

Barrie Gunter is Professor of Mass Communication, Department of Media and Communication, University of Leicester. His research interests are the psychological effects of the mass media, particularly in areas such as violent and sexual behaviour, health and consumerism. His most recent books include the co-authored *Alcohol Advertising and Young People's Drinking* and the forthcoming *Celebrity Capital: Assessing the Value of Fame.*

MEDIA AND THE SEXUALIZATION OF CHILDHOOD

Barrie Gunter

Routledge
Taylor & Francis Group

LONDON AND NEW YORK

First published 2014
by Routledge
2 Park Square, Milton Park, Abingdon, Oxon OX14 4RN

And published by Routledge
711 Third Avenue, New York, NY 10017

Routledge is an imprint of the Taylor & Francis Group, an informa business

British Library Cataloguing in Publication Data
A catalogue record for this book is available from the British Library

Library of Congress Cataloging in Publication Data
Gunter, Barrie.
Media and the sexualization of childhood / Barrie Gunter.
pages cm
Includes bibliographical references and index.
1. Mass media and children. 2. Sex in mass media. 3. Children and sex.
4. Children--Sexual behavior. 5. Mass media--Influence. I. Title.
HQ784.M3G86 2014
302.23083--dc 3
2013046158

ISBN: 978-1-138-01519-7 (hbk)
ISBN: 978-1-138-02544-8 (pbk)
ISBN: 978-1-315-77430-5 (ebk)

Typeset in Bembo
by Taylor & Francis Books

Printed and bound in the United States of America by
Edwards Brothers Malloy

CONTENTS

INTRODUCTION

This book examines the issue of the sexualization of childhood in relation to the role played by mediated experiences in children's lives. There has been growing concern in different parts of the world about the increased infiltration of sexual themes and attributes into a wide range of child experiences. This debate is multifaceted. It has been articulated within contexts such as consumerism and materialism; feminism and the status of women as citizens; crime and personal security; the status of the economy and the emergence of under classes and poverty ghettoes; and the impact of rapidly evolving communications technologies that have economic, political, social, cultural and psychological implications for the well-being of children.

The debate about 'sexualization' in childhood had adopted a stance that it represents a phenomenon that is characterized by a distortion of childhood socialization. Sex and sexuality are core aspects of human character and their manifestations take different forms in different settings and are linked throughout to gender. The psychological development of children is underpinned by their inherited biological make-up and their learning from their social experiences. Boys and girls learn how to behave in different settings, and expectations about behaviour can take on common forms for both genders as well as being gender specific.

Over time, a sexual aspect to their development becomes increasingly apparent as they approach adulthood. There is nothing abnormal about this process. The rate at which physical and social development takes place can vary from child to child, and this includes the age at which the onset of sexual characteristics emerges.[1] Sometimes, adult-like sexual attributes can begin to emerge long before a child reaches his or her teens. The concerns that have been raised about the 'sexualization of childhood' are grounded in a belief that environmental factors can conspire to introduce sexualized themes into a child's life too early. In effect, there is an intervention that might change the natural rate of sexual maturation for most children. Thus, children's attention is drawn unnecessarily to sexual themes, inviting them to adopt adult-like styles of appearance and behaviour before they have matured sufficiently in a physical and psychological sense to be able to cope with social pressures and risks that might follow on from this intervention.[2]

The notion of 'sexualization', which has been adopted with different meanings by various theorists, social commentators and political protagonists, has been extensively debated in the mainstream media in the UK and in a number of other countries, including the United States, Canada and Australia.[3] In these countries, a number of major reviews of academic and non-academic research evidence have been carried out and published. The debates and concerns for children's well-being in these countries have frequently conflated 'sexualization' with 'commercialization'. This conflation reflects the allegedly increased prevalence of commodities targeted at children.

Primarily, the debates and concerns linked to sexualization focus on the premature imposition of sexual themes in the lives of young children. Although it is widely acknowledged that sexual awareness develops as a natural process throughout childhood socialization, it becomes more acute as children enter puberty and reach physical and sexual maturity as a function of normal biological changes. Despite this fact, the concerns that attach specifically to the sexualization of childhood have centred on the very early introduction into a child's life of sexual references that convey social messages about their personal image and identity, norms of sexual behaviour, and other gender-related beliefs and attitudes. Such material has been held responsible for promoting distorted or deviant social learning about self-image, interpersonal relations, and the manifestation of sexuality in everyday life.[4]

There have been accusations that when marketers tune in children's minds to consumerism from a very early age by introducing them to brands, there are often sexual themes running through the branding campaigns and the commodities themselves. Such themes can be found in children's fashions (clothes and accessories), toys and games, and in other areas of entertainment. The impression often given is that children are surrounded by a social and cultural environment permeated with 'sexual' messages. They are introduced to such themes even before they start school and are then bombarded with them subsequently. These experiences, which are embedded within a wide range of socialization experiences, embrace consumerism, interpersonal relations, and the ways in which children then present themselves to the world and perhaps also in the ways they formulate self-identities. There is even a view that children are encouraged to see themselves as 'brands' and their commoditized personalities are shaped by an early sexual awareness.[5]

The presence of 'sex' in commercialism and consumerism is nothing new and can be traced back over many years in relation to adult targeted brand marketing. The first ever recorded use of sexual imagery in advertising was the use of a naked 'maiden' on the pack cover of Pearl Tobacco in 1871. Within the next 20 years, other tobacco companies followed suit in using sexual images of young women on pack covers, trading cards and other promotions.[6] It is the link between sexuality in marketing and children and childhood that raises concern because of the risk that they represent inappropriate messages that if widely disseminated could potentially normalize ideas about sexual activity in childhood.

The acute sensitivity to the use of child actors to promote commodities that may be child appropriate but through campaigns that are not was brought into sharp focus when Calvin Klein used 15-year-old Brooke Shields to advertise their jeans in a sexually provocative way. In a print version of this famous advertisement, Shields is depicted lying down wearing tight jeans and a T-shirt saying, 'Want to know what gets between me and my Calvins? Nothing.'[7]

Likewise, children, and most especially girls, have long been shown wearing more adult-like clothes and cosmetics as they approach, but have not yet reached, the stage at which they mature physically into women. While the notion of 'sexualization' as a process that occurs during childhood has been characterized as a form of deviancy, it might be conceived as part of a broader suite of socialization dynamics that have historically featured in the lives of children as they enter adulthood.[8] Trying on adult styles has been a part of growing up. Concern arises where 'trying out' being a grown-up is encouraged or occurs at a very early age, long before natural maturation processes have reached a point at which such curiosity might be expected to occur.

Sexual themes also characterize adult-oriented entertainment appearing originally in literature before being embraced by more modern media, including magazines, newspapers, music, cinema, radio, television and, most recently, the online world of the internet. The widely debated concerns about the use of sex to sell or the sale of sex itself have been accompanied by claims that it has become more prevalent throughout mainstream media and consumerism, that its presence and use are all too often gratuitous, and that with the relaxation of boundaries of taste in relation to regular media and the growth of online media that have opened up access for children to previously restricted access content, children of all ages have greater exposure to sexual material.[9]

According to critics, including some prominent political figures, this phenomenon has drawn undue attention of young children to sexual issues before they are physically mature or psychologically ready.[10] Furthermore, certain types of sexual portrayal have become not only more visible and explicit, but might create a new distorted set of norms about the place of sex in people's lives that cultivate social perceptions, beliefs and even values that result in anti-social behaviour that place at risk the well-being of children.[11]

As already noted, there have been a number of national inquiries into this subject over the past ten years, most notably in the United States, the UK and Australia. They have been sponsored by governments and have drawn the attention of policy-makers and the public to the increasingly premature exposure of children to sexual themes before they have reached a stage of sexual maturity. There is a growing volume of research in the social sciences that has documented the nature and prevalence of sexualization in different domains of children's experience and that has also begun to explore the short-term or lasting psychological effects it can have on them.

There are additional concerns not just about the impact of widespread sexual material in the media on the dispositions of individual media consumers, but also on the rights and status of women compared with men in society. Liberal feminist activists have lobbied for women to receive the same political and economic rights as men. Socialist feminists have joined this debate and located the source in inequality in capitalism which has allegedly oppressed women in economic terms. Radical feminists have extended the debate to gender inequalities driven by male patriarchy, arguing that men have acquired and sought to retain socially, politically and economically advantageous positions *vis à vis* women. These historical precedents lay at the root of not only economic inequalities where women are often paid less than men for doing the same job, but also more overt forms of power display such as sexual oppression of women, justification for sexual violence and child sexual exploitation.[12]

Concerns about 'sexualization' where this idea includes the use of sexual themes to define children's commodities, the appearance of sexual themes in brand promotions, the reporting of the sexual lives of famous people, the depiction of simulated sex in various kinds of popular entertainment for children and adults, and the increasing availability of real sex (including illegal sexual practices) on the internet can be found in other parts of the world. Concerns about the exposure of children to sexualized material do not just centre on the use of sex to sell commodities, but also in relation to the presentation of 'sex' as a commodity. The latter concerns have centred on children's access to pornography through digital communications technologies that young people have enthusiastically adopted. Studies from around the world have assessed the extent to which children are or might be exposed to pornographic material online.

There are two further important dimensions to debates about this topic that cannot be ignored. The first of these is that discussions of sexualization have given far more attention to the experiences of girls than of boys. Yet, socialization linked to sexual development is an equally important feature of the lives of both. Boys can be the subjects as well as targets of sexualized messages, as well as girls. For each gender, there are outcomes that can be manifest in terms of distorted self-images and 'other' images.[13]

Another linked dimension is the focus on the 'victims' of sexualization. Children are often regarded as helpless victims here and this has led to debates about the protection of children from perpetrators or pedlars of sex – from the adult world – who seek either to benefit themselves in some selfishly and often illegally gratifying way in relation to warped urges or who use sex to sell commodities for personal financial benefit. Yet, there is also a concern about the socially conditioning effects of normalizing 'sex' in children's lives in the way they perceive themselves and members of the opposite sex and in the nature of interpersonal relations and eventual sexual relations that emerge as they reach puberty. The latest mobile digital media are frequently invoked in public debates about the way in which teenagers become sexually active and the treatment of girls by boys and also the use of digital media (and especially social media) to communicate private and intimate details about sex and real sexual relations in the public arena. Despite the powerfully made arguments of government-sponsored inquiries into the sexualization of childhood, critics have challenged the idea that children are invariably innocents at risk.[14]

Structurally, the book begins by examining the general positions that have been adopted by governments, professional bodies and lobby groups as articulated mainly through government inquiries and consultations and other privately backed reviews of research. At the outset it visits historical debates and evidence about the presence of sex and sexual themes in children's lives. This represents an important context for the examination of current and recent discussions and debates about the way in which children are exposed to sexual themes by adults and then adopt these themes in terms of self-identity formation, relations with others and, more broadly, in the ways they perceive the world around them.

Gender differences in these experiences and children's responses will be reviewed at the outset and then revisited in subsequent chapters in relation to the different areas of experience with sexual content and sexual themes that enter children's lives. Thus, the concept of childhood will be defined along with varying definitions of 'sexualization' that have driven contemporary social, cultural and political concerns about the well-being of children. This will serve the important purpose of defining the topic that this book will examine.

Having set out the principal concerns that have surfaced, the book will then take a systematic look at evidence from a number of experiential domains. These will include child fashions, products aimed at children, magazines, music, film and television, advertising, pornography and interactive digital media. International evidence is reviewed from each of these areas concerning the use of sexual themes and the extent to which children are exposed to them and might be influenced by this exposure. As already indicated, a great deal of the most popularly cited research evidence has derived from Western developed countries and most especially from the United States, the UK, and from Australia and Canada.[15]

There has been further research about exposure to sexually themed content across Europe and other work on the presence of sexual themes in advertising and specific mass media outputs (usually television drama programmes) in other parts of the world, most notably in the Far East (mainly from China, Hong Kong, India, Japan and Singapore) and a small amount from Africa and the Middle East.[16] It is not my aim to provide a detailed analysis of cross-cultural values differences linked to sexual attitudes and behaviour, gender relations and equality, or media regulations. All of these factors could have a place in debates about the sexualization of childhood. Some reference to comparable or comparative research in relation to the representation of sexual themes in specific media or commodity promotion practices will be made where this serves to enhance debates about impact and control.

The book concludes that although the risk associated with some sexualization experiences has been exaggerated, there are some areas of childhood experience where introducing sex into their lives at an early stage of development may not be a good idea. Most seriously, there are legitimate reasons to be concerned about the use of the internet and mobile phones by children, both to access explicit sexual material and to send and receive sexualized images of themselves.

Chapter 1 begins by examining the issues around childhood sexualization that have been widely debated in different parts of the world and that have focused, in particular, on the role of mediated experiences. One aim of this review is to examine definitions of sexualization and to clarify the nature of the phenomenon that this book will examine. By mediated experiences here is meant the experiences of children in relation to commodities and related activities targeted at them (e.g. brand marketing) and their use of media such as magazines, music, television and digital media. There are a number of texts that have discussed the place of sex in children's lives that provide a range of theoretical perspectives and different levels of practical advice. Some of these texts have also discussed the history of the subject, which is helpful in positioning current debates and social concerns about the premature introduction of sex into children's lives or inappropriate representation of sex in mediated outputs.

Much of the empirical evidence that has informed this debate has been crystallized in a number of inquiries sponsored by national governments and professional bodies. Their reports have identified a growing social problem that stems, in part, from the increased prevalence and accessibility of explicit sexual materials targeted at adults, the infiltration of sexual themes into fashions, products and entertainment aimed at children, and the use by young people of new technologies to exchange sexual images of themselves and their friends. There are associated worries about early sexual activity among children resulting in increased prevalence of unwanted pregnancies and sexually transmitted diseases, as well as attitudes towards sex that denigrate women.

This chapter sets the scene in terms of where the concerns can be found. The remainder of the book then examines sexualization themes in a number of areas of childhood experience. These reports have been important in informing government policy positions in relation to marketing and media regulation. However, they have been dominated by specific research perspectives that have adopted largely quantitative research methodologies. It is important also to include the voices of children (and their parents) through the use of qualitative research and this work will be cited in this scene-setting chapter.

One of the earliest experiences of sexualized themes in childhood involves clothing choices. Chapter 2 will examine historical reviews of sex and children in relation to commodities targeted at children and then move on to examine contemporary representations of sexualized themes that have attracted closer scrutiny in relation to recent public debates. Concerns here have centred on fashions for very young children that emphasize outer appearance and frequently draw attention to sexual attributes that they do not yet possess. This pattern of sexualized experience is further exacerbated by the growth in popularity of beauty pageants for children as young as two. In these events, children are dressed up by their mothers and paraded in front of live audiences and panels of judges who evaluate them in terms of their attractiveness. Although a lot of focus is placed on girls in relation to these events, boys can and do also compete.

This chapter examines how prevalent sexualization of children's clothing fashions has become and whether there is evidence that exposure to such items can produce unwanted psychological side-effects. One concern is that such fashions can lead to an unhealthy preoccupation with appearance and body shape both among girls and boys, and this, in turn, can lead to unfavourable self-perceptions and behaviour patterns designed to engineer a specific body shape. As well as reviewing empirical research that attempts to examine the impact of sexual themes upon children, this chapter will allow children and parents to speak for themselves on this issue by reviewing relevant anecdotes from media reports and covering relevant qualitative inquiries that engaged both in open discussions.

Chapter 3 will turn to other merchandise designed for children that is characterized by sexual themes. As well as clothes, there are many other products targeted at children where sexual themes have been found. These include dolls aimed at girls that come with accessories and mature body shapes that children can dress up to look sexy. There are other products for children with brands associated with adult sexual themes, such as *Playboy*.

There are also games that have sexual themes. Playing with these products can draw children's attention to sex and again emphasize its centrality to human experience and, more significantly, to the way in which people can be judged. Electronic games with sexual themes can play a part in shaping narrowly defined attitudes about girls and women among boys in which females are objectified in a sexual way. There has been a growing literature about children and electronic games; but this is examined within this chapter rather than elsewhere because it forms part of children's play experiences that evolve alongside the use of other play-related products. While an argument might be made for treating electronic games as a separate category for review, there is also an equally strong argument for conceiving of it as an extension of play and its role in children's development.

Much of the work with computer games has focused on the theme of violence and aggression with theory generalized from the mass media violence effects literature. However, the latter theories have attempted to explain the effects of mediated experiences over which consumers have little direct control. With computer games – with which players interact, control on-screen events and engage with other players – this could be conceived as a direct rather than a strictly mediated experience and also as an experience with an interpersonal dimension. Mass communication theory may not always be the appropriate foundation on which to establish the effects of the electronic games experience.

As Chapter 4 will aim to show, sexual themes have been found to permeate magazines that are read by children. These include publications that are targeted at younger readers as well as those targeted at adult markets but which have also established a market presence among children. Magazines contain sexualized images, especially of women, and feature content that deals with sexualized themes.

Magazines targeted at teenage and pre-teenage girls often publish articles on themes that have a sexual nature, such as looking good to attract boys and how to keep your boyfriend keen or happy. These publications also have features that cover the lives of famous performers and even when aimed at pre-teen girls, often draw attention to their physical attributes in a sexualized way. Sports magazines have been found to treat female and male athletes differently and sexualized evaluations are much more likely to occur in relation to female sports performers.

Magazines aimed at young men feature numerous sexually objectified images of nubile and voluptuous young women in various stages of undress. A frequent impression flowing from this content is that these young women are sexually available and that they are typical of other women of their age. Empirical evidence has emerged that this type of content can shape young men's attitudes towards young women in an unflattering way.

There are important issues of gender socialization and orientation to be considered in this context. Magazines are aimed at male and female markets and can present varying representations of sexual themes in each case. This distinction will be examined in this chapter to establish whether the potential effects of exposure to sexual themes via magazines are different and operate through different social and psychological mechanisms for each gender.

Television remains the most ubiquitous medium and children turn to it as a major source of entertainment. Chapter 5 discusses research evidence accumulated from different parts of the world that television programmes and movies frequently display women in highly stereotyped ways and that the sexual objectification of women today occurs more often than it used to.

Exposure to this content has been found to shape infants', pre-teenagers' (or 'tweens') and teenagers' self-perceptions in terms of their own sexual attractiveness, the perceptions that boys hold about girls, and that girls hold about boys and themselves, and has been linked to early onset of sexual behaviour amongst teenagers.

Television can provide a valuable source of information about sex for teenagers, but it can also cultivate socially unhealthy attitudes about sex and sexual relations. In addition to a gender dimension, there is also an age-related developmental dimension that needs to be examined in this area. This chapter will draw upon qualitative and quantitative research, but the evidence both perspectives have provided will need to be interpreted in terms of what is known about the limits to their understanding of media outputs and the social circumstances of children as they pass through different stages of cognitive development.

Chapter 6 will turn attention to sexual themes in popular music. A great deal of popular music consumed by children is characterized by sexual relationship themes. The growth of music videos has meant that these themes have become increasingly visualized. There is growing concern about the sexual objectification of women featured in music videos as well as in the lyrics of many songs. Exposure to this material has been linked to the emergence of lowered self-regard among some girls and to sexist attitudes and beliefs amongst boys. This evidence is reviewed here.

In this chapter, the evidence that will be examined derives from studies of representations of sexual themes in music – both orally and visually – and the reactions of girls and boys to music outputs. This analysis will take into account the position of music in the lives of young people in developed countries, where most sexualization and music concerns have emanated. It will consider what we know from young people themselves when they talk openly about their experiences with music and also from studies that have established more contrived designs in which exposure and reactions to music are measured through fixed metrics designed to facilitate statistical tests of causal or correlational connections.

Chapter 7 examines what is known about the nature and effects of sexual content in advertising. Advertising is everywhere and children are exposed to it on a daily basis. Sexual themes are widely used in the belief that 'sex sells'. There is considerable research evidence that sex is a prevalent aspect of advertising and also that women have frequently been depicted in highly sexist ways within these themes. Research with young consumers has found that exposure to sexist themes and sexual content in advertising can influence attitudes towards girls and women. Women can be seen more as sex objects by boys and young men who have experienced a regular diet of sexualized advertising.

As with other areas of mediated experience, the reactions of children to advertisements can evolve over time as they grow older and their levels of cognitive and social maturity change. These developmental factors cut across genders. In addition, studies of sexual themes in advertising have identified a number of distinct potential social and cultural messages that can be conveyed to each gender. There is a wealth of quantitative research concerned with analyses of causal links between exposure to sexual material in advertising and sexual attitudes, beliefs and behaviours. There is also much interesting qualitative research that provides a different range of insights into the way in which young people engage with advertising and respond to it. Both types of evidence will be reviewed in this chapter.

There has been growing concern about the distribution of sexually explicit material. This is material that makes no pretence to be anything other than sexual in nature and often contains graphic depictions of sexual behaviour. Chapter 8 examines the concerns about pornography and children. The internet has emerged as a prominent factor in this phenomenon and its widespread adoption by children has put them at increased risk of exposure. There is ample evidence that teenage and pre-teenage children have seen pornography online. They can display differing reactions to it.

Some youngsters are offended and upset by such material, while others are intrigued by it and a few might even develop an appetite for it. There is also considerable evidence that women and men, and girls and boys can be influenced by explicit depictions of sex. Attitudes about female sexuality can be distorted by this material and it has even been identified as playing a role in triggering sexually deviant behaviour. This evidence is reviewed here and the risk that pornography poses for children is discussed.

This chapter will review evidence concerning how both genders have described their experiences with pornography, and how each has responded to this material. Evidence about exposure patterns will be reviewed alongside historical changes in the amount and nature of such material and where it can now be accessed.

Chapter 9 turns to the latest developments to affect children's involvement with sexualized material. The widespread use of the internet by young people in relation to many different aspects of their lives has rendered them targets of purveyors of sexualized content. One particularly worrying phenomenon is the emergent use of new communications technologies to create and distribute self-made sexual images. These can be posted onto personal websites, blogs or social media networks and circulated through mobile phones. This behaviour can also adopt a threatening tone when disgruntled boyfriends circulate sexually explicit images of their girlfriends online. This often happens after relationships have broken down.

Girls can proactively post up such images of themselves and in doing so can put themselves at risk of unwanted approaches from sexual predators. Another growing trend is in cybersex, in which participants engage in sexualized message exchanges with strangers online. All of these developments pose important questions about premature exposure to sexual content and about the effects of such content not only on the attitudes and beliefs of recipients, but also on the extent to which young people now place themselves at risk as a result of conformity with social pressures to display sexual maturity.

There are more pressures being placed on infrastructure providers and search engines to play an active part in the control of problematic content and behaviour in the digital communications world. Governments have spoken about introducing legislation to place tighter restrictions on children's activities in this environment, especially in relation to the reception and trafficking of sexual content. These political debates will be set alongside the empirical evidence concerning what we known about children's behaviours in the digital world and how they respond to sexualized content that they find there.

Notes

1 Steingraber, S. (2009) 'Girls gone grown-up: Why are U.S girls reaching puberty earlier and earlier?,' in S. Olfman (Ed.) *The Sexualization of Childhood*. Westport, CT: Praeger.
2 Olfman, S. (2009) 'The sexualization of childhood: Growing older younger/growing younger older', in S. Olfman (Ed.) *The Sexualization of Childhood*. Westport, CT: Praeger.
3 American Psychological Association (2007) *Report of the APA Task Force on the Sexualization of Girls*. Washington, DC: American Psychological Association; Australian Senate (2007) *Inquiry into the Sexualization of Children in the Contemporary Media Environment*, http://www.aph.gov.au/Senate/committee/eca_ctte/sexualisaiton_of_children, accessed 14 November 2012; Commonwealth Parliament, Senate Standing Committee on Environment, Communication and the Arts (2008) *Inquiry into Sexualization of Children in the Contemporary Media*, 1.25; Papadopoulos, L. (2010) *Sexualization of Young People*. London, UK: Home Office; Phoenix, A. (2011, January) *Review of Recent Literature for Bailey Review of Commercialisation and Sexualization of Childhood*. London, UK: Childhood Wellbeing Research Centre for the Department of Education.
4 White, H. (2012) 'Child sexualization "imposes" adult sexuality on young children: MEP at E meeting', 11 June, www.lifesitenews.com/child-sexualization-imposes-adult-sexuality-on-young-children; Belgutay, J. (2011) 'War against the sexualization of childhood', *Times Education Supplement*, 5 August, www.tes.co.uk/article.aspx?storycode=6107531, accessed 7 August 2013.
5 Levin, D. and Kilbourne, J. (2008) *So Sexy So Soon: The New Sexualized Childhood and What Parents Can Do to Protect Their Kids*. New York, NY: Ballantine; Durham, M. G. (2008) *The Lolita Effect: The Media Sexualization of Young Girls and What You Can Do About It*. New York, NY: Overlook; Lamb, S. and Brown, L. M. (2006) *Packaging*

Girlhood: Rescuing Our Daughters from Marketers' Schemes. New York, NY: St Martin's Press.

6 Beigelman, V. (2012) 'Column: Why sex sells', *The California Aggie*, 9 February, www.theaggie.org/2012/02/09/cokun-why-sex-sells, accessed 6 August 2013.

7 Sischy, I. (2008) 'Calvin to the core', *Vanity Fair*, April, www.vanityfair.com/culture/features/2008/04/calvin200804?CurrentPage=7, accessed 7 August 2013.

8 Egan, R. D. (2013) *Becoming Sexual: A Critical Appraisal of the Sexualization of Girls*. Cambridge, UK: Polity.

9 Palmer, S. (2006) *Toxic Childhood: How the Modern World is Damaging Our Children and What We Can Do about It*. London, UK: Orion; Palmer, S. (2007) *Detoxing Childhood: What Parents Need to Know to Raise Happy, Successful Children*. London, UK: Orion.

10 BBC News (2010) 'Sexualized products for children facing age curb plan', 6 December, www.bbc.co.uk/news/uk-11923107; Curtis, P. (2011) 'David Cameron backs proposals tackling sexualization of children', 6 June, *The Guardian*, www.guardian.co.uk/society/2011/jun/06/david-cameron-children-sexualization-commercialisation, accessed 25 June 2013.

11 Attwood, F. (2009) *Mainstreaming Sex: The Sexualization of Western Culture*. London, UK: I. B. Tauris; Attwood, F. (2010) *porn.com: Making Sense of Online Pornography*. New York, NY: Peter Lang Publishing.

12 Atmore, C. (1996) 'Cross-cultural mediations: Media coverage of two child sexual abuse controversies in New Zealand/Aotearoa', *Child Abuse Review*, 5, 334–345; Bray, A. (2008) 'The question of intolerance', *Australian Feminist Studies*, 23(57), 323–341; Duschinsky, R. (2010) 'Feminism, sexualization and social status', *Media International Australia*, www.academia-edu/1489600/Feminism_Sexualization_and_Social_Status, accessed 6 August 2013.

13 Levy, A. (2005) *Female Chauvinist Pigs: Women and the Rise of Raunch Culture*. New York: NY: Free Press; Durham, M. G. (2008) *op. cit*; Palmer, S. (2010) *21st Century Boys: How Modern Life Is Driving Them off the Rails and How We Can Get Them Back on Track*. London, UK: Orion.

14 Ringrose, J. and Renold, E. (2012) 'Slut-shaming, girl power and "sexualisation": Thinking through the politics,' *Gender and Education*, 24(3), 333–343; Clark, J. (2013) 'Passive, heterosexual and female: Constructing appropriate childhoods in the "Sexualization of Childhood" debate', *Sociological Research Online*, 18(2), 13, www.socresonline.org.uk/18/2/13, accessed 29 October 2013.

15 American Psychological Association (2007), *op. cit*. Commonwealth Parliament, Senate Standing Committee on Environment, Communication and the Arts (2008), *op. cit*. Papadopoulos, L. (2010) *op. cit*. Jaffer, M. S. B. and Brazeau, P. (2011) *The Sexual Exploitation of Children in Canada: The Need for National Action*. Standing Senate Committee on Human Rights, November, www.parl.gc.ca/Content/SEN/Committee/411/ridr/rep/rep03nov11-e; Commissioner for Children and Young People Western Australia (2012, March). *Sexualisation of Children*. Issues Paper 9. Available at www.ccyp.wa.gov.au.

16 American Psychological Association (2007) *op. cit*.

1

IS CHILDHOOD BEING SEXUALIZED?

Concern about the premature introduction of children to sexual themes has attracted increasingly vociferous debate since the turn of the millennium. There is wide acceptance by governments and childhood activist, charity and lobbying groups in different parts of the world that consumer culture has become sexualized and that this phenomenon has infiltrated not just commodities and associated marketing targeted at adults, but also that aimed at children.[1] This phenomenon is, it has been argued, manifest in film and television entertainment, music videos, advertising, and commodities including accessories, clothing, cosmetics and toys. Wrapped up with sexualized content are messages that seek conformity to centralized standards of physical attractiveness and beauty that often create unrealistic or unattainable targets for young people.

There has been extensive public debate about the sexualization of childhood in many countries. This debate has been informed by diverse forms of research into the nature of sexualization in the media, marketing, fashion and commodities targeted at children. Public debate has been further fuelled by high-profile media coverage of sexualization issues that has focused increasingly on the role being played by the digital media that have become so widespread and popular among children. Criticisms have centred on the sexual content in magazines targeted at pre-teenage and teenage children, in music videos, films and television programmes to which children can gain access, and in electronic games that many children play offline and online, and on styles of clothing aimed at children, and especially at teenage and pre-teenage girls, that attempt to make them look sexually mature when they are not.[2]

More interactive communications systems such as online social media sites and mobile telephones have attracted much attention because of their use to convey sexual messages and images by children themselves. Sexual themes in media, marketing and children's commodities and sexual interactions via digital communications media have been identified as placing children at risk of sexual abuse or creating a generation of young people with warped values and for whom sex has a casual social currency.[3] There have been specific concerns about the effects mixed messages put out by sexualized material have on the self-images of girls as they are growing up. Clothing fashions and cosmetics products targeted at girls, even before they are sexually mature, encourage them to 'look sexy', while making themselves look sexy runs the risk of criticism for being promiscuous. Exposure to explicit sexual content in online pornography reinforces the view that women (and therefore girls) enjoy wild sex, even when it is mixed with violence, which leaves both boys and girls uncertain how to proceed as they become sexually active in their teens.[4]

These mediated public debates seldom provide a clear definition of 'sexualization' but often presume that we all intuitively know what it means. There is a further presumption that children are passive receptacles of messages about sex in different media and that exposure results in psychological changes that are manifest in the way in which children perceive themselves, how they interact socially and sexually with others, and the beliefs, attitudes and values they hold about sexual matters. 'Sexualization' formed part of the lexicon of early 20th-century psychoanalysis and was used to describe the feelings someone felt about an object of erotic desire. During the second half of that century, this sexual desire was not only seen as a source of pleasure but also as a force for the relief of anxiety.[5] Sexualization also became conceived as an aspect of socialization that was linked to the adoption of cultural gender norms. There was also a sense in this context that sexualization could lead to behaviours that were not deemed normal in terms of usual cultural and social expectations. In part, this perspective on sexualization identified the parameters that should ensure that relations between parents and their children, while loving, should not adopt an erotic or sexual tone.[6]

There is also frequently an implicit proposition that 'sexualization' is not only a bad thing but a new contemporary issue about which something must be done. There was growing attention given in the late 20th century to the idea that contemporary culture had become increasingly 'sexualized' and that this trend had, in particular, characterized the way in which women and girls were treated by the media and by consumer commodity markets. This emergent cultural phenomenon was acutely manifest in the distribution of toy cosmetics products for pre-teenage girls, which invited them to engage in grown-up behaviours and to adopt a more adult-like appearance that in the case of adult women generally signals greater sexual attractiveness. In this setting, therefore, 'sexualization' was labelled as a social problem.[7]

The proposition about a need for action, however, presumes that there is a healthy ideal that can be achieved in terms of being sexually aware and active and also in terms of the way in which sexual matters are covered by the media or used in relation to commodities aimed at non-adult (e.g. under-18s) markets. There has also been a political dimension to debates about sexualization. For some feminists, for example, the sexualization of young girls was regarded as a plot by male-dominated politics and industry to undermine the progress that had been made in gender equality and which had resulted in women becoming more independent, powerful and successful in their own right. The focus on the need to be sexually attractive to be socially successful was a distraction designed to challenge the newfound self-confidence of women.[8]

In fact, this type of debate conveniently ignores the diverse nature of sex in terms of the ways in which it is socially and culturally defined, the moral standards that construct parameters around its occurrence in different settings, and the way it emerges during children's psychological and social development. This type of debate also fails to acknowledge that concerns about sex and children date back over many generations and predate not only the digital media but also the earlier analogue mass media.[9]

Observations were made about the use of sexualized images of children and adolescents in paintings and book illustrations in the 19th century.[10] It was during this period that the age of sexual consent was only 12 and pre-teenage prostitutes were prevalent.[11] During the first half of the 20th century, arguments were made for closer attention by society to the protection of childhood, which came to be regarded as a stage of innocence. A conception of vulnerability emerged whereby society could source many potentially corrupting influences that could prey on children that resembled the contemporary accusations of 'sexualization risks' linked to media, marketing and children's commodities in the 21st century.[12]

Sexualization is part of a wider suite of social concerns linked to the general psychological development of human beings, normative standards of appearance and body form, and more specifically the emergence of sexual identity. Sexuality is an integral part of human nature. Sexual relations are critical to the survival of the species. The definition of our personal identity is closely linked to our gender or our 'sex' and this, in turn, underpins how each of us relates socially to others. Social relations are influenced by the social judgements we make about ourselves and others with whom we interact. These social judgements can be shaped by both our own physical and psychological characteristics and those of others. Hence, physical appearance and personality are critical factors that underpin 'self-identity' and 'other' identity.[13]

In this wider span of social identity development, appearance and body shape play a key part in determining how we evaluate each other. The degree to which our appearance conforms to contemporary cultural standards of attractiveness or beauty can affect our popularity and success in life. Attractiveness in this context often means 'sexual attractiveness'. Sexual attraction drives the development of close and intimate interpersonal relationships that form the foundation of partnerships, family life, and more extended social communities. We tend to develop social bonds more often than not with others in whom we perceive attractive qualities. These may not always be 'sexual' qualities; but at some point sexual attraction must be present as the glue that binds together social relationships.[14]

Our ideas about sex can therefore vary depending upon the ways in which we have been introduced to it, the ideas about sex that circulate within our families and among our peer groups, and sexual representations that we experience else-where, including the media, marketing and commodities with which we engage. It might be premature to presume that we internalize all of these impressions about sex as they were initially experienced and without any further process of internal negotiation in terms of the meanings or values we might attach to them.[15]

We use appearance to make all kinds of judgements about other people. Their body shape, hair style, facial attributes, skin tone and posture can all reveal something about the type of person we believe them to be. In addition, the clothes they wear and accessories they carry around with them can provide further insights into their personality, social status, and the kind of lifestyle they enjoy.

With the growth of consumerism in modern societies, branding has emerged as an increasingly important barometer signifying social status and taste and, in turn, attractiveness. The growth, too, of the mass media has created a global apparatus for the promotion of brands to mass consumer markets. The importance of associating brands with cultural and social values that have currency in specific markets is also well recognized by marketers.

Among the cultural standards that marketers seek to connect to their brands are norms concerning physical and, more specifically, sexual attractiveness. We are often told that 'sex sells'. This means that if consumers believe that their use of a specific brand will enhance their personal attractiveness, that brand will accrue social capital and become more desirable.

It is against this background that advertisers utilize sexualized imagery and messages to promote brands. For some industries, such as fashion, the idea of attractiveness enhancement is an integral quality of the products they distribute. For other product ranges, such as motor vehicles that may be less immediately connected to a person's physical appearance, sex might still be used to sell the product by creating a brand social status that is believed to enhance personal and sexual attractiveness of anyone who uses that brand.[16]

The use of sex to sell becomes a problem when it is targeted at inappropriate markets. Full sexual development is associated with reaching adulthood. The use of sexuality messages to promote products that are targeted at young consumers who have not yet reached a stage in their development when sexual drives have emerged runs the risk of exposing them to messages about personal identity and the nature of social interactions that they are not ready to assimilate. Some feminist theorists have argued in this context that the use of sexualized images of young girls in commercial promotions represents a form of corporate exploitation of children that cannot be separated from outcomes such as child abuse because they function to create an impression of social norms through which young childhood sexuality is regarded as acceptable.[17]

Such early and repeated exposure to sexualized messages is also believed to cause children to grow up too quickly and potentially to place them at risk if they become preoccupied with their own sexuality before they reach physical maturity.[18]

Critics have claimed that it can cause children to become sexually active before they are ready, focus their attention on the significance of looking sexually attractive, putting them at risk of unwanted attention from paedophiles, and distort their self-images in a way that can result in low self-confidence.[19] Most of the blame for these social effects has been attached to the advertising, broadcasting, magazine and music publishing and fashion industries.[20] In effect, media and marketing practitioners have created an overly sexualized child and youth culture that treats sex as a casual commodity rather than as an integral part of loving and committed romantic relationships.[21]

Two different pathways to premature sexualization can be broadly identified. The first pathway represents a form of direct sexual socialization that occurs when children are dressed or made up in ways that draw attention to sexual attributes they have not yet developed. The second pathway takes the form of less direct sexual socialization that follows from children's experiences of specific products, such as toys that have sexual features, or from their exposure to marketing campaigns and media outputs that have sexual themes. It has also been observed that sexualization as a socialization process entails defining self and others primarily in terms of their sexual appeal and places centre-stage the physical attractiveness of people as the primary attribute by which they are judged.[22]

Critics of early sexualization of children have been challenged for holding old-fashioned attitudes; but there are genuine reasons for concern because of evidence that drawing the attention of children to sexual features too soon can place them at risk in terms of their psychological well-being and personal security. Beauty pageants for the under-fives on the surface may seem like harmless fun, but might also instil in infants internalized social pressures always to focus on how they look that can create unwanted and chronic anxiety conditions, especially if they feel they fail to live up to the expectations of their parents or of society in general in terms of their personal attractiveness.[23] Alternatively, dressing up young girls to make them look sexy may place them at risk of unwanted and inappropriate sexual attention from older boys or men with a predisposition to engage in sexual activity with under-age females.

Although these concerns are serious and deserve close attention, it is important to ensure that the prevalence and availability of offending commodities and associated marketing messages is not overstated. Evidence emerged from within the UK that indicated that the number of sexualized goods aimed at children was small.[24] Further, not all the evidence has shown that exposure to such goods necessarily has harmful effects on young consumers.[25]

Much of the debate about the sexual socialization of consumerism has centred on concerns about the impact of 'sexualized goods' on young girls' self-perceptions and effects on their mental and physical well-being. Linked to this focus on young females are additional questions about the impact of these products upon young boys' perceptions of girls and, ultimately, upon their behaviour towards the opposite sex. Hence, what at first seems a narrow area of concern is actually linked to wider debates about body image, gender stereotyping, and general health and well-being, as well as with the sexual socialization of young people.[26]

One of the major issues of concern has been the tendency to sexually objectify women. As we will see, research has shown, for instance, that women photographed in sexually provocative poses are seen as objects rather than as people. This empirical evidence has been backed up by the experiences of well-known female celebrities. The actress Jessica Alba once complained that she was treated in a sexualized way early in her career and believed that her physical appearance played a bigger part than her acting abilities.[27]

Although the sexual objectification of women in the media has been regarded as encouraging men to see women as sex objects, evidence has also emerged that women perceive their own gender in a similar way. Interestingly, the same effect does not occur with sexy-looking men, with both sexes seeing them as people rather than as objects.[28] Research led by Belgian academic Philippe Bernard presented participants with photographs of men or women in underwear shown either the right way up or upside down. Immediately after this initial presentation, participants were shown a pair of pictures, one of which depicted the same person as they were shown earlier. They had to correctly identify which of the two they had seen before.

Previous research had shown that with physical objects, people are readily able to recognize the complete object when previously they had only seen part of it. The same result did not so readily recur with facial recognition. In other words, object recognition involves a different way of processing shape information than person recognition.

The participants recognized the right-side up men better than upside-down men. This indicated that in the upside-down mode, men were seen as less human and therefore not so easily recognizable. With pictures of women, however, this difference did not occur and participants performed equally well in the recognition task regardless of whether the target women had originally been shown right side up or upside down. The researchers argued here that it was as easy to recognize women in underwear irrespective of which way up they had initially been shown and that this tendency was consistent with the idea that sexy women are seen more as objects than as people. What we need to know now is whether this experience of women in mediated settings transfers to how they are treated in everyday life.

While often regarded as placing women at a disadvantage socially and professionally, female sexual attractiveness has also been used as part of women's armoury to gain social and political advantage. In some cultures, young women have proactively used their sexuality in an aggressive way to promote women's rights. India has witnessed the rise of so-called 'aggrimbos'. These pro-feminist TV and film starlets have exposed their flesh to demonstrate that a woman should not be embarrassed about showing off her physical body.[29]

Extensive academic research on gender stereotyping and body image has placed the spotlight on the role of the mass media in this aspect of socialization.[30] There has been much interest in the impact of the media upon the development of distorted gender-linked perceptions and body self-image on young people's behaviour patterns. Gender stereotypes can act to limit the aspirations of young people (especially girls) and can shape the way in which they behave interpersonally. Body image distortions can underpin unhealthy eating patterns and obsessions with dieting among girls. Meanwhile, overemphasis on the female body form can result in girls and women becoming objectified, and this, in turn, can influence the beliefs and attitudes formed about them by boys and men that may eventually shape the way in which the former are treated by the latter. This work will be revisited in later sections of this book in connection with different media and marketing experiences of young people.

A related sphere of research has been the study of media representations of sexual behaviour. Overt depictions of sexual behaviour have been found to influence male attitudes and beliefs towards women in the context of sexual relationships and may also shape preferences for specific types of sexual relationship or encounter. As with research into gender stereotyping, an extensive body of research has accumulated that has focused on the effects of media depictions of sexual conduct, including the influences of sexual imagery in magazines, in films, on television and on the internet.[31] One significant part of the research on media representations of sex and sexuality has focused on discourses and, more especially, images used in the marketing of commodities.

Research conducted across the 20th century reported that advertising regularly deployed stereotyped gender images that were particularly disadvantageous to women. Other research indicated that preferences for very slender female body shapes in advertising could influence the body image perceptions of girls and young women and, in some cases, have knock-on effects on their eating habits, sometimes with serious health consequences.[32] There were also frequent observations of the regular sexual objectification of women by advertisers.[33] The cultivation of an objectified self-image in women as a result of the way in which they are treated socially can trigger a number of subsequent mental health risks.[34]

There has been relatively limited research carried out on the role played by goods and commodities on the socialization of young people. There is a well-developed research literature on the relationships between advertising and children's consumer socialization.[35] This literature also extends into issues concerning children's understanding of money, the price of commodities, and the role played by consumerism in shaping self-image and social status.[36] There is a wider literature on sexual socialization as one aspect of social–psychological development; but research concerned specifically with the part played by commercial goods in this context is limited. Taking a wider perspective, there has been growing interest within the sphere of the 'sociology of childhood' in children and consumption and children's fashion consumption.[37]

The sexualization of childhood debate centres on a premise that the mass media are promulgated by images that place emphasis on the sexual attributes of young people, even before they are sexually mature. Mediated sexuality can take many forms, including depictions of sexual themes in television programmes that attract large child audiences, music videos with sexual themes, celebrities with a large child fan base who dress in sexually provocative ways, and magazines targeted at children that focus on sexual issues. These mediated images and messages are reinforced further by the prevalence of sexualized products aimed at children.[38] These include products that are overtly characterized by sexuality, such as dolls with full female figures and provocative dress styles, clothing and cosmetics aimed at pre-teenage girls that encourage them to dress as if sexually mature before they are, and the extensions of sexualized brands to merchandise (e.g. accessories and clothing) aimed at children.[39]

Sexualization is seen to be a serious problem where it affects young people, and especially girls and young women, at those stages in their lives in which their self-identities are becoming formed.[40] The sexual aspect of development becomes particularly acute during adolescence when girls display physical sexual characteristics and experience hormonal changes that awaken their sexual desires. Although sex is an integral aspect of human existence and sexuality represents a defining part of human character, it is important that this attribute alone is not the primary defining attribute of young women's personal identities or, indeed, of the way in which they are perceived by others. The emphasis on sexualization can become even more problematic where it attaches to children before puberty in settings in which young girls are presented in ways that emulate adult sexual appeal. At the other end of the age spectrum, sexualization can also be a problem where it creates cultural norms that put pressure on women always to look young and sexy.[41]

During the 21st century, governments of countries such as Australia, the UK and the United States acknowledged that premature sexualization of children was a matter of growing concern that warranted comprehensive and systematic investigation. Large-scale reviews of the subject were undertaken by the American Psychological Association in 2007 and by the Commonwealth of Australia in 2008.[42] In the UK, the Home Office under the Labour government commissioned a major review led by psychologist Linda Papadopoulos which was published in 2010. This was followed a year later by a report produced by Reg Bailey entitled *Letting Children Be Children* that was produced for the UK's Department for Education, having been commissioned by the new Conservative–Liberal Democrat coalition government. These reviews were triggered by growing government concerns about the premature sexual socialization of children and also the use of sexual connotations in association with products targeted at young people and the way in which such products are promoted. These reviews provide an excellent starting point for a new review of the impact of 'sexualized commodities' upon young people. A third review of this field in the UK was undertaken at this time by the Scottish Parliament.[43]

American Psychological Association (APA) Task Force

The American Psychological Association mounted a task force to review evidence on the *Sexualization of Girls*, which reported in 2007.[44] The inquiry examined 'the psychological theory, research, and clinical experience addressing the sexualization of girls via media and other cultural messages., including the prevalence of these messages and their impact on girls and the role and impact of race/ethnicity and socioeconomic status' (p1).

The APA identified four conditions that define the occurrence of 'sexualization': the centrality of sex appeal or sexual behaviour in defining a person's value; the application of narrow standards of physical attractiveness; the objectification of a person for other sexual gratification and amusement; and the inappropriate imposition of sexuality upon a person. The final condition was particularly relevant in relation to the sexualization of childhood because it conveys the concern about treating children in an adult-like sexually defined way.

The APA immediately identified a variety of different media and cultural forms as purveyors of sexualization content, mostly linked to representations of women. This phenomenon has been identified in films, videos and television programmes, in print media, in music lyrics, in many different forms of advertising, in computer games and across the internet. It also occurs in fashion and other commodity fields, and especially in products aimed at children.

The APA concluded that the media are permeated with sexual images of women; that sexualized content in advertising has increased; that the media work alongside parents and peer groups in influencing girls' decisions about whether or not to adopt a sexy appearance; and that exposure to these pervasive sexualization images can affect girls' self-perceptions, attitudes and beliefs about their gender, and their sexual behaviour. Sexualization effects can also occur among boys who develop sexist attitudes, adopt narrow ideas about female attractiveness, and experience difficulties establishing healthy relationships with girls.

The report has been regarded as presenting a comprehensive review of relevant research evidence and also criticized for taking a largely non-critical orientation to this evidence.[45] There were a number of weaknesses in the nature of the evidence presented about sexualization and its alleged effects on girls and boys. A lot of the cited research did not examine 'sexualization', but instead touched on other issues such as body dissatisfaction that might be related to sexualization but cannot represent it. The APA review focused on girls when there are equally important questions about how boys might be affected by exposure to sexualization images and messages.

The definition of sexualization adopted by the APA was very broad. While recognizing that healthy sexuality is central to positive intimate relations, sexualization is present when:

- a person's value comes only from his or her sexual appeal or behaviour, to the exclusion of other characteristics;
- a person is held to a standard that equates physical attractiveness (narrowly defined) with being sexy;
- a person is sexually objectified – that is, made into a thing for others' sexual use, rather than seen as a person with the capacity for independent action and decision-making; and/or
- sexuality is inappropriately imposed upon a person.

The report goes on to state that sexualization occurs when any one of these conditions is present – it is not necessary that all four occur together. The definition does not help in determining when an image can be deemed sexual, however, because each of the conditions outlined requires further definition in order to be consistently applied. From the research literature that has examined the representation of 'sex' (which is a form of behaviour) and 'sexualization' (which is a form of social learning linked to attitudes, beliefs and values that might be attached to objects through their association with sexual activity), there is a lack of consistency or standardization across studies in the way in which sexual content or sexualized content was coded.

Most of the research reported by the APA was, understandably, given the profession it represents, based on psychological studies of media and marketing effects. Other perspectives including ones provided by anthropology and sociology can help to shed light on the extent and nature of the varying definitions of sex and sexualization and varying standards of acceptability that might be adopted by different social and cultural communities. The absence of detailed historical analysis meant that there was no examination of representations of sex and sexuality in societies over time or of the degree to which contemporary concerns differ greatly from those voiced before the mass media became widely established. The APA also adopted a position that mediated sexual images could and will have specific effects on young people and that these effects will cause them to depart from an ideal of sexual health. That ideal or norm was not defined, however, and it may be impossible to do so anyway.

The Australia Institute Inquiry

Other national inquiries followed the one conducted in the United States. In Australia, in 2008, an inquiry was launched by the Commonwealth Parliament, Senate Standing Committee on Environment, Communication and Arts into *Sexualization of Children in the Contemporary Media*. The committee sought to investigate three areas: first, 'the sources and beneficiaries of premature sexualization of children in the media'; second, 'the short- and long-term effects of viewing or buying sexualising and objectifying images and products'; and, third, 'strategies to prevent and/or reduce the sexualization of children in the media and the effectiveness of different approaches in ameliorating its effects'.[46]

The Australian Committee on Environment, Communication and the Arts viewed sexualization as follows:

> ... a continuum from the explicit targeting of children with images, attitudes, and content that inappropriately and prematurely seek to impose a sexual identity on a child, through the presentation of one-dimensional and stereotypical images of children and young people, predominantly girls, in content, products and advertising directed at them, to what might be described as the 'background noise' of society at large where products, advertising and other materials made for and directed at adults are readily accessed by children and reinforce the sexualising messages they are receiving.[47]

The Australian inquiry acknowledged that children are consumers and represent a 'legitimate commercial market', but that there are good reasons to have concerns about some of the products and promotional formats that are directed at them. The Standing Committee also concluded, however, that the empirical evidence about specific alleged effects of the media on the premature sexualization of children remained inconclusive. Such was the importance of this issue, though, that the committee recommended there should be a major longitudinal study carried out into the effects of premature and inappropriate sexualization of children.

Following on from the initial inquiry, a further review was launched by the Senate Legal and Constitutional Affairs References Committee of the National Classification Scheme to determine whether more could be done by government or by the contemporary media to address the issue of sexualization of children and to revise the nature and implementation of relevant codes of practice in this context. The major outcomes from this were to continue monitoring relevant industry action and its impact and to seek to establish a better consumer complaints system.[48]

The UK Home Office Inquiry

In the United Kingdom in 2009, the Home Office commissioned Dr Linda Papadopoulos, a psychologist at London Metropolitan University, to undertake a fact-finding review of evidence linked to the sexualization of teenage girls.[49] This inquiry formed part of a wider consultation being undertaken by the Home Office Violent Crime Unit on violence against women.[50]

The Papadopoulos report acknowledged that sexualization is part of everyday life and can, at appropriate moments and in appropriate ways, form an integral and perfectly healthy aspect of childhood socialization. Nevertheless, a Western society such as the UK has become permeated with 'hyper-sexualized' images and products that place too much emphasis on looking 'sexy' and in promoting sexual appeal or attractiveness as a core aspect of identity definition even for very young people who have not yet reached a stage of development where they are becoming sexually active. Because this imagery can be found extensively across the mass media that children and teenagers consume, and in environments that they frequent, they receive repeated exposures from which it can be difficult to escape. The emergence of new digital technologies and their applications, with the internet and World Wide Web being centre stage here, has meant that children – who are enthusiastic early adopters – can access material of the most extreme sexual nature that can make them upset or confused and even lead them astray.

Papadopoulos found evidence from academic research literature in different parts of the world that confirmed that young people were often exposed to sexually themed material that was inappropriate for them, invited to become engaged with sexual themes through toys and games, and encouraged through child fashions to develop an excessively sexualized identity. This exposure to an environment permeated by sex in which sexual attractiveness or sexual activity were linked closely to childhood could place them under unreasonable pressure to conform prematurely to identity norms relevant only to adults and contribute to the development of restrictive stereotypes, antisocial and even criminal behaviours usually directed at girls and women.

The UK Bailey Review

In 2010, the new coalition government in the UK launched a further committee of inquiry to seek ways of protecting children from excessive commercialization and premature sexualization.[51] This inquiry was led by Lord Bailey, chief executive of the Mothers Union. The Bailey Review built upon the work of a number of earlier reviews. It also sought submissions from various stakeholder groups, including lobbyists, businesses, charities and parents. A national survey of parents was also commissioned which was supplemented by further in-depth interviews and focus groups with participants who were parents.

The Bailey Review confirmed many of the concerns identified by Papadopoulos. Parents, in particular, voiced concerns about the prevalence of sexualized imagery that provided an almost constant backdrop to children's lives. It could be found in the products they consume, the clothing they wear, advertising to which they were exposed, the magazines they read, as well as the music they listened to (and watched on music videos), as well as on television and in films. Much of the sexualization embraced gender stereotyping that placed girls and women at a disadvantage socially by cultivating distorted perceptions of attractiveness and its centrality to female identity definition. There were further concerns that premature exposure to sexual imagery put children under pressure to adopt a sexually charged identity for themselves that did not provide a good fit psychologically for pre-pubescent youngsters and that brought unreasonable social pressures on teenage girls to become sexually active before they were personally ready.[52]

Scottish Parliament Equal Opportunities Committee Inquiry

A further UK review was undertaken by the Scottish Parliament's Equal Opportunities Committee between 2008 and 2010.[53] This investigation examined the prevalence of sexualized products marketed at children. There was no specific definition of sexualization provided for this context. Instead, products were presented to parents for their opinions that appeared to researchers to represent relevant attributes. The views of children were also sought. In addition, the research carried out here included an audit of products marketed to children in 32 retail outlets.

All the data from children in this investigation were collected in their classroom settings at school. They were invited to design and pitch a product for a specified age group and to indicate whether there were things about it that their parents might like or dislike. They then engaged in a fictional shopping exercise in which they were shown a booklet that contained a range of products targeted at either ten-year-old boys or girls. They had to choose products for the boy and for the girl and give their reasons for their selections. Finally, they were asked to look again at the shopping booklet and identify products they thought were 'sexy' or 'sexualized'.

The 12- to 14-year-old children questioned by the Scottish Parliament were aware that some goods are designed to make children look sexy, but they did not have a problem with this, did not think they were innocent victims waiting to be duped, and believed they should be given opportunities as consumers to make up their own minds about the kinds of things they liked to buy. Some of these respondents were aware that wearing sexy clothes might put other children and teenagers at risk by making them appear older, but they were not unduly anxious about this for themselves.

Sources of concern

There are many reasons for the concerns about early exposure of pre-pubertal children to sexual images. Drawing their attention to sexual themes early in their lives could put children at risk by encouraging them to focus on their physical attributes and those of other children and to judge both themselves and others in these terms. This can, in some cases, lead to a loss of self-esteem about their own appearance, and encourage them to take steps to change the way in which they look either by excessive dieting or becoming preoccupied in later life with cosmetic surgery as solutions. Insofar as mediated or merchandised sexual themes also encourage social judgements about others based on their sexuality, they might also encourage girls to associate social capital with a sexually provocative appearance and encourage young boys to regard girls as sex objects.

The effects of sexualization messages can become manifest in terms of short-term and longer-term influences. Pre-teenage girls begin by dressing up dolls in sexually provocative fashion before adopting such fashions for themselves as they shift their attention as consumers from toys to personal appearance. The fashion industry feeds this drive by providing clothing styles that emphasize adult sexuality before children themselves have reached a stage of full physical and accompanying psychological maturity. As they grow up, therefore, girls are surrounded by social pressures to focus on their appearance as the main determinant of self-worth and their wider social standing among their friends and peers.

As girls enter adolescence and mature physically into women, their sexual attributes become visually more apparent and hormonal changes push them into becoming sexually active. Girls start to develop identities as women. What is critical at this stage of development is whether their new emergent identities are defined primarily by their sexual appeal. If this norm of sexualized identity definition has already become established, there can be enormous peer pressure for young teens to emulate older teens and young adult women who represent their primary role models. Such pressures could lead young teens to imitate their slightly older role models in both appearance and behaviour.[54] This means that 13-, 14- and 15-year-olds set out to look and act sexy. They may regard this behaviour as perfectly acceptable and ignore or be oblivious to risks that can follow on from it.

There is also a gender dimension to the sexualization of childhood in that most of the public and political concern along with most of the empirical research has focused on girls. Boys can also be targets of sexualization messages and have both their self-images and impressions of others – most particularly, girls – affected in consequence.[55] With girls, however, anti-sexualization arguments have accused the media, marketers and manufacturers of colluding in a corporate conspiracy to preserve through subtle social conditioning a world dominated by a patriarchal ethos in which women are politically, economically and sexually subjugated by men.[56]

There is ample evidence that many young women in their teens and early-20s are preoccupied with the way in which they look, and display dissatisfaction with their facial features and body shapes. One UK survey of 25,000 respondents found that nearly half the women surveyed said they had missed a meal to lose weight, while 8 per cent admitted to bulimic tendencies. In the same survey, over half of girls aged 12 to 16 years believed that their body image prevented them from getting a boyfriend. Although acknowledging that a curvy female body shape was probably the best body shape to have, despite the prevalence of skinny size-zero models in fashion magazines, it was still the case that almost half of all women wanted to change their own bodies and over one in ten said they actually 'hated' their physical appearance.[57]

Dissatisfaction with personal appearance was also found amongst pre-teenagers as well as teenagers. A UK investigation by the Children's Society found that one in six of all children aged 10 to 15 surveyed (18 per cent) said they were unhappy with their appearance. Girls (22 per cent) were much more likely than boys (13 per cent) to express such concern.[58] An American survey by OTX Teen Topix and the Intelligence Group reported that 68 per cent of 13- to 17-year-olds were happy with their looks and 58 per cent were happy with their body. This left significant minorities apparently not happy with these personal attributes.[59] There is considerable evidence also that exposure to mediated images in movies, television shows and advertisements that depict idealized women in terms of appearance can lead insecure women to become even more questioning about their own body image, which they perceive to be different from an ideal favoured by men.[60]

More serious concerns about the sexualization of girls stems from possible links of materialism to sexual abuse. Placing sexual objectification centre-stage in marketing and media outputs and merchandising aimed at children and teenagers can put young female consumers under pressure to appear sexually alluring and available. This can, in turn, lead to girls placing themselves at risk by conceding to social pressures to become sexually active at an early age and might also encourage adult child abusers' antisocial urges. Further public concerns about the objectification and commodification of female sexuality have identified links between this social trend and the occurrence of domestic sexual violence.[61]

Sexualization can cause particular complications when it occurs among girls as they are developing into women. At this time of life, they are insecure about their identity and are constantly seeking cues from others about how to appear and how to behave. They may be encouraged to look 'sexy' before they have become sexually awakened and know how to make sensible decisions about the use of their sexual attractiveness and the kinds of sexual relationships to engage in.[62]

Contestations of government sexualization inquiries

The major inquiries produced and/or sponsored by various government organizations in Australia, the United Kingdom and United States have not gone unchallenged. These inquiries have successfully raised public anxieties about serious issues but have, according to some critics, adopted and debated contested concepts such as 'sexuality' and 'sexualization' and failed to provide comprehensive reviews of relevant evidence that have resulted in key concepts that are too narrowly defined.[63] Moreover, these inquiries have added unhelpful emotionality to discussions of childhood sexualization through the use of terms such as 'corporate paedophilia' to describe specific types of offending and potentially harmful media and marketing content, and child-targeted commodity designs.[64]

Despite the concerns raised by these national inquiries,[65] the debates themselves can be reconceptualized as one-dimensional and biased in their almost exclusive focus on girls as victims, girls as innocents, and risks that are confined largely to heterosexual scenarios. The recent wave of publicity about the sexualization of childhood, manifest primarily in relation to girls as victims, has given an impression that this is a newly emergent issue and social problem, when it is not. Scholars have investigated the phenomena of texts that convey adult-themed discourses about sex and sexuality to children for many years.[66]

There have been a number of presumptions made about the status of young girls that underpin the moral panics and public anxieties about exposure of pre-adults to sexually themed materials. One presumption concerns the innocence and sexual maturity of children as reaching specific thresholds at particular ages or stages of development, when there are diverse individual differences among children of the same age in their relative psychological development and when this development does not always follow a generic linear path for all children. Girls reach womanhood in terms of their physical and psychological maturity at different ages and their reactions to the same sexualized content can vary. It could, indeed, be true that the presence of sexually themed commodities targeted at children could blur certain boundaries between childhood and adulthood,[67] but we cannot presume that all children respond in the same way to these experiences or necessarily interpret materials defined by their critics as unsuitably sexualized in a sexual way.[68]

The major government-backed inquiries have also been found wanting in that they have not included in their reviews any or sufficient consideration of more qualitative research evidence that has indicated that mediated sexualization messages are not invariably accepted at face value or internalized by children in a verbatim fashion. Instead, in-depth discussions with children about these issues can often reveal that there is a complex process of negotiation of sexualization that occurs and a renegotiation of sexual messages purportedly communicated by the media or by child-targeted commodities.[69]

The vulnerability of children to social and personal influences of sexualized materials tends to emerge from an oversimplified concept of their relative innocence and passivity in these contexts.[70] Regardless of any value judgements that might be attached to such behaviour, teenage girls use social media proactively to engage in highly sexualized discourses with others and to put themselves on sexual display. Within these online communities, such behaviour can attract the disapproval of others, but can also be worn as a badge of identity within their closest social cliques.[71]

Understanding sexualization

A number of theories have been developed to help us understand the psychological mechanisms that come into play to shape the way in which mass media can influence our social perceptions, beliefs, attitudes and behaviour in the context of sexualization. Sexualization is an aspect of socialization. Socialization comprises a range of experiences that include formal and informal learning about social values, moral codes, and ways of feeling and behaving. The socialization process is designed to instil in all of us an internal discipline over how we ought to behave towards others and how we should present ourselves so as not to cause harm or offence.

The effects of being brought up in a sexualized environment can be felt at a number of levels that shape the way in which we think about ourselves, evaluate others, and behave in our interpersonal relationships. Socialization in a highly sexualized environment places sexuality at the forefront of the codes and scripts that we learn and which set the parameters on how we ought to behave in different social settings. Social scientists have developed a number of explanations of socialization that can be invoked to help us understand better how we might all be influenced by a sexualized environment.

There are socialization theories that focus on the way we learn specific behaviours or rules about behaviour. This 'social' learning can take place by simply observing the actions of others. Actions in this context can mean both overt behaviours and speech. Speech provides verbal representations of internal thoughts and feelings that we can interpret in the form of knowledge, beliefs and attitudes.

There is often a strong sexual element running through a lot of social learning because many of the codes or rules that are established by the society or culture in which we live are linked to gender. Thus, children learn ways of behaving that are deemed by prevailing social and cultural codes as most appropriate and acceptable for their own sex.[72] Initial social learning theory focused on the learning of specific observed actions. Later theoretical developments in 'cognitive' theory in psychology examined more closely how rules about overt behaviours could be internalized and stored away (or remembered) for future reference.[73]

This process can proceed in early infancy in relation to learning about the social behaviour expectations attached to females and males. Rather than simply observing the behaviour of others and then copying it immediately afterwards as conceived by initial social learning theory, children can remember the sequences of behaviour they have seen performed by others and store them away in memory as behaviour 'scripts'. Cognitive theories have therefore proposed that children are constantly internalizing incidents and episodes they have witnessed in their own lives in which specific behaviours have occurred. It is not just the overt behaviour sequences that are internalized, however, but also further observations concerning the social settings in which the behaviours took place, the circumstances under which they occurred (i.e. interpretations of the motives of the actors) and the consequences and outcomes for those involved. In this way, sets of rules are encoded that indicate that specific behaviours may be appropriate on specific occasions where certain outcomes are desired. Over time, we may encounter some scripts or variants of them frequently. Such repetition allows us to rehearse those behaviour sequences in our heads without performing them. Nevertheless, that repetition and rehearsal can lead some scripts to grow stronger and to become primary choices in terms of how we behave in specific social settings.[74]

Cultivation effects and sexualization

Another manifestation of socialization, particularly where it derives from our exposure to the mass media, is the cultivation effect. This theory posits that our social perceptions and beliefs can be influenced by messages from the media about different aspects of society. These messages can derive from fictional drama, news reports, advertisements, and other mediated content. The media can provide us with a lot of information about different types of people, defined by their gender, age, ethnicity, occupation, social status, religion, politics, and so on. The media can also represent a source of information about ways of behaving in different social settings. The media might also regularly combine specific social groups with specific patterns of behaving. Hence, television dramas with law enforcement themes might provide representations of the work of the police or lawyers. These fictional representations may provide true reflections of these occupations or highly distorted depictions of them. If they are our only source of information about these occupations, however, we may internalize beliefs about them based on inaccurate media depictions. In other words, the media can cultivate beliefs about the police and lawyers that we commit to memory and which shape our expectations about them.[75]

Similar cultivation effects have been observed to occur in relation to the genders. If men and women are depicted in the media in different ways – in terms of their personality attributes and abilities, social roles and occupational roles – various ideas and beliefs can be cultivated and attached to each gender as being typical of it. As we will see later in this book, such gender stereotyping has been well documented in magazines, movies, newspapers, television programmes, and advertising messages. This stereotyping can influence our beliefs about each gender and is an aspect of socialization that can begin during early childhood.[76]

Cultivation effects have been observed to occur in relation to our perceptions of our bodies. The media have been implicated as sources of stereotyping about ideal body shapes and standards of physical attractiveness.[77] In this context, concern has arisen most especially about the way in which women are physically represented in the media. Movie and television producers and advertisers have exhibited clear preferences for women with slender body shapes in lead roles and as product demonstrators and endorsers. Much published empirical research evidence has emerged to show that these media representations of body shape can influence beliefs about standards of beauty and attractiveness. Young people become more strongly attracted to feminine models of thinness and masculine models of muscularity.[78] Furthermore, exposure to these media representations can influence how girls and young women perceive themselves and their general levels of satisfaction with their own body shape.[79]

Turning to interpersonal relationships, romance, marriage and sex, the media can cultivate further distorted perceptions of social reality. Television drama, for example, has been found to present its own distinctive view of the world in terms of the amount of sexual activity that occurs between people, how often marital relationships break down, and the prevalence of casual and apparently unprotected sex. These representations of sexual relations might impart social scripts to young people that they subsequently call upon to guide their own sexual relationship choices.[80]

Sexual objectification

As we have seen, psychologists have offered a number of explanations of how sexualization effects and their consequences can be explained for girls and women, as well as for boys and men. The influences of sexualization can change the way in which girls perceive themselves. This, in turn, can influence how they perform in different situations. Repeated experiences in which girls are treated in a sexualized way can condition longer-term changes that can impact upon personality and general mental and physical health. Girls may begin to see themselves as sexual objects rather than as human beings. These perceptions of girls may be shared by boys. Associated with this 'objectification' effect are other qualities concerning ideal body shapes, facial appearance and skin tone.

Aspirations to attain an ideal appearance as a core aspect of personal attractiveness and contingent social status can result in the adoption of distorted behaviour patterns and treatments that carry spin-off risks.[81] These responses may not only attach to individuals in terms of how they perceive themselves, but can be generalized in the form of stereotypes to the entire gender. Sexual stereotypes of girls and women can result in a narrowing of social and economic ambitions and of associated rights and opportunities. Standards of beauty and attractiveness pinned to youthfulness can impact upon lasting anxieties of older women who continually seek to conform to such social ideals, often with unrealistic expectations and unsatisfactory outcomes.[82]

One important factor in the development of sexualized orientations among girls is modelling. As they grow up and become women, they acquire personal identities based on internalized social experiences and observations.[83] In sexual matters, girls learn from observing the behaviour of older girls and women and by talking to them, and also by picking up illustrations on how to behave second hand via the media.

One of the major concerns linked to the learning experiences that arise out of exposure to sexualized content is the risk that young people will develop distorted beliefs about human sexuality and sexual relations as a result of the treatment of women (and, increasingly, men) as sex objects. Objectification theory was formulated to explain how this influence occurs and the consequences it can have.[84]

Self-objectification can result in young women performing less well in cognitive tests. Frederickson and his colleagues had young women try on either a swimsuit or a sweater on their own in a changing room. While they waited for a few minutes wearing the garment, they were given a maths test. The women wearing the swimsuit performed less well than the ones wearing sweaters. The same differences did not occur when these tests were conducted with young men. The researchers concluded that the young women may have been caused to think more about their physical selves while wearing the swimsuit and that this disrupted their mental functioning.[85]

This tendency to constantly monitor one's own body shape as a side effect of sexual objectification has been shown by numerous studies.[86] Social comparison theory has emerged as another theoretical model that has been used to explain how idealized perceptions about body shape can become internalized. This process can act as a powerful mediator of mass media effects of body shape beliefs and satisfaction. It has also emerged that not all of us demonstrate social comparison tendencies to the same extent. Those people who do regularly make comparisons between their own appearance and that of other people (including celebrity role models seen on television and in magazines) are particularly susceptible to the influences of media representations of the thin ideal for women.[87]

Women who were found to make comparisons between themselves and others in terms of their body weight and shape were not only more likely to exhibit low self-esteem about their own body shape, but also thought that other people were as preoccupied as they are with such things.[88] Furthermore, women who have body shape-related anxieties and who are in the habit of making social comparisons were more likely to perceive well-known celebrities as being thinner than they really are. Women who were satisfied with their own bodies were much less likely to misjudge celebrities in this way.[89]

A further dimension to social comparison is the extent to which those of us who engage in such activity regularly detect a discrepancy between what we see in ourselves and the standard of attractiveness we would ideally like to attain. Hence, people who readily make social comparisons not only compare themselves with other people, they also compare the person they believe themselves to be (or their actual self) with an ideal they would like to achieve (their ideal self). The bigger the gap between the actual self and ideal self, the less satisfied we tend to think and feel about ourselves.[90] This type of body dissatisfaction can motivate those who experience it to take radical steps, including extreme dieting behaviour.[91]

Self-discrepancy has been observed as a chronic condition that persists over time and as a temporary state that can come and go with a person's current mood.

Those who experience self-discrepancy (i.e. evaluate their actual self as inferior to the ideal self they would like to attain) have also been found to show greater susceptibility to media influences on body self-perceptions.[92] Media depictions of physically attractive models can trigger temporary self-discrepancies that can give rise to unfavourable evaluations of our own body shape.[93] These effects can occur among men as well as women. For example, exposure to pictures of muscular male models in the media can lead men to feel less favourably about their own body build. The tendency of the media to focus on specific body parts can result in the self-discrepancy effect being focused on a particular aspect of our own physique than our overall body shape. A woman might say she does not like the size of her bottom or a man might express dissatisfaction with a flabby stomach.[94]

Obsession with the body

In May 2012, male officials managing Great Britain's preparations for the 2012 London Olympics were accused of putting female athletes under pressure about their size by telling them to lose weight. This pressure led one international standard female athlete to develop an eating disorder. Matters came to a head when Jessica Ennis, Britain's leading heptathlete, was described as 'fat' by an athletics official. Anyone who has seen Ennis would know that she is as far from being fat as you can be. Such pressures led one leading athlete to quit before she had reached her full potential. Hollie Avil, a triathlete who competed for Britain in the 2008 Olympics in Beijing, quit at the age of 22 to set up a charity to support young athletes faced with similar accusations.[95]

A substantial amount of published research, using samples of girls and young women from around the world and different methodologies, has shown that the media not only draw girls' and women's attention to body shape issues, but can contribute to their dissatisfaction with their own body shape. Although the media do not act alone in shaping women's body self-esteem, they represent a constant presence in their lives that exerts a persistent influence with women who are most anxious about their bodies being the most susceptible.[96]

Cosmetic surgery

For many years, women have turned to plastic surgery to combat the effects of ageing. More recently, teenage girls have increasingly turned to this solution in pursuit of a more attractive body image. With teenagers, how they look is central to how they feel about themselves. Anecdotal clinical evidence has indicated girls as young as 11 seeking cosmetic surgery to improve the way they look.[97] One survey of British teenagers undertaken by a popular magazine found that more than four in ten said they had considered surgery. The most widespread uses of cosmetic surgery were tummy tuck, thinner thighs, breast enlargement and breast reduction.[98]

This apparent drive for body sculpting was corroborated by evidence released by the American Society of Plastic Surgeons that around one third of 1 million

American adolescents aged 18 years or under underwent plastic surgery in 2005. Most of these procedures comprised chemical peels or laser hair removal, but breast enlargements were also among the most popular types of cosmetic surgery.[99]

Problem sexual behaviour

The exposure of children to sexual images in media and marketing has been linked by some clinicians to problematic sexual behaviour among children themselves. In Australia, this type of behaviour has been observed to occur as early as seven years of age.[100] Although such behaviour is usually linked to disrupted family lives or early histories of abuse and neglect, as many as one in five of these cases did not have this type of disadvantaged background.[101] Instead, sexual imagery present in the social environments of these children has been identified as playing a part in shaping their attitudes towards sex and propensity to become involved in premature sexual activity.[102]

A study of teenagers in North Carolina tracked whether there were any statistical links between how much media sex they were exposed to and early onset of sexual behaviour.[103] In this investigation, more than 1000 teenagers aged between 12 and 14 years when first recruited were interviewed on two occasions separated by two years. Soundings were taken initially about whether they were sexually active at the start of the inquiry and also about their reported consumption (over a previous month) of television, movies, music albums and magazines. Lists of programmes, films, albums and magazines were provided and the teenage respondents were asked to indicate the frequency with which they consumed each one. Those media outputs that were endorsed by at least 10 per cent of respondents were located and analysed by the researchers for the amount of sex they contained. By multiplying between reported use of these media and this sex content quantification, it was possible to produce a unified measure of the amount of mediated sex each respondent had been exposed to. All respondents were asked if they had ever had full sexual intercourse and the age at which this had first taken place, or, if not, whether they had engaged in a range of other sexual behaviours leading up to intercourse (e.g. kissing, touching in intimate places, oral sex and so on).

Two years later, those teenagers who had been exposed to the most sex in the media they had consumed were more than twice as likely to have had sexual intercourse than those who had had the least exposure to such content. This finding survived controls for the kinds of families they came from. Splitting out sub-groups of respondents defined by their gender and race, this relationship was found to disappear for black teenagers after controlling for parental disapproval of teenage sex and the sexual permissiveness of their peer group. Exposure to sex in the media also predicted degree of sexual activity, other than full intercourse, but only for white teenagers and not for black teenagers.

Although providing some evidence that teenagers' exposure to sex in the media was linked to early onset of sexual activity up to and including intercourse, these effects of the media were confined to one ethic group – white teenagers. With black teenagers, sexual behaviour was more strongly influenced by family background and peer group factors and these swamped any influences of media. A limitation of this work by Jane Brown and her colleagues is that they were not able to separate out distinctive effects of different media. Can we assume without question that sex in music lyrics, sex discussed in magazines and sex depicted in films and television programmes are all one and the same in terms of their respective influences on young people?

The British family support charity Family Lives considered the issues raised by the report produced by Lord Bailey that we looked at earlier, one year on from its publication. One of its principal observations was that debates about the sexualization of childhood, particularly in the context of the conditioning of young people as consumers, have focused on girls and given much less attention to boys.[104] This is a critical omission. Boys are targeted by marketers as much as girls and are also susceptible to messages that draw attention to sexualized attributes of each gender. While there is little doubt that the consumer environment is filled with images that emphasize the physical features of girls in a sexualized way, it is not only young girls who might be influenced in terms of their self-perceptions, but also young boys.

Sexualized images and messages and commodities can contribute to a form of hyper-masculinity among boys in which they develop distorted beliefs about girls. Their human qualities can be subverted beneath an objectified impression of the other gender. There is the added concern that such cognitive effects can become manifest in the way in which boys behave towards girls. Family Lives' own helpline received over 40,000 calls between April 2011 and March 2012 of which over 1200 (3 per cent) concerned children's sexual behaviour. One-third of the latter calls dealt with under-age sex and mostly involved teenagers aged 13 to 15.

Further interesting work was conducted by David Buckingham that examined the role of commercialism in children's lives in the UK and the impact it has upon their well-being.[105] Evidence was reviewed that indicated commercialism can pose risks and bring benefits to children. Evidence for the harm of commercialism needs to be examined carefully and not taken at face value. At the same time, extensions of marketing campaigns from usual sites in the mainstream media to other venues such as inside schools or other public spaces occupied by children where commercialism is not normally expected need to be monitored closely.

When thinking about 'well-being' here, attention was directed towards the physical and mental health of young people. Evidence was collected from a wide range of sources. Commercialism can take many different forms and occurs in many different settings. Although it has changed in its nature over time, so, too, has society more generally. The children's commercial marketplace has grown in monetary value and in terms of the number and ranges of commodities targeted at children. The rapid developments in media and communications systems in the new millennium have also opened up opportunities to marketers and expanded the range of experiences of children.

Any evidence must be evaluated in terms of whether it has been effective in its measurement of key variables and the ability to demonstrate causal connections between them. A lot of social scientific research on the effects of marketing on children has reported degrees of correlation between alleged exposure to marketing messages and the beliefs, attitudes and behaviours of children. The word 'alleged' is critical here. Very often marketing exposure is based on broad estimates reported by survey respondents answering questionnaires or participants in extended face-to-face interviews. The accuracy of these self-reports is rarely validated in relation to real behaviour. Researchers are also restricted by the rules of research ethics in terms of whether they can seek to measure actual causality. Relationships based on correlations do not demonstrate causality. However, causal tests may be forbidden in some research contexts in which researchers attempt to manipulate children's reactions to marketing messages. Hence, the investigation of cause–effect relations between commercial message exposure and commodity purchase and use or more general values associated with commercialism can end up being a contested field.

There is much disagreement between researchers about research methods, modes of measurement of commercialism and consumer behaviour, and causality. There has been further disagreement about the 'effects' of commercial messages. Effects can occur in different forms, including immediate emotional responses, memories for commodity attributes, more persistent beliefs about and attitudes towards commodities, intentions to purchase, and actual purchase and use.

The Buckingham report acknowledged that there has been vocal public concern about the sexualization of children and, in particular, about the roles played by marketing and media in this context. One of the key areas of concern centres on the depiction of female body shapes in the media with a focus on a slender shape as ideal. In addition, there is concern about the use of sexual content in media and marketing outputs targeted at children, as well as in relation to certain children's products. Sexual themes in children's commodities include sexually mature body shapes of dolls, children clothing fashions and cosmetics that place a focus on accentuating sexual attributes even among very young pre-pubertal children, and also extensions of sex brands (e.g. *Playboy*) to accessories and clothing sold to children.

Buckingham made important observations that the issue of the sexualization of childhood is not new even though recent high-profile media debates give a different impression. Children and teenagers have been represented as sexual objects in literature and the visual arts long before the modern media were available. Moreover, the age of consent for heterosexual sex was still only 12 in the 19th century. During that time, child prostitutes as young as eight or nine were also not unusual. Hence, the concept of sexualization of childhood is not a consequence of modern consumerism.

Concerns about body image are linked to wider observations about sexualization of childhood. It has been observed that cultural industries frequently focus on the physical bodies of women. It is not only that stereotyping of ideal body shapes allegedly occurs with a slim shape being promoted as the ideal, but also that women are frequently used in a highly physical way within commercial messages with a focus placed on their physical form. To draw further attention to this, there is extensive use of nudity and other sexualized imagery with women in marketing and media. For some critics, this pattern represents a sexual objectification of women where they are use as objects of (mainly male) titillation regardless of the relevance of such imagery to informing consumers about the brands being promoted.

The use of these images has been identified as having profound effects on the way in which girls perceive themselves and on the way they are perceived by boys. These representations can, in turn, place girls under pressure to think about themselves and to present themselves in a sexualized way before they have reached physical maturity. Even for young physically developed teenagers, these representations might encourage them to give undue prominence to their physical attributes in determining their self-worth. The use of digital smoothing techniques to alter the appearance of even the most beautiful models can set unrealistic and unattainable benchmarks of attractiveness (and success) for young girls, leading them to question their own attractiveness. This can, for some, cause them to be more susceptible to social pressures to become sexually active to prove their worth to themselves and others, with many unwanted side effects.

In theory, therefore, there are many unwanted potential effects of sexualized content in commercial settings. In practice, sound evidence is needed that these effects actually occur. Research evidence is unfortunately less than clear cut here because of fuzzy definitions of key concepts such as 'sexual', 'sexualized' and 'objectification'. At what point does an image of an attractive young woman in an advertisement warrant the label 'sex object'? Would it be socially healthier if all female nudity in advertisements was banned? How confident can we be that the relevant empirical research on the effects of female body shapes on the body shape ideals and self-confidence of teenage girls has produced evidence that such effects really happen?

A number of major reviews of research have concluded that media and marketing play a significant role in cultivating childhood sexualization.[106] Put simply, media producers and marketing executives are regarded as instruments of influence upon children, drawing undue attention to sexual themes and attributes in children's everyday lives. This influence becomes manifest through the treatment of young women as sexual objects, the glorification of a narrow range of mediated and technologically altered standards of feminine beauty, and the integration of sex with children's commodities. These influences can leave children, and especially girls, at risk of low self-esteem, premature sexual awareness, and unwanted and inappropriate attention from boys and men.

Much of the evidence here has focused on the nature of media themes and images, which may not tell us exactly how children or adults respond to these outputs. One might argue that it is inappropriate to depict young girls under the age of eight in revealing costumes and full facial make-up, but we need to know whether the girls themselves are psychologically changed or whether exposure to them triggers inappropriate sexual responses among adult males and how widespread such reactions might be. The restrictions of research ethics mean that it is impossible for researchers to construct studies that directly measure these influences before they occur. Instead, researchers are restricted to assessing *post hoc* cases where such images have apparently been linked to self-perceptions or the behaviours of others.

We need to look more closely at emergent evidence that young women's psychological states can be altered by exposure to sexually objectified images of their own gender. Do such images really reduce their self-esteem? Can they trigger depression? Do they cause girls and young women to adopt extreme eating habits to sculpt an idealized body shape? Can such images also influence boys' perceptions of girls? Do they affect boys' beliefs about sexual relationships? Can they encourage boys to see girls as sexual objects rather than human beings?

Researchers have tried to engage with young people to assess their verbal reaction to media representations of sex, love and relationships.[107] This research found that children often encountered sexual material in the media. Sex occurred in many different settings and was presented in different ways. Young people regarded the mass media as valuable sources of information about sex and relationships. They would consult with teenage magazines on issues they were too embarrassed to ask their parents about.[108]

Although youngsters used the media for information about sex and relationships, they did not trust everything they read or saw. They often engaged in making complex judgements about sexual themes presented to them in the media. In fictional settings, the impact of a character's own relationship dilemmas on young viewers depended upon how much they identified with that character. Teenagers could be very critical of media representations of sexual relationships. This finding flies in the face of evidence marshalled by some critics to show that mediated representations of sex put young people at risk.

Sexualization is closely tied to concepts of the body. Body images feature prominently in many media that are targeted at young people and also in marketing campaigns. The female body is used extensively by some product sectors, including cosmetics, diet, fitness and fashion sectors. Young, beautiful models with slender body shapes are generally preferred. Even where the female body shape on display is not thin, it will frequently have been digitally altered or 'airbrushed' to alter the model's original shape or to change the skin texture or tone. These techniques are increasingly used with male models as well, creating a media environment populated by unrealistic role models targeted at both genders.

There are a number of issues that need to be investigated. How frequently occurring is sexualization? Where does it occur and in what forms? Are particular media or settings prominent in the conveyance of sexualization messages? Is sexualization integrated with consumerism? What types of impact upon girls and young women can sexualization messages have? Do girls and women accept sexualization messages and internalize them? How do sexualization effects become manifest? How serious are these effects and what can be done about them? Should we be concerned about the effects of this type of environment on young people? Research in the United States has indicated that exposure to a high level of sexual imagery may increase the likelihood of early onset of sexual activity among teenagers.[109]

Other American research found that exposure to sexual content not just on television but also in films, magazine and music was associated with increased likelihood of sexual activity among 12- to 14-year-olds. Exposure to this content is also linked to beliefs about sexual relationships.[110] This research also revealed that girls who consumed sexually themed media content more often also endorsed more strongly stereotyped beliefs about women as sex objects. This content can also affect the beliefs that boys hold about girls and the kinds of relationships they have with the opposite sex.

Sexualization and social risks

The rise of sexualization messages in media and marketing, and as expressed in sexual features that have become integrated with fashion commodities and products and games targeted at children and adolescents has raised many important questions about their societal implications. Repeated exposure to mediated and commodified sexualization can result in exaggerated attention being drawn to sex amongst young people before they are psychologically and physically ready to become sexually active. Sexualization messages can cultivate a normative view that sex is and should be central to the way in which we evaluate ourselves and others.

Although a sexual aspect is integral to forming and maintaining close interpersonal relationships that are essential both to social cohesion and the maintenance of the species, the version of sex promoted by the mass media and in consumer markets is at odds with the type of sexual relationship most likely to promote healthy companionship. Sex is treated as a commodity that can be cheaply traded. In this context, female and male sexualities are objectified as well, and distorted beliefs can become cultivated and internalized about the appropriateness of different sexual activities in different social settings.

In this sexualized world, there is a gender divide that usually tends to place women at a disadvantage in terms of their social position. Sexualized messages encourage girls (and eventually women) to develop self-identities that are founded on a narrow idea of the ways in which they ought to present themselves as sexual beings. In the sexualized world, women have been treated as sex objects whose primary purpose is to service the sexual urges of men. The sexualized world has also increasingly placed men under pressure in terms of expectations related to their sexual performance. Sexualization messages can introduce girls to a world that appears to be normatively defined in terms of sex. This means that social status is often intimately bound up with appearing sexy and with being sexual.

For boys, these messages can impart distorted ideas about female sexuality and also about how to behave in a sexual way towards girls. The sexualized world places high value on physical appearance but also sets the standards for the ideal physical identity. Constant exposure to messages about outer appearance can mean that internalized values become usurped by sexualized priorities. The sexual objectification of women by fashions that emphasize sexual allure, magazines that present women unclothed, films and television programmes that depict women entering into casual sexual relationships, and burgeoning pornographic outputs that represent women as available to satisfy any male sexual fantasy can create beliefs about female and male sexuality that undermine men's abilities to enter into and develop selfless and committed intimate relationships.[111] It can also undermine the confidence of young women as sexual beings and result in distorted self-impressions that represent a potential vulnerability that could also put them at risk.[112]

As we will see later in this book, the sexualization message is not one that is promulgated by dominant males who seek to cultivate a submissive sexual self-identity among women. Women have become active perpetrators of sexualization messages about women. In the worlds of music and fashion, female celebrities have proactively presented highly sexualized images of themselves. Actresses such as Demi Moore and Sharon Stone have played sexualized starring roles in mainstream movie releases in which they portrayed characters who were both sexually available but also sexually empowered. One of the world's most famous female celebrities, Madonna, has presented a sexualized media image since the start of her career through her music, concert appearances, film roles and culminating in her book, entitled *Sex*, that featured many explicit nude portraits of her. The sexualized mantle adopted by Madonna has more recently been taken up by other female artists such as Britney Spears and Lady Gaga.[113]

In all of these cases, these artists have flaunted their sexual allure in highly exposed and explicit ways, but on their own terms.[114] Such sexual empowerment might be regarded as a positive development for women, but it has the downside of continuing to seek to define women in sexually objectified ways. Controlled sexualization might be an effective marketing tool for popular female celebrities who possess the authority and power to be sexual in an open way that they can control, but it could still cultivate distorted beliefs about female sexuality among boys and young men and could place women who do not possess that degree of control over their lives at a social disadvantage.[115] These iconic displays of female sexuality can also influence young women. Scenes of female celebrities engaging in public displays of sexuality towards other women (e.g. kissing each other on the lips) have created a fashion trend among young women more generally – a phenomenon that has been labelled 'lesbian chic' or 'bisexual chic'. In other words, these overt sexual displays represent a fashion statement rather than a sign of genuine emotional involvement.[116] We turn our attention first to the role of fashion in the transmission of sexualization messages to children and teenagers. This is an area of potential influence that is perhaps closest to home because it stems from the clothing styles and choices that are presented to young people and the impressions of themselves they are encouraged to put on display through the way they dress.

Notes

1 Atwood, F. (2010) 'Introduction: Porn Studies: From social problem to cultural practice', in F. Attwood (Ed.) *Porn.com:Making Sense of Online Pornography*. Oxford, UK: Peter Lang; Buckingham, D., Bragg, S., Russell, R. and Willett, R. (2010) *Sexualized Goods Aimed at Children: A Research Report*. Edinburgh, Scotland: Scottish Parliament.

2 Belgutay, J. (2011) 'War against the sexualization of childhood', *Times Education Supplement*, 5 August, www.tes.co.uk/article.aspx?storycode=6107531, accessed 7 August 2013. White, H. (2012) 'Child sexualization "imposes" adult sexuality on young children: MEP at E meeting', 11 June, www.lifesitenews.com/child-sexualization-imposes-adult-sexuality-on-young-children.

3 Martin, D. (2012) 'Young teenagers "turned into criminals by sex texts"', *Daily Mail*, 12 December, p12.

4 Figes, K. (2013) 'Pawns in a new age of porn', *The Sunday Times*, Festival of Education Supplement, 26 May, pIII.

5 Kohut, H. (1971) *The Analysis of the Self*. New York, NY: International Universities Press.

6 Finkelhor, D. and Browne, A. (1985) 'The traumatic impact of child sexual abuse: A conceptualisation', *American Journal of Orthopsychiatry*, 55(4), 530–541.

7 Schiro, A. M. (1981) 'Play cosmetics for children: Dissenting voices are heard', *New York Times*, 21 February.

8 Levy, A. (2005) *Female Chauvinist Pigs: Women and the Rise of Raunch Culture*. New York: NY: Free Press; Roberts, Y. (2003) 'Cheated out of childhood: While liberals remain nervous about discussing rules and standards, they fail today's children', *The Observer*, 21 September, http://www.guardian.co.uk/society/2003/sep/21/children-protection.comment, accessed 18 December 2012.

9 Egan, D. and Hawkes, G. (2010) *Theorizing the Sexual Child in Modernity*. New York, NY: Palgrave Macmillan; Renold, E. (2005) *Girls, Boys and Junior Sexualities*. London, UK: Routledge.

10 Kincaid, J. (1992) *Child Loving: The Erotic Child and Victorian Culture*. London, UK: Routledge; Kincaid, J. (1998) *The Culture of Child Molesting*. Durham, NC: Duke University Press; Higonnet, A. (1998) *Pictures of Innocence: The History and Crisis of Ideal Childhood*. London, UK: Thames and Hudson.

11 Kehily, M. J. and Montgomery, H. (2002) 'Innocence and experience: A historical approach to childhood sexuality', in M. Woodhead and H. Montgomery (Eds.) *Understanding Childhood: An Interdisciplinary Approach*. Chichester, UK: Wiley.

12 Egan, R. D. and Hawkes, G. L. (2007) 'Producing the prurient through the pedagogy of purity: Childhood sexuality and the social purity movement', *Journal of Historical Sociology*, 20(4), 443–461; Egan, R. D. and Hawkes, G. L. (2008a) 'Endangered girls and incendiary objects: Unpacking the discourse on sexualization', *Sexuality and Culture*, 12, 291–311; Egan, R. D. and Hawkes, G. L. (2008b) 'Girls, sexuality and the strange carnalities of advertisements', *Australian Feminist Studies*, 23(57), 307–322; Hawkes, G. and Egan, R. D. (2008) 'Developing the sexual child', *Journal of Historical Sociology*, 21(4), 443–465.

13 Ricciardelli, L. A. and Mellor, D. (2012) 'Influence of peers', in N. Rumsey and D. Harcourt (Eds.) *The Oxford Handbook of the Psychology of Appearance*, Chapter 20, pp253–72. Oxford, UK: University of Oxford Press.

14 Smolak, L. (2012) 'Appearance in childhood and adolescence', in N. Rumsey and D. Harcourt (Eds.) *The Oxford Handbook of the Psychology of Appearance*, Chapter 12, pp123–137. Oxford, UK: University of Oxford Press.

15 Buckingham, D. and Bragg, S. (2004) *Young People, Sex and the Media: The Facts of Life?* London, UK: Palgrave; Buckingham, D. and Bragg, S. (2005) 'Opting into (and out of) childhood: Young people, sex and the media', in J. Qvortrup (Ed.) *Studies in Modern Childhood, Society, Agency and Culture*. London, UK: Sage, pp59–77.

16 Gunter, B. (2002) *Media Sex: What Are the Issues?* Mahwah, NJ: Lawrence Erlbaum Associates.

17 Rush, F. (1980) *The Best Kept Secret: Sexual Abuse of Children*. New York, NY: McGraw-Hill; Bray, A. (2008) 'The question of intolerance', *Australian Feminist Studies*, 23(57), 323–341; Gill, R. (2008) 'Empowerment sexism: Figuring female sexual agency in contemporary advertising', *Feminism and Psychology*, 18(1), 35–60.

18 Levin, D. and Kilbourne, J. (2008) *So Sexy So Soon: The New Sexualized Childhood and What Parents Can Do to Protect Their Kids*. New York, NY: Ballantine; Papadopoulos, L. (2010) *Sexualization of Young People*. London, UK: Home Office.

19 Durham, M. G. (2008) *The Lolita Effect: The Media Sexualization of Young Girls and What You Can Do About It*. New York, NY: Overlook; Lamb, S. and Brown, L. M. (2006) *Packaging Girlhood: Rescuing Our Daughters from Marketers' Schemes*. New York, NY: St Martin's Press; Levin, D. and Kilbourne, J. (2008) *ibid*.

20 Levin, D. and Kilbourne, J. (2008) *ibid*.

21 Warren, L. (2011) 'Childhood in danger from sex culture, warn parents', *Daily Mail*, 11 April, p26.

22 American Psychological Association (2007) *Report of the APA Task Force on the Sexualization of Girls*. Washington, DC: American Psychological Association; Australian Senate (2007) *Inquiry into the Sexualization of Children in the Contemporary Media Environment*, http://www.aph.gov.au/Senate/committee/eca_ctte/sexualisaiton_of_children, accessed 14 November 2012.

23 Tozer, J. and Horne, M. (2011) 'Cocktail parties in stretch limos, catwalk shows and fake tattoos – the disturbing sexualization of little girls revealed', *Daily Mail*, 26 February, pp40–41; Witheridge, A. (2012) 'The toddler whose mother gives her a fake tan every month', *Daily Mail*, 16 June, pp32–33.

24 Buckingham et al (2010) *op. cit*.

25 Phoenix, A. (2011) 'Review of recent literature for the Bailey Review of commercialisation and sexualization of childhood', January, Childhood Wellbeing Research Centre.

26 Frost, L. (2001) *Young Women and the Body: A Feminist Sociology*. London, UK: Palgrave; Hayward, K. and Yar, M. (2006) 'The "chav" phenomenon: Consumption, media and the constitution of a new underclass', *Crime, Media, Culture*, 2(1), 9–28; Dittmar, H., Halliwell, E. and Ive, S. (2006) 'Does Barbie make girls want to be thin? The effect of experimental exposure to images of dolls on the body image of 5- to 8-year-old girls', *Developmental Psychology*, 42(2), 283–292.

27 Leake, J. and Grimston, J. (2012) 'Look harder, you'll see she's a woman', *The Sunday Times*, 20 May, p12.

28 Bernard, P., Gervais, S. J., Allen, J., Campornnizzi, S. and Klein, O. (2012) 'Integrating sexual objectification with object versus person recognition', *Psychological Science*, 3 April, DOI:10.1177/0956797611434748.

29 Smith, N. (2012) 'Aggrimbos inflame India', *The Sunday Times*, 6 May, p22.

30 Gunter, B. (1995) *Television and Gender Representation*. London, UK: John Libbey; Wykes, M. and Gunter, B. (2005) *The Media and Body Image*. London, UK: Sage; Grogan, S. (1999) *Body Image: Understanding Body Dissatisfaction in Men, Women and Children*. London, UK: Routledge.

31 Gunter, B. (2002) *Media Sex: What Are the Issues?* Mahwah, NJ: Lawrence Erlbaum Associates.

32 Grabe, S., Ward, L. M. and Hyde, J. S. (2008) 'The role of the media in body image concerns among women: A meta-analysis of experimental and correlational studies', *Psychological Bulletin*, 134, 460476.

33 Halliwell, E., Malson, H. and Tischner, I. (2011) 'The effects of contemporary framings of women in advertising on weight-concern and self0objectification', *Psychology of Women Quarterly*, 35, 38–45.

34 Frederickson, B. L. and Roberts, T. A. (1997) 'Objectification theory: Toward understanding women's lived experiences and mental health risks', *Psychology of Women Quarterly*, 21, 173–206.

35 Gunter, B. and Furnham, A. (1998) *Children as Consumers: A Psychological Analysis of the Young People's Market*. London, UK: Routledge; Gunter, B., Oates, C. and Blades, M. (2005) *Advertising to Children on TV: Content, Impact and Regulation*. Mahwah, NJ: Lawrence Erlbaum Associates.

36 Furnham, A. and Argyle, M. (1997) *The Psychology of Money*. London, UK: Routledge; Gunter, B. and Furnham, A. (1998) *op. cit.*

37 Martens, L., Southerton, D. and Scott, S. (2004) 'Bringing children (and parents) into the sociology of consumption: Towards a theoretical and empirical agenda', *Journal of Consumer Culture*, 4(2), 155–182; Boden, S., Pole, C., Pilcher, J. and Edwards, T. (2005) 'New consumers: Children, fashion and consumption', *Sociology Review*, 15(1), 28–32.

38 Buckingham, D., Willett, R., Bragg, S. and Russell, R. (2010) *Sexualized Goods Aimed at Children: A Report to the Scottish Parliament Equal Opportunities Committee*. Edinburgh, Scotland: Scottish Parliament Equal Opportunities Committee.

39 Brooks, K. (2008) *Consuming Innocence: Popular Culture and Our Children*. Queensland, Australia: University of Queensland Press; Edwards, T. (2011) *Fashion in Focus: Concepts, Practises, Politics*. London, UK: Routledge.

40 Arnett, J. J. (2000) 'Emerging adulthood: A theory of development from the late teens through the twenties', *American Psychologist*, 55, 469–480.

41 Cook, D. T. and Kaiser, S. B. (2004) 'Betwixt and between: Age ambiguity and the sexualization of the female consuming subject', *Journal of Consumer Culture*, 4, 203–227.

42 American Psychological Association (2007) *Report of the APA Task Force on the Sexualization of Girls*. Washington, DC: APA, www.apa.org/pi/wpo/sexualization.html; Commonwealth of Australia (2008) *Standing Committee on Environment, Communications and the Arts: Sexualization of Children in the Contemporary Media*, June. Parliament House, Canberra: Senate Printing Unit, www.aph.gov.au/senate/committee/eca_ctte/index.htm.

43 Buckingham, D., Willetts, R., Bragg, S. and Russell, R. (2010) *op. cit.*

44 American Psychological Association (2007) *op. cit.*

45 Buckingham, D., Willetts, R., Bragg, S. and Russell, R. (2010) *op. cit.*

46 Commonwealth Parliament, Senate Standing Committee on Environment, Communication and the Arts (2008) *Inquiry into Sexualization of Children in the Contemporary Media*, 1.25.

47 Commonwealth Parliament, Senate Standing Committee on Environment, Communication and the Arts (2008) *ibid*, 1.28.

48 Commonwealth Parliament, Senate Legal and Constitutional Affairs References Committee (2011) *Review of the National Classification Scheme: Achieving the Right Balance*, June, www.aph.gov.au/Senate/committee/legcon_ctte/classification_board/report/index.htm, accessed 20 December 2012.

49 Papadopoulos, L. (2010) *Sexualization of Young People*. London, UK: Home Office.

50 Home Office (2010) *Together We Can End Violence Against Women and Girls: A Strategy*. London, UK: HM Government.

51 Kempsell, R. and Bailey, R. (2010) *Bye Buy Childhood: A Report into the Commercialisation of Childhood*. London, UK: Mothers' Union, www.muenterprises.org/wp-content/themes/byebuymu/files/bye-buy-childhood-report, accessed 30 March 2013; Bailey, R. (2011) *Letting Children Be Children: Report of an Independent Review of the Commercialisation and Sexualization of Childhood*. London, UK: Department of Education and HMSO Stationery Office.

52 Phoenix, A. (2011) *op. cit.*

53 Scottish Parliament, Equal Opportunities Committee (2010) *External Research on Sexualized Goods Aimed at Children*. Edinburgh, Scotland, SP paper 374.

54 Bussey, K. and Bandura, A. (1984) 'Influence of gender constancy and social power on sex linked modelling', *Journal of Personality and Social Psychology*, 47, 1292–1302; Bussey, K. and Bandura, A. (1992) 'Self-regulatory mechanisms governing gender development', *Child Development*, 63, 1236–1250.

55 Palmer, S. (2010) *21st Century Boys: How Modern Life Is Driving Them off the Rails and How We Can Get Them Back on Track*. London, UK: Orion.

56 Walkerdine, V. (1997) *Daddy's Girl*. Cambridge, MA: Harvard University Press; Lamb, S. and Brown, L. M. (2006) *Packaging Girlhood*. New York, NY: St Martin's Press; Gill, R. (2008) *op. cit.*

57 BBC News (2007) 'Young "hung up on their bodies"', 20 February, http://www.news.bbc.co.uk/1/health/6376367.stm, accessed 23 March 2009.
58 Blake, H. (2010) 'Superficial society makes children unhappier about appearance than anything else', 27 January, http://www.telegraph.co.uk/health/children_shealth/7078935, accessed 28 January 2010.
59 PRNewswire (2012) 'New research shows 81% of teens are happy', March, www.prnewswire.com/news-release/new-research-shows-81-of-teens-are-happy-57121087.
60 Wykes, M. and Gunter, B. (2005) *The Media & Body Image*. London, UK: Sage.
61 Travis, A. (2009) 'Jacqui Smith to tackle "sexualisation" culture', Guardian.co.uk., 9 March, http://www.guardian.co.uk/society/2009/mar/09/jacqui-smoth-sexualisatiin-teenagers, accessed 23 March 2009.
62 Collins, W. A. and Sroufe, L. A. (1999) 'Capacity for intimate relationships: A developmental construction', in W. Ferman, B. B. Brown and C. Feiring. (Eds.) *The Development of Romantic Relationships in Adolescence*, pp125–147. Cambridge, UK: Cambridge University Press; Tolman, D. L. (2002) *Dilemmas of Desire: Teenage Girls Talk about Sexuality*. Cambridge, MA: Harvard University Press.
63 Clark, J. (2013) 'Passive, heterosexual and female: Constructing appropriate childhoods in the "Sexualization of Childhood" debate', *Sociological Research Online*, 18(2), 13, www.socresonline.org.uk/18/2/13, accessed 29 October 2013.
64 Rush, E. and La Nauze, A. (2006) 'Corporate paedophilia: Sexualization of children in Australia', Discussion Paper No 90, Australia Institute, www.tai.org.au/documents/dp_fulltext/DP90.pdf.
65 American Psychological Association (2007) *op. cit*; Papadopoulos, L. (2010) *op. cit*; Standing Committee on Environment, Communications and the Arts (2008) *op. cit*; Bailey, R. (2011) *op. cit*; Buckingham, D. et al (2010) *op. cit*.
66 Thorne, B. (1993) *Gender Play: Boys and Girls in School*. Buckingham, UK: Open University Press; Walkerdine, V. (1997) *Daddy's Girl: Young Girls and Popular Culture*. London, UK: Verso; Renold, E. (2005) *Girls, Boys and Junior Sexualities*. London, UK: Routledge; Egan, D. and Hawkes, G. (2010) *Theorizing the Sexual Child in Modernity*. New York, NY: Palgrave Macmillan.
67 Walkerdine, V. (1999) 'Violent boys and precocious girls: Regulating childhood at the end of the millennium', *Contemporary Issues in Early Childhood*, 1(1), 3–23.
68 Driscoll, C. (2002) *Girls: Feminine Adolescence in Popular Culture and Cultural Theory*. New York, NY: Columbia University Press; Attwood, F. and Smith, C. (2011) 'Lamenting sexualization: Research, rhetoric and the story of young people's "sexualisation"', in UK Home Office Review, Special Issue: Investigating Young People's Sexual Cultures, *Sex Education*, 11(3), 327–337; Gill, R. (2009) 'Beyond the "sexualization of culture" thesis: An intersectional analysis of "six packs", "midriffs" and "hot lesbians" in advertising', *Sexualities*, 12(2), 137–160.
69 Holland, J. and Thomson, R. (2010) 'Revisiting youthful sexuality: Continuities and changes over two decades', *Sexual and Relationship Therapy*, 25(3), 342–350; Thomson, K. (2010) 'Because looks can be deceiving: Media alarm and the sexualization of childhood – Do we know what we mean?', *Journal of Gender Studies*, 19(4), 395–400.
70 Coy, M. (2009) 'Milkshakes, Lady Lumps and growing up to wait boobies: How sexualization of popular culture limits girls' horizons', *Child Abuse Review*, 18(6), 372–383; Lerum, K. and Dworkin, S. (2009) '"Bad girls rule": An interdisciplinary feminist commentary on the Report of the APA Task Force on Sexualization of Girls', *Journal of Sex Research*, 46(4), 250–263.
71 Renold, E. and Ringrose, J. (2011) 'Schizoid subjectivities: re-theorising teen girls' sexual cultures in an era of sexualization', *Journal of Sociology*, 47(4), 389–409.
72 Bem, S. L. (1981) 'Gender schema theory: A cognitive account of sex typing source', *Psychological Review*, 88(4), 354–364.
73 Bussey, K. and Bandura, A. (1999) 'Social cognitive theory of gender development and differentiation', *Psychological Review*, 106, 676–713.

74 Huesmann, L. R. (1998) 'The role of social information processing and cognitive schema in the acquisition and maintenance of habitual aggressive behaviour', *Human Aggression: Theories, Research and Implications for Social Policy*, 73–109.

75 Gerbner, G., Gross, L., Morgan, M. and Signorielli, N. (1994) 'Growing up with television: The cultivation perspective', in J. Bryant and D. Zillmann (Eds.) *Media Effects: Advances in Theory and Research*, pp17–41. Hillsdale, NJ: Lawrence Erlbaum Associates.

76 Gunter, B. (1995) *Television and Gender Representation*, London, UK: John Libbey; Gunter, B. (2002) *Media Sex: What Are the Issues?* Mahwah, NJ: Lawrence Erlbaum Associates; Gunter, B. and McAleer, J. (1997) *Children and Television*. London, UK: Routledge.

77 Wykes, M. and Gunter, B. (2005) *The Media and Body Image*. London, UK: Sage.

78 Harrison, K. (1997) 'Does interpersonal attraction to thin media personalities promote eating disorders?', *Journal of Broadcasting & Electronic Media*, 41, 478–500; Bartlett, C. P., Vowels, C. L. and Saucier, D.A. (2008) 'Meta-analyses of the effects of media images on men's body-image concerns', *Journal of Social and Clinical Psychology*, 27, 279–310.

79 Harrison, K., (2000) 'Television viewing, fat stereotyping, body shape standards and eating disorder symptomatology in grade school children', *Communication Research*, 27 (5), 617–640; Harrison, K. and Cantor, J. (1997) 'The relationship between media consumption and eating disorders', *Journal of Communication*, 50(3), 119–143.

80 Sapolsky, B. S. and Tabarlet, J. G. (1991) 'Sex in prime time television: 1979 vs 1989', *Journal of Broadcasting and Electronic Media*, 34, 505–516.

81 Grogan, S. (2008) *Body Image: Understanding Body Dissatisfaction in Men, Women and Children*, 2nd edition. London, UK: Routledge; Wykes, M. and Gunter, B. (2005), op. cit.

82 Huston, A. C. and Wright, J. C. (1998) 'Mass media and children's development', in W. Damon, L. E. Sigel & K. A. Renninger (Eds.) *Handbook of Child Psychology: Vol 4. Child Psychology in Practice*, pp999–1058. New York, NY: Wiley.

83 Bussey, K. and Bandura, A. (1992) 'Self-regulatory mechanisms governing gender development', *Child Development*, 63, 1236–1250; Bussey, K. and Bandura, A. (1999) 'Social cognitive theory of gender development and differentiation', *Psychological Review*, 106, 676–713.

84 Frederickson, B. L. and Roberts, T. A. (1997) 'Objectification theory: Toward understanding women's lived experience and mental health risks', *Psychology of Women Quarterly*, 21, 173–206; Frederickson, B. L. and Harrison, K. (2005) 'Throwing like a girl: Self-objectification predicts adolescent girls' motor performance', *Journal of Sport and Social Issues*, 29, 79–101.

85 Frederickson, B. L., Roberts, T., Noll, S. M., Quinn, D. M. and Twenge, J. M. (1998) 'That swimsuit becomes you: Sex differences in self-objectification, restrained eating, and math performance', *Journal of Personality and Social Psychology*, 75, 269–284.

86 See Wykes, M. and Gunter, B. (2005), op. cit.

87 Heinberg, L. J. and Thompson, K. (1992) 'Social comparison: Gender, target importance ratings and relation to body image disturbance', *Journal of Social Behaviour and Personality*, 7, 335–344; Smolak, L., Levine, M. P. and Gralen, S. (1993) 'The impact of puberty and dating on eating problems among middle school girls', *Journal of Youth & Adolescence*, 22, 355–368; Streigel-Moore, R. H., Silverstein, L. R. and Rodin, J. (1986) 'Toward an understanding of risk factors for bulimia', *American Psychologist*, 41, 246–263.

88 Beebe, D. W., Hornbeck, G. N., Schober, A., Lane, M. and Rosa, K. (1996) 'Is body focus restricted to self-evaluation? Body focus in the evaluation of self and others', *International Journal of Eating Disorders*, 20, 415–422.

89 King, N., Touyz, C. and Charles, M. (2000) 'The effects of body dissatisfaction on women's perceptions of female celebrities', *International Journal of Eating Disorders*, 27(3), 341–347.

90 Thompson, J. K. (1990) *Body Image Disturbance: Assessment and Treatment*. Elmsford, NY: Pergamon Press.

91 Forston, M. T. and Stanton, A. L. (1992) 'Self-discrepancy theory as a framework for understanding bulimic symptomatology and associated distress', *Journal of Social and Clinical Psychology*, 11, 103–118; Strauman, T. J., Vookles, J., Berenstein, V., Chaiken, S. and Higgins, E. T. (1991) 'Self-discrepancies and vulnerability to body dissatisfaction and disordered eating', *Journal of Personality and Social Psychology*, 61, 946–956.

92 Bessenoff, G. R. (2006) 'Can the media affect us? Social comparison, self-discrepancies and the thin ideal', *Psychology of Women Quarterly*, 30, 239–251; Dittmar, H. and Halliwell, E. (2008) 'Think "ideal" and feel bad? Using self-discrepancies to understand negative media effects', in H. Dittma (Ed.) *Consumer Culture, Identity and Well-Being: The Search for the 'Good Life' and the 'Body Perfect'*, pp147–172. Hove, UK: Psychology Press.

93 Dittmar, H. and Halliwell, E. (2008), *ibid.*

94 Blond, A. (2008) 'Impacts of exposure to images of ideal bodies on male body dissatisfaction: A review', *Body Image*, 5, 244–250; Dittmar, H. and Howard, S. (2004) 'Thin-ideal internalization and social comparison tendency as moderators of media models' impact on women's body-focused anxiety', *Journal of Social and Clinical Psychology*, 23(6), 768–791.

95 Mansey, K. (2012) '"Fat" athletes pushed towards anorexia', *The Sunday Times*, 27 May, p11.

96 Grabe, S., Ward, L. M. and Hyde, J. S. (2008) 'The role of the media in body image concerns among women: A meta-analysis of experimental and correlational studies', *Psychological Bulletin*, 134(3), 460–476.

97 BBC News (2003) 'Teens going "under the knife"', 21 November, http://www.bbc.co.uk/1/hi/magazine/3227396.stm, accessed 28 January 2010.

98 BBC News (2004) 'Third of teens want cosmetic ops', 26 August, http://news.bbc.co.uk/1/hi/health/3601200.stm, accessed 28 January 2010.

99 National Research Center for Women and Families (2010) *Women's Health: Teens and Breast Implants*, http://www.center4research.org/teenimplants.html, accessed 28 January 2010.

100 Staiger, P., Kambouropoulos, N., Evertsz, J., Mitchell, J. and Tucci, J. (2005) *A Preliminary Evaluation of the Transformers Program for Children Who Engage in Problem Sexual Behaviour*. Australia: Australian Childhood Foundation and Deakin University.

101 Tucci, J. and Goddard, C. (2008) *Joint Submission to the Senate Inquiry into the Sexualization of Children in the Contemporary Media Environment*.

102 Bailey, R. (2011) *Letting Children Be Children*. London: Department for Education.

103 Brown, J. D., L'Engle, K. L., Pardun, C. J., Guo, G., Kenneavy, K. and Jackson, C. (2006) 'Sexy media matter: Exposure to sexual content in music, movies, television and magazine predicts black and who adolescents' sexual behaviour', *Pediatrics*, 117, 1018–1027.

104 Family Lives (2012) *All of Our Concern: Commercialisation, Sexualization and Hypermasculinity*, June, www.TeenBoundaries.co.uk.

105 Buckingham, D. (2011) *The Impact of the Commercial World on Children's Wellbeing: Report of an Independent Assessment*. Department for Children, Schools and Families and the Department for Culture, Media and Sport.

106 American Psychological Association (2007) *Report of the APA Task Force on the Sexualization of Girls*. Washington, DC: APA; Rush, E. and La Nauze, A. (2006) *A Corporate Paedophilia: Sexualization of Children in Australia*. Canberra, Australia: The Australia Institute.

107 Buckingham, D. and Bragg, S. (2004) *Young People, Sex and the Media: The Facts of Life?* London: Palgrave.

108 Steele, J. R. (1999) 'Teenage sexuality and media practice: Factoring in the influences of family, friends and school'. *Journal of Sex Research*, 36(4), 331–341.

109 Collins, R. L., Elliott, M., Berry, S., Kanouse, D. E. and Hunter, S. (2003) 'Entertainment television as a healthy sex-educator: the impact of condom-efficacy information in an episode of *Friends*', *Pediatrics*, 112, 1115–1121; Collins, R. L., Elliott, M., Berry, S., Kanouse, D. E., Kunkel, D., Hunter, S. et al (2004). 'Watching sex on television predicts adolescent initiation of sexual behaviour'. *Pediatrics*, 114(3), 280–289.

110 Brown, J. D., L'Engle, K. L., Pardun, C.J., Guo, G., Kenneavy, K. and Jackson, C. (2006) 'Sexy media matter: Exposure to sexual content in music, movies, television and magazines predicts black and white adolescents' sexual behaviour', *Pediatrics*, 117(4), 1018–1027.

111 Kimmel, M. (1996) *Manhood in America*. New York, NY: The Free Press; Kindlon, D. and Thompson, M. (1999) *Raising Cain: Protecting the Emotional Life of Boys*. New York, NY: Balantine Books; Pollack, W. (1998) *R Teal Boys: Rescuing Our Sons from the Myths of Boyhood*. New York, NY: Random House.

112 Tolman, D. L. (2002) *Dilemmas of Desire: Teenage Girls Talk about Sexuality*. Cambridge, MA: Harvard University Press.

113 Lippert, B. (2005) 'From sexy to sleazy', *Adweek*, 1 March, 8–10.

114 McNair, B. (2002) *Striptease Culture – Sex, Media and the Democratisation of Desire*. London, UK: Routledge.

115 Brooks, G. (1995) *The Centerfold Syndrome: How Men Can Overcome Objectification and Achieve Intimacy with Women*. San Francisco, CA: Jossey-Bass.

116 Kinnick, K. (2007) 'Pushing the envelope: The role of the mass media in the mainstreaming of pornography', in A. C. Hall and M. J. Bishop (Eds.) *Pop-Porn: Pornography in American Culture*. Westport, CT: Praeger.

2

FASHION AND SEXUALIZATION

The sexualization of childhood can start early and this often happens in terms of the way in which children dress and present themselves to the world. Clothing products that are targeted at children, and increasingly at pre-teenage girls, use adult-oriented marketing strategies and promotional claims to attract young consumers. In February 2007, a catalogue for children's clothes published by No Added Sugar was criticized by the UK's Advertising Standards Authority (ASA) for showing images featuring a young girl in sexually suggestive poses. Two images respectively displayed a pre-teenage girl on all fours on a chest of drawers and lying down in the back seat of a car. Another image of a young boy in low-slung jeans pushing a car was also criticized for containing sexualizing connotations. The firm was instructed to desist from using these images.[1]

Adults around children can also become role players in the sexualization conditioning process. Parents can encourage their children, particularly girls, to attach social status to being physically attractive. Some parents engage in this behaviour by encouraging their children to enter beauty contests; at the extreme, others even pay for their children to have cosmetic plastic surgery.

Among girls, as they approach their teens, pressures arise from within their peer group to adopt adult-like standards of attractiveness. Girls encourage each other to wear clothes more appropriate for young adult women and to accentuate their sexual appeal through the application of make-up. In a sense, they engage in self-objectification activities in defining their identities primarily in terms of the way they look.[2] If girls are continually bombarded with products that are backed up by pervasive marketing and media messages about 'being sexy', there is a risk that their self-identity will become prematurely dominated by the belief that this is the only thing that matters in life. More than that, the objectification of sex and of female sexuality will mean that sexual activity is seen as little more than another commodity to be traded for superficial pleasures, rather than as a level of intimacy between partners with a deep emotional attachment and long-term commitment to each other.[3]

It is not unusual for girls to think of themselves in sexually objectified ways. In fact, debate about the societal implications of young girls being in a hurry to adopt a more adult outer appearance can be traced back at least 50 years. *Life* magazine published an article entitled 'Boys and Girls: Too Old Too Soon' on 10 August 1962 (pp58–65) that bemoaned the trend of girls as young as 11 and 12 wearing make-up and making out with boys on their bedroom floors.[4] Research evidence has long confirmed that girls sometimes do treat their own bodies as objects which they can dress up to attract attention. If this behaviour is successful in gaining them the attention and social feedback – often in the form of reassurances about their attractiveness or sexiness – they can internalize self-perceptions through which they think of themselves more as objects than as people.[5]

The emergence of the pre-teen market as a distinct consumer category – and one that at its older end has an ambiguous sexual identity – has been traced back to the clothing industry in the 1930s and 1940s. Observations were made during this period that standard children's sizes were not always big enough for children in the 11- to 13-age bracket, nor had they yet reached the more adult proportions more prevalent among teenagers aged 14 and above. This meant that there was a distinctive market for these 'sub-teens' or 'pre-teens' as they were labelled by the clothing trade between the 1940s and 1970s, or 'tweens' as they came to be known later.[6]

The tendency of the 'tween' market to identify more with older age groups than with the younger ones they had left behind, combined with signs of early physical maturity, particularly among girl tweens, facilitated a downward trickle of clothing design features that embraced adult qualities that included features that might be considered to be sexualized.[7] Female tweens were discovered to display a sexualization ambiguity that had less to do with finding a sexual orientation than with deciding whether they were sexual or non-sexual as individuals.

As Daniel Cook of the University of Illinois and his colleague Susan Kaiser of the University of California Davis have noted, interviews with girls aged 13 to 15 years indicated that they admittedly switch identities on some occasions, dressing to look older, on others dressing to look younger or to look their age, as they see it at the time.[8] This identity ambiguity was recorded much earlier in media advice columns in which mothers reported how their teenage daughters wanted to wear adult clothes and make-up even as 'tweens', but how mothers would usually negotiate a delay in approving of this until their girls were in the mid-teens.[9]

Some feminist theorists have described the sexualization of girls, particularly through fashion, as a response by male-dominated media and marketing industries to the emergent emancipation of women and their rise to prominence in fields such as business and politics. The cultivation of a preoccupation with physical appearance and sexual attractiveness among girls represents a ploy to induce ambiguous feelings in women about their identity and choice of life roles.[10] Counter-feminist arguments have emerged that girls and women are not that easily duped by male marketing campaigns and that their decision to wear sexually revealing clothes stems from a need to demonstrate their independence and self-confidence in their own sexual identity.[11] A different perspective again has challenged the 'girl power' notion of girls choosing to be sexy in what they wear if they want to and not because they are conditioned into doing so by men and positioned these fashion choices as outcomes of commercial marketing of 'sex' as a fashionable brand attribute. Girls' fashion and associated beauty product choices have less to do with exercising their independence of thought than they are a response to consumer trends.[12]

The pre-teen beauty industry

One growing phenomenon that has been regarded as a source of sexualization is the involvement of very young children in adult-style pageants. A beauty industry has emerged that aims its commodities at primary school-age children. Marketing campaigns encourage young girls to have facials and manicures. They tempt them with facial and body cosmetics, including temporary tattoos. Young children and their parents are encouraged to get involved in parties at which these products are openly demonstrated and marketed, and to take part in fashion competitions and beauty pageants that involve making up pre-teenage girls to look far older than their years and to accentuate sexual features.[13]

In June 2012, Savanna Jackson from Michigan, US, was depicted with blond hair perfectly coiffed, wearing lip gloss and eyeliner, wearing a frilly pink top and bottom, bare mid-riffed, hands on hips in a pose which for an adult female would be classed as sexually alluring. She was an almost exact human replica of the pictured Barbie doll next to her.[14] Savanna was just three years old. We also learn that Savanna's mother, Lauren, frequently paid for her daughter to be fake-tanned for child beauty pageants.

Child beauty pageants have been popular in the United States for a long time and recently they have also begun to spread to other countries. American TV shows such as *Toddlers and Tiaras* have popularized them more than ever, and the UK held its first pageant for very young children in May 2012 for the prize of Mini Miss Princess UK.

As a leading UK newspaper reported, one contestant, Lexci Turner, was entered aged just three by her mother Emma (age 21) in the inaugural UK competition. The same event included further contests for entrants under one year (Baby Princess) and others aged over one (Tiny Princess). A Little Princess category took entries from children aged two and three years. According to Emma Turner, there was nothing to worry about with these competitions even though children under five were paraded in high heels, skimpy clothes and make-up: 'Little girls wear bikinis on the beach every day, so I don't see what the difference is between that and a sparkly two-piece for a pageant. Lexci often tries on my shoes, so hopefully she'll be able to manage in heels.'[15]

Another mother, Michelle Naylor (42), saw entry into the Miss Princess UK competition for her nine-year-old daughter Jade as the first step towards a modelling career. Jade herself had apparently said she 'might want to be a topless glamour model when she's older' (p39). She was already a veteran of childhood modelling, having appeared in billboard advertisements for clothing companies.

In these child beauty competitions, girls under six parade in high heels on catwalks in front of admiring audiences. For the serious and more successful competitors – and their mothers – it becomes a business in which they acquire an entourage of make-up artists, hair stylists and talent coaches who rival those of the best-known adult catwalk models. Their mothers will argue that there is no harm in these pageants and that they can instil self-confidence in girls from an early age.

The mother of the four-year-old winner of the Miss Glitz Sparkle pageant held in 2012 in the small provincial city of Lincoln in the UK claimed that participating had been 'confidence building and [a showcase] for her beauty'. It was her follow-up remark, however, that was perhaps more revealing. 'People take it far too seriously – it's just a bit of fun. She [her daughter] wasn't wearing false eyelashes or false nails or fake tan or hair extensions, like some of the other girls. I was so proud of her. And she was proud of herself.'[16] The tell-tale remark here was 'like some of the other girls', who clearly were wearing all kinds of physical enhancements normally associated with adults and usually linked to enhancement of physical (and sexual) attractiveness.

In a further comment in response to the criticism that such events are prematurely introducing very young children to sexual themes, the same young mother retorted: 'The idea of sexualization does not cross anyone's mind in that room.' She then related the fact that her daughter had worn a one-piece sailor costume and full make-up for a dance show and this was not a problem because wearing stage make-up is quite usual for performers. The question is whether this is a relevant comparison and defence for what happens in a quite different setting such as a beauty pageant where children are not being judged for their performance abilities but for their appearance. What also undermined this mother's defence was a large photograph of her daughter which dominated the article in which she was depicted in a one-piece pink bathing costume, with trendy sun-glasses, apparently wearing lipstick and walking with her hand on her hip.[17] Critics will argue that these competitions place too much emphasis on an idealized standard of beauty and focus the attention of very young girls far too early on their physical attributes – some of which are deliberately exaggerated in ways that are inappropriate for ones so young.

Beauty pageants are not restricted to girls. Equivalent competitions have emerged for boys aged 4 to 12, with titles such as Mr English Beauty. Once again, an emphasis is placed on being valued in terms of specific standards of appearance and attractiveness. Here boys who have barely started school wear fake tan, expensively styled haircuts, tuxedos and even false eyelashes or teeth.[18]

Do beauty pageants for children have any short-term or lasting psychological effects? One study of this issue conducted extensive tests with a number of women who had participated in beauty pageants as children and compared them with similar women who had not taken part in these kinds of contests. It emerged that the women who had been regular beauty pageant contestants displayed greater dissatisfaction with their bodies as adults and were more inclined to distrust other people and to be more impulsive. Childhood beauty pageant participants did not exhibit any other self-esteem problems or greater proneness to depression when compared with similar women who had not been entered in these competitions when younger.[19]

The 'Honey Boo Boo' phenomenon

As a contrast with the middle-class infant beauty pageant queens that have caused so much debate about childhood sexualization, an even more controversial working-class infant icon emerged in the United States via a television reality show in the shape of six-year-old Alana 'Honey Boo Boo' Thompson. She and her family live in a shack in rural Georgia. Alana and her overweight mother June Shannon acquired celebrity status through the TLC cable channel's series *Here Comes Honey Boo Boo*. They had both previously appeared on the widely criticized reality series about child beauty pageants called *Toddlers and Tiaras*. Despite early criticisms of the show, audiences and TV critics gradually warmed to the fact that June was a hands-on mother and that Alana and her older sisters Anna (17), Jessica (15) and Lauryn (12) all got along with each other and laughed a lot. Despite their lack of education, unhealthy diet and obesity, the family displayed no pretensions and the show avoided the temptation succumbed to by other reality series of excessive scripting interference from the producers. In some ways, therefore, despite the context of her introduction to celebrity status, Honey Boo Boo's subsequent TV career presented an antidote to the commercialized sexualization themes that have become so ubiquitous.[20]

Fashion and the projection of sex appeal

Girls are encouraged to express their individual identity through what they wear. There may be nothing intrinsically wrong with this because identity definition is part of growing up and clothing has for a long time played an important part in this process. Problems arise when girls are enticed into adopting inappropriate identities *per se* or identities that they are not yet mature enough to cope with. Clothing fashions may encourage teenage girls to show off their rapidly developing figures. This trend may be acceptable to a point, but designers sometimes push the boundaries to extremes. More serious problems can occur if these fashion trends spread to pre-teenage girls and in the process place an emphasis on self-worth determined by outward appearance. Further, if clothes, cosmetics and accessories are targeted at very young girls, there may result an inappropriate focus on feminine beauty based on sexuality. The growing prevalence and popularity of beauty pageants for pre-teenage girls and even for infants has further underlined a trend that is manifest in little girls being presented made-up in ways that would normally be associated with fully developed women.

Sexy clothing for children is not hard to find. The children's departments in many leading retail stores contain clothes for children that would be seen as designed primarily to enhance sexual attributes if adult versions were worn by grown women. Lingerie lines are targeted at under-sevens. Thongs and other clothing items worn by strippers have been aimed at 'tweens' (8s to 12s).[21] In the United States, even Halloween costume manufacturers got in on the act. Costume ranges aimed at girls played on creating an attractive and sexualized physical appearance underlined by brand names such as 'Sexy Devil'.[22]

Elsewhere girls aged between six and ten years were depicted in the *New York Times Magazine* dressed in adult-styled clothes, with mature hair styles and sexy poses. At the turn of the century, clothing merchandise with sexualized themes was already being marketed to girls as young as six that included G-strings, padded bras, shorts with handprints on the back, and T-shirts with slogans such as 'wink wink' and 'eye candy'.[23] Some social commentators questioned: although these sexually themed garments may be seen as appropriate for adult consumers, should pre-teenage children be introduced to such themes? Of course, these fashions might all be harmless fun for children, but do they run a risk of drawing to young children undue attention from adults who would prey under-age youngsters for sexual ends?[24]

The same points have been made in regard to sexualized fashions aimed at teenagers. Stripper-inspired merchandise for teenage girls has been popular for some time. Adolescents have embraced these products as fun and also regard them as a light hearted way to express themselves sexually as they reach a stage of sexual maturity. Potential problems lie in the nature of the clothing that not only draws attention to the sexual attributes of physically developing teenage girls, but encourages them to project a sexual identity to others in ways that might put them at risk.[25]

In the UK, actress and model Liz Hurley was roundly criticized for sexualizing young girls with her range of bikini products targeted at youngsters aged up to 13 years. The product line included the 'Mini Cha Cha Bikini' aimed at under eights and the 'Collette Bikini' targeted at girls slightly older. The website promoting these products contained photographs of child models wearing these products, including a very young child demonstrating the leopard skin Mini Cha Cha Bikini standing with hands on hips and smiling into the camera.[26]

Intriguingly, while clothing aimed at pre-teen girls may be printed with adult slogans such as 'eye candy', the same kinds of products targeted at young women often contain child-like cartoon images and referents. Thus, the association of sexualized items with children occurs not only among merchandise being sold to children, but also on that aimed at adults.

It was noted earlier in this chapter that there are explicitly sexualized clothes targeted at children. Adult styles of clothing, including underwear, high heel shoes and clothes that accentuate a womanly appearance even in girls as young as five, have been sold widely in developed countries.[27] The sexualized nature of these items is further accentuated by the materials that are used, which include fur, leather and rubber. Some items, such as lacy bras and pants and G-strings, are not just modelled on adult garments but are closely associated with the sex industry.[28] Sexualized clothes have been manufactured for boys as well as girls and tend further to reinforce the sexuality of each gender by drawing attention to the sexual differences between them.[29]

Emma Rush and Andrea La Nauze of the Australia Institute made the following observations about the potential sexualization influences of children's clothing fashions:

> Clothing that emphasises specific parts of the body, often at the expense of inhibiting movement or comfort, can have a sexualising effect. For girls, examples include: bolero crossover tops and low necklines, both designed to emphasise the breasts of adult women; 'crop tops' which draw attention to the waist and navel area; dangling jewellery from necks, ears or wrists, dangling belts from the hips or waist, and rings on the fingers, again designed to attract attention to sexually differentiated features of adult women, and some styles of dress or skirt, most particularly very short skirts, and dresses held up by thin straps. For boys, examples include suit jackets designed to emphasise the shoulders of adult men (p7).[30]

The fashion industry has always used child models to promote clothing and linked accessories targeted at children. The sector has also used more young models and portrays young girls, in particular, with more adult-like facial expression and poses.[31] Risks posed by using more sexualized images of pre-teenage girls include the triggers they can provide to paedophiles who use not only child pornography, but also catalogue images of young girls for sexual gratification. The sexualization of girls in advertisements can be used by paedophiles to justify their own sexual thoughts about them.[32]

Sexually attractive models are used to promote women's and men's products. With women's products, their usual aim is to create benchmarks in terms of appearance or success that are associated with the advertised brands. With men's products, they are used either to demonstrate the probability of enhanced sexual success associated with the brand or simply to attract initial visual attention to the brand. The image of a nude woman may not convey useful information about the premium value linked to a brand of car, but male consumers otherwise not in the market for a vehicle nevertheless turn their attention to the ad to ogle at the girl.

The use of children in sexually alluring poses has been criticized as socially irresponsible. Frequently, pre-teenage models are depicted in clothing catalogues and in clothing advertisements in mainstream magazines for this age group in poses typically adopted by adult female models. In the case of girls, these poses include the frontal pose with head slightly tilted to one side, the over the shoulder pose with a coy glance at the camera, and the downcast eyes pose that draw attention to the model's body. Pre-teenage boy models adopt the more dominant and self-confident poses that characterize adult male models with legs apart, thumbs in pockets and fingers outside pointing toward the genital area.[33] It is seen as wrong to be drawing children's attention to sexual matters before they have had the opportunity to live their lives as children and to pass through earlier stages of cognitive, emotional and physical development. It also blurs the distinction between children and adults, which could play into the hands of adults who might wish to groom children for sexual purposes.[34]

As well as clothing brands, cosmetic products have long been targeted at teenage girls but are now also increasingly aimed at the pre-teens market. For women, cosmetics represent a core part of their arsenal in making themselves look more sexually appealing. This market has been getting younger and younger. Spa kits are sold for pre-teen girls to hold spa parties in which they experiment with different kinds of cosmetic makeovers. Flavoured lip glosses and eye make-up are sold to pre-teens. Initially, the cosmetics industry introduced itself to children via toy cosmetics sets; but subsequently, cosmetics have been sold to girls in the same way as they are targeted at the adult market.[35] Perfume products are also increasingly aimed at this younger female market. Well-known names such as Givenchy and Dior have targeted this age group with extensions of their major brands. Girls from age 12 have been found to report using fragrances at least several times a week.[36]

The risks for children and teens of excessive 'sexing up' of clothing fashions is that clothes could play an important part in their wider socialization. When girls as young as five, six or seven (and sometimes even younger than this in beauty pageants) are encouraged to wear clothes or cosmetics that highlight female sexual attractiveness, they are being asked to pretend to be something they are not. While pretend play can be and often is a healthy part of childhood development, this is true so long as it remains within the realms of fantasy. In the clothes they wear in their everyday lives, assuming they are not 'fancy dress' for a party, the pretending is not restricted to a fantasy world.

Wearing 'sexy' for real runs a risk of establishing sets of norms by which girls see themselves and by which others perceive them. It places being sexy centre stage in terms of how best to gain social status and be well regarded by others. It might also socialize boys into seeing and evaluating girls in purely appearance-based and sexual ways, and in later life when girls and boys become grown up and sexually mature this could influence their attitudes towards each other and how they treat each other in close personal relationships. The other risk of sexualizing pre-teenage girls is that it might encourage them to seek sexual activity prematurely or to encourage boys and men to seek to engage with them in a sexual way before they are ready and when such behaviour is deemed illegal by society.

Anecdotal evidence has emerged that mothers have voiced growing concern over their pre-teenage and teenager daughters' clothing choices. Some mothers have observed that their daughters have taken to wearing suggestive clothing not just around the house but also in public. When mothers object to this behaviour, their sulky offspring respond by saying that 'everyone is doing it'.[37] Young girls now present themselves voluntarily as sex objects in the belief that it is normal to do so. Teen icons such as Britney Spears and Lindsay Lohan cavort even as adults in little girl outfits that are physically revealing, which combined with a celebrity lifestyle enhances the appeal to teens of this type of fashion package.

Sexualized children's products

There are plentiful observations of fashion products aimed at children that have explicit sexual attributes or that are characterized by more subtle sexualized overtones; but what kinds of products are found in retail outlets that children are known to frequent? This was a question addressed by a study conducted by David Buckingham and his colleagues for the Scottish Parliament in stores in Scotland in 2009.[38] This investigation sought to provide a clear framework for understanding the nature of sexualized goods. It also examined the views of children and parents about these goods. Evidence emerged that children are not automatically or passively taken in by marketers' promotions, including when they are sexualized. They construct their own meanings of brands upon which they reflect before making purchase and consumption commitments.

Buckingham and his colleagues audited 32 retail outlets in city centres in Glasgow, Perth and Inverness in Scotland. The stores they examined included specialist children's shops, general stores with children's departments, and other general stores that made no distinctions between adults' and children's products except for the presence of a school clothing section or displays of children's toys and games.

As well as visiting stores and examining the children's products they had on display, these researchers also spoke to retail industry experts and examined relevant retail websites. They made 38 observational visits to stores. The researchers acknowledged that their analysis of retail outlets in terms of the presence of sexualized goods targeted at children was challenging not least because of the difficulty reaching a clear, concise and inclusive definition of 'sexualization' with which consumers would identify.

They identified five different types of goods that had potentially sexual connotations. These were goods that made references to sexual practices whether through explicit descriptions or more subtle innuendo; goods with attributes that held implicit links to sexual settings (e.g. sexy clothing items); goods that could be applied to different parts of the body and which in adults are designed to accentuate sexual characteristics; high fashion goods described in adult language with sexual implications; and goods that referred to gender stereotypes with sexual overtones. Buckingham and his co-workers found a number of sexualized products aimed at children and these were mostly clothing and cosmetics brands.

Among the most explicit sexualized goods that were identified in specialist children's stores or departments were confectionery such as *Hello Kitty Sexy Little Mints*; *Playboy* branded T-shirts for boys and girls, accompanied by pictures of semi-nude young women in provocative poses; *Money Genes*, low-slung jeans for boys and girls; *'Kylie' leopard skin print boxers* and *'Kylie' sequined boob tube dress*, both targeted at girls aged 9 to 13; *Glitter Butterfly Bikini* for girls aged 9 to 15; *Hannah Montana Bikini* for girls aged 3 to 13; *Glamour Heart Cosmetics Case* for girls from age 4; '*1 Night Stand*' *temporary hair colour, 'Raunchy Red*'; and very short skirts and tight leggings for girls aged 4 to 12 years.

What emerged from this analysis was that some retail stores were instrumental in promoting sexuality as an aspect of children's clothing. This was evidenced not just in terms of products with explicit sexual attributes, but also through adult brand extensions and the positioning of children's products adjacent to sexualized adult products in stores targeting cross-generational markets.

Sexualization potential of clothing

Clothes are important tools for the expression of self-identity. The clothes we wear say a great deal about the type of person we are. Clothes can give off signals about our affluence, and also our taste and fashion sense. Clothes can provide insight into the wearer's personality. They can indicate how self-confident we are or, indeed, how uncertain we are of ourselves.[39] Clothes can also be used to enhance our appearance and attractiveness, particularly in the case of women to display their sexuality. One of the ways in which women can express their sexual allure is through the clothes they put on. Sexualized clothes generally enhance the sexual qualities of their wearer to the extent that they reveal the shape of her body or expose her flesh. Concern has arisen about sexualization of clothes because styles have been developed for pre-teenage girls that are modelled on the fashions designed to show off the sexually mature female form.

The worlds of fashion and marketing have played an important part in creating an environment in which concern about appearance and being responsive to the latest fashion trends is encouraged not only among adult consumers but also among children. Marketers have distinguished a number of child consumer markets. In the field of clothing products, distinctive products have been developed for children and for teenagers. With teenagers, as they reach physical maturity it is understandable that products are marketed that resemble those available to adult markets. The teen market in its attempt to be more grown up has a taste for adult styles, but with a distinctive twist that sets them stylistically apart from adults, and especially from their parents. Teenage girls have reached a stage of consumer awareness at which brand consciousness has usually become firmly established. As with adult women, clothes are critical items through which they define and project a specific self-identity.[40]

By the 1950s, marketers had already begun to distinguish another distinctive consumer category among pre-teenage children.[41] By the 1990s, this age group had become labelled the 'tweens'. Clothing brands were developed for this consumer category that encouraged them to be more like older girls who were reaching sexual maturity. The sexualization messages that were increasingly being used to market clothes to women and teenage girls were also adopted to market clothes aimed at pre-teenage girls.[42]

One of the principal concerns of this marketing development was that the dividing line between sexually innocent childhood and sexually aware adulthood was being blurred. Clothing advertisers played along with this childhood sexualization theme. Pre-teen girls were depicted in sexually knowing poses and wearing clothing styles that were normally used with adult women to draw attention to their sexual attributes. Sexually mature young women were dressed to look like pre-teen girls creating a hybrid girl–woman image.[43]

Systematic analysis of clothes marketed to the female pre-teen market in the United States has indicated that although sexualization themes do not dominate the sector, they are prevalent. Girls' clothes presented on the websites of 15 major national stores were examined and classified in terms of whether they were 'sexualized' in any way. Sexualized clothes were defined as 'clothing that revealed or emphasised a sexualized body part, had characteristics associated with sex, and/or had sexually suggestive writing' (p1).[44]

Sexualized body parts included the chest, waist, buttocks and legs. Thus, any clothing that revealed or drew attention to these body parts was classified as sexualized. Such clothes might include bikini swimwear, short skirts, cropped tops and tight jeans. The material and colours used in the clothing was also an aspect of sexiness, especially if they were associated with sex in equivalent adult clothing (e.g. black lacy underwear). The presence of sexualized words that appeared as prints on garments was another sexualization attribute. Coders were trained to evaluate images of clothes on these websites and to determine whether they were sexualized or not. Four broad categories were defined here: childlike, definitely sexualizing, ambiguously sexualizing, and adult-like.

The results showed that nearly seven out of ten (69 per cent) of 5666 clothing items were coded as having only 'childlike' characteristics. One in four (25 per cent) were judged to have a mix of childlike and sexualizing attributes, and just a small proportion (4 per cent) were classed as having only sexualizing qualities. The most frequently occurring types of definitely sexualized clothes aimed at pre-teen girls were bras (9 per cent) and pants/trousers (9 per cent). Among ambiguously sexualized clothes, the most prevalent were swimsuits (64 per cent) and dresses (52 per cent). From this analysis, while it is apparent that most of the clothes marketed at pre-teens by leading American clothing retailers had childlike qualities, a significant minority of these garments were sexualized. In most cases of sexualized clothing, the sexualization attributes were combined with childlike attributes. This is perhaps the most important finding here. We know that clothes are used to differentiate the genders in adult markets and that in this context women are sexualized far more often than men.[45] The current evidence indicates that this process gets under way during childhood with the direct linkage of 'sex' to 'childhood' in pre-teen clothes marketing and retail presentations.

Sensitivity to sexualized themes in fashion has been observed to emerge long before teen years when girls begin to turn into women. Christine Starr and Gail Ferguson of the Department of Psychology, Knox College, in Illinois conducted an experiment with girls aged between six and nine years in which paper dolls dressed in different styles were evaluated. Two sets of dolls were presented to the girls that were identical in many ways except that one set were defined as 'sexy' and were dressed in skin-tight and revealing clothes such as short skirts, low-cut tops and bare midriffs, while the other set had most of their bodies covered in more modest clothes.

The girls were asked to evaluate the dolls in terms of which set they felt they looked like, which set they would like to look like, which set would be most popular, and which set they would like to play with. Although there was no difference in the extent to which the girls said they felt they looked more like one set of dolls or the other, they were significantly more likely to choose the sexy looking dolls as role models for their own appearance and as being most popular. These differences were weakened if the children attended dance classes, had mothers who talked to them about the things they saw on television (enhanced media literacy) and had mothers who had stronger religious beliefs. It is possible, then, that more involvement in physical activity that possibly enhanced their own body self-esteem, greater media literacy that led to more critical appraisal of commodities, and living in a household in which beliefs systems weakened the value attached to physical appearance could counter the attraction of young girls to sexually themed products aimed at their age group.[46]

Fashion and body image

Another aspect to the sexualization potential of clothing is the attention it may draw to our physical form. As we will see later in this chapter, how we dress can send messages to others about the type of person we are.[47] Sexually provocative clothes send out sexual messages and will be received in this way. Clothing that sends out sexual messages about teenage and pre-teenage children might therefore convey impressions to others that are inappropriate and place the wearers at risk.[48] In addition, clothes make statements about us that we internalize and that play an important part in our developing self-identity as young people.

There is no denying that marketers the world over target children legitimately as potential consumers. Children represent a large consumer market. There are many perfectly worthy and beneficial commodities designed for children, that support their psychological development. In relation to fashion, children, like everyone else, must wear clothes. Moreover, there are different types of clothes for different occasions.

The fashion market is populated by many different suppliers who compete legitimately, as do other businesses, for market share. This means that within any specific clothing range for children, many brands are available to choose from. Brands must compete with each other. They can do this on price, but will also tend to present images that convey messages about value for money or 'brand value'. This means that while one brand may cost more than another, its advertisers will argue that it also delivers more value in terms of longevity, quality, versatility or simply in terms of being more fashionable. Thus, a brand is traded on offering premium value over others.

The fashion sense of consumers is often played on in relation to premium brand value and this is done through association of the brand with highly valued social or lifestyle attributes. In relation to clothing which provides an outer cover for consumers, it can be used to convey messages about the type of person we are. By linking a brand to an attractive lifestyle we may believe that through association with that brand, a similar lifestyle will follow for us. Similarly, by using attractive models or actors to demonstrate or promote the brand, we may hope to attain some of their intrinsic physical appeal. In the latter context, sex is a key selling ingredient.

Wrapped up with sex is the physical attractiveness of the model depicted in an advertisement. This physical attractiveness is rarely totally natural in advertising images today. Not only do advertisers carefully select particular types of models for promotional purposes, but they also digitally alter the original photographic or video images captured of them. With female models, there has been a propensity to select models on the basis of their body shape. In some markets, skin tone is also an important feature. In all markets, once a model has been selected and photographed, whether they are a well-known celebrity or someone with no significant public profile, media producers will tend to use technology to digitally change the original photographic images. Body shape, facial features and skin texture and tone may be altered using computer software. Waists are slimmed down further, wrinkles are removed, and skin tone is lightened. Hence, unnatural and usually unattainable images of beauty are created, but nevertheless are presented as role models to young consumers.

What is of particular concern in the context of sexualization of childhood is when pre-teenagers are depicted in sexually adult-like poses and are used to advertise child versions of adult clothing lines such as lingerie. Such children may be further embellished with the application of adult cosmetics to their faces. An important question here is whether children are influenced psychologically by this type of advertising. Does exposure to these images promote greater anxieties among pre-teenage girls about their own physical appearance? Do they worry about their body shape? Do they become preoccupied with their facial appearance? Does this advertising encourage them to pester parents to purchase clothes or make-up that enhances their outward appearance? Does the emergence of these consumer behaviours enhance the probability of other more serious clinical conditions, such as dieting at a crucial time of their physical development?

Fashion and girls' overall well-being

We have examined evidence that many clothes aimed at child markets are sexualized in terms of their design and the ways in which they are presented and promoted. What does this mean in terms of how the wearers of these clothes, or others who see teenage and pre-teenage children dressed in this way, respond? Can provocative clothing lead to the sexual objectification or sexualization of children?

Clothes have a number of purposes that are linked to many fundamental human needs. They keep us warm when the climate is cool and they protect our modesty by keeping hidden from others areas of our bodies that we regard as private. The latter purpose has a sexual aspect in that 'protection of modesty' generally means covering up those parts of our body that define our gender and that are involved in sexual activity. Being put in a position in which the clothes we wear leave us physically exposed can cause us to focus more on ourselves as objects and result in a feeling of uncertainty, especially when we already experience low body self-esteem. When male and female American college students of varied ethnicities were invited to complete a series of tests in a psychology laboratory while wearing a swimsuit or a sweater, those in the swimsuit condition generated more statements about their bodies in an exercise in which they described the kind of person they were, displayed higher rates of shame about their bodies, and performed more poorly on a mathematics test.[49]

Clothes can also make social statements about our affluence and taste and reflect different aspects of our personalities. Clothing styles also reflect current cultural norms and values about self-representation and attractiveness or beauty.[50]

Our clothing forms part of who we are, and as an outer cover our clothes are critical to the initial impressions we make on others.[51] These impressions can be social and affect whether we are regarded as friendly and approachable.[52] Clothes can influence how we are perceived in business and professional settings. Wearing the right kinds of clothes in a business environment can determine the degree to which others rate us as competent and reliable.[53] There are often socially conditioned sets of expectations that stipulate the need to dress appropriately for the status of job a person occupies.[54]

We noted earlier that clothes are used to protect our (sexual) modesty, but clothing can also be used to project sexual messages. Wearing sexually revealing clothes can make women seem more sexually available. When men and women were shown film clips of a social interaction between a man and woman, they rated the woman as being more intent on seeking a sexual relationship when she wore revealing clothes.[55] In a work context, wearing sexy outfits can be judged as relevant and advantageous in some jobs, but as entirely inappropriate and disadvantageous in others. Thus, women working in some environments as hostesses or waitresses might be more popular with male clientele and get better tips when they appear sexy. In formal office settings, however, short skirts and low-cut tops might get a woman noticed, but not always in the right way.[56]

The effects of provocative clothing worn by women can become particularly acute in situations where violence is involved. Evidence has emerged from studies of date rape that rape victims are seen as more culpable if the clothing they wore was regarded as sexually revealing and provocative.[57]

Women who dress in a sexualized way are judged differently not only by men but also by their own gender. In one controlled study of women's reactions to three well-known female sports stars in the US who had appeared in a men's magazine in full body shots wearing minimal clothing, not only did these images render the sports women in question as more sexually desirable and experienced as compared to standard sports images of them, but it also caused women observers to rate them less favourably in terms of their sporting competencies and degree of self-respect they seemed to have.[58] Female athletes – as we will see in Chapter 4 – represent important role models for girls in that they provide examples of strong independent women who are successful. Yet, media treatments of female high sports performers tend to be more sexualized than those given to male counterparts. The choice of some female sports stars voluntarily to present themselves as sexual objects, especially in settings where they deliberately target men, can result in a loss of respect from their own gender.

Parents have been found to be quite circumspect in their opinions about sexualized clothes. Buckingham and his colleagues conducted a series of focus group interviews on the subject with parents in Scotland.[59] Parental views about children as consumers and the sexualization of products aimed at children were obtained. The sample of 43 parents was not representative and comprised mainly mothers (n = 35), but nevertheless yielded some interesting insights into parental concerns. What was interesting was the extent to which these parents acknowledged that children need to be allowed to develop their own tastes and understanding as consumers. Moreover, their tastes are likely to change as they mature. Once they get into their teens, it is natural that adolescent girls and boys want to be seen as more grown up. This phenomenon is nothing new and the parents were able to recall going through this stage of development themselves.

Evidence has emerged that parental concerns centred more on the growth of commercialism than on the sexualization of products. The trend towards target marketing very young children meant that materialistic values were being encouraged from an early age, which often had a spin-off effect of putting pressure on parents to comply increasingly with children's purchase requests. Brand awareness emerged early on and was often defined not simply by marketing messages but by the interpretations of children's own peer group sub-culture, which developed its own rules about which brands were 'in' and why they were fashionable.

Turning specifically to sexualization, this was regarded by these Scottish parents as a gendered issue. In other words, it was a more significant matter in relation to girls than boys. One concern was that girls were becoming sexual too soon and that sexualization in the media and in children's goods might contribute to this outcome. Nevertheless, pre-teenage girls often sought to acquire products – clothes and cosmetics, for example – that were sexualized for reasons other than appearing sexually attractive to boys. More usually, these items were consumed to make appropriate fashion statements to other girls of their own age. Despite these reasons, there was no getting away from the fact that for sexually maturing girls in their mid-teens, many highly fashionable clothing brands were very revealing.

Some clothes were not invariably sexualized and much depended here on how, when and where they were worn. Wearing leggings that comprehensively covered the legs had the effect of de-sexualizing very short skirts. For girls with busts, bras were an essential for comfort, but when visibly seen because of the design of outer clothing, their sexualization quotient could increase beyond acceptable levels. Certain brands caused a problem if they were extensions of sexualized adult brands such as *Playboy* or when they had a name that made a clear sexual reference, such as a hair colorant called 'One Night Stand'.

There were fewer concerns about how boys would respond to sexualized clothes and accessories. The brands targeted at boys were not generally seen to be problematic. As they grew older, however, some parents indicated that they hoped their own sons would not form warped ideas about female sexuality from seeing girls wearing sexualized clothes or applying sexualizing products such as make-up to their bodies. Parents with daughters were aware of the risks that teenage and pre-teenage girls could run if they flashed the flesh too much and made themselves up to look older than their years. Banning their children from using these products was not seen as a workable solution. Instead, instilling the right values in their children while also talking to them in a non-restrictive way about being conscious of social risks were far more significant actions in this context.

Buckingham and his colleagues also conducted research with small samples of children aged 12 to 14 years, and as well as interviewing them about their consumer behaviour some were also given shopping exercises to carry out, including designing new products for specific categories, selecting products appropriate to children of different ages, and indicating what they regarded as sexy or sexualized products.

The children acknowledged that they were sensitive and responsive to consumer trends underpinned by their peer groups' current tastes but that they were not readily duped by marketing messages. They were able to define which products were designed for their own age group or for other child age groups. They were aware that 'sex' is used to sell, but were not invariably swayed in their own choices by this attribute, recognizing that marketers often try to force sexualized messages onto young consumers in the mistaken belief that they will not be able to resist. Some fashion styles – traditionally classed as sexy or sexualized – could become trendy for reasons defined by the consumer culture of which children and teenagers were a part and these reasons would often have nothing to do with sex. Furthermore even with explicitly sexy brands such as *Playboy*, the brand logo might be adopted as fashionable after its meaning had been renegotiated by their peer group.

The 'tweens' and 'teens' interviewed by Buckingham felt that they were already constrained in clothing choices, most especially in terms of what they could wear at school, so that in other settings they ought to be given freedom to choose their own brands and styles of dress. Sometimes this might mean that they would choose sexualized products that would make them look older. For many teenage girls, having the freedom to dress to look older is very important even though their parents might express concerns about their daughters adopting excessively sexual appearances.[60] This was regarded as a critical aspect of natural development and self-expression. If there were consequences of dressing provocatively, then they should be given the opportunity to learn these lessons for themselves.

In drawing our examination of fashion and sexualization to a close, there is ample evidence that sexual themes are present in clothing styles that have been targeted not only at sexually maturing teenagers, but also at pre-teenage children who have not reached that stage of development. Concerns about sexualized themes in childhood are not new, but they have become crystallized in increasingly explicit forms in respect of fashion trends in children's clothing and beauty pageants that take sexually themed styles of dress to the greatest extreme. Of course, girls want to look attractive as much as women do. For girls, looking 'sexy' is often treated as a normative objective that is significant in terms of their self-image and personal identity.

The term 'sexy' here may carry different connotations among teenage and pre-teenage girls. For older children, who have reached puberty and begun to develop mature physical attributes and urges, the term may be used in a more literal sense whereas among pre-teenagers and especially the under tens, it has a more innocent meaning. Nonetheless, an emphasis on physical appearance and the conversion of this feature into a competitive attribute – as occurs in child pageants – can convey the message that being 'sexy', however this is interpreted by the child, is an important aspect of one's character and social standing. Where such social conditioning occurs at a critical stages of development, it may be internalized to a point where it can have longer-term effects on the facets of themselves (and others) that children adopt as being the most significant in terms of the way in which people are judged.

There is a wider concern about the undesirable side-effects of putting young children on display in a sexualized manner. In presenting children in an adult-like sexual fashion, such images of under-age sexuality represent potential triggers to unwanted adult attention that is sexually motivated. What is also unclear is the degree to which sexualization in fashion can combine with other childhood sexualization triggers that occur through other media to place children at greater sexual risk. In the next chapter, we turn our attention to another area that can bring sex-ualization close to home, and that is the presence of sexual attributes and themes in the games and toys that children play with.

Notes

1 BBC News (2007) 'Children's catalogue "suggestive"', 7 February, http://www.news. bbc.co.uk/1/hi/uk/6337373.stm, accessed 23 March 2009.
2 Eder, D. (with Evans, C. C. and Parker, S.) (1995) *School Talk: Gender and Adolescent Culture*. New Brunswick, NJ: Rutgers University Press.
3 Sarracino, C. and Scott, K. M. (2008) *The Porning of American: The Rise of Porn Culture, What It Means and Where We Go From Here*. Boston, MA: Beacon.
4 See Cook, D. T. and Kaiser, S. B. (2004) 'Betwixt and between: Age ambiguity and the sexualization of the female consuming subject', *Journal of Consumer Culture*, 4, 203–227.
5 Frederickson, B. L. and Roberts, T. A. (1997) 'Objectification theory: Toward understanding women's lived experience and mental health risks', *Psychology of Women Quarterly*, 21, 173–206; McKinley, N. M. and Hyde, J. S. (1996) 'The Objectified Body Consciousness Scale', *Psychology of Women Quarterly*, 20, 181–215; Salter, A. and Tiggemann, M. (2002) 'A test of objectification theory in adolescent girls', *Sex Roles*, 46, 343–349.
6 Cook, D. T. and Kaiser, S. B. (2004). *op. cit.* Donnally, T. (1999) 'In tune with tweens', *San Francisco Chronicle*, 24 August, E1–2.
7 Davis, F. (1992) *Fashion, Culture and Identity*. Chicago, IL: University of Chicago Press.
8 Cook, D. T. and Kaiser, S. B. (2004) *op. cit.*

9 Paoletti, J. and Kregloh, C. (1989) 'The children's department', in C. Kidwell and V. Steele (Eds.) *Men and Women: Dressing the Part*, pp22–41. Washington, DC: Smithsonian Institution Press.

10 Wolf, N. (1990) *The Beauty Myth*. London, UK: Chatto and Windus; Weeks, J. (2007) *The World We Have Won: The Remaking of Erotic and Intimate Life*. London, UK: Routledge.

11 Duits, L. and van Zoonen, L. (2006) 'Headscarves and porno-chic: Disciplining girls' bodies in the European multicultural society', *European Journal of Women's Studies* (1392), 103–117; Duits, L. and van Zoonen, L. (2007) 'Who's afraid of female agency? A rejoinder to Gill', *European Journal of Women's Studies*, 14(2), 161–170.

12 Gill, R. C. (2007) 'Critical respect: The difficulties and dilemmas of agency and "choice" for feminism', *European Journal of Women's Studies*, 14(1), 69–80; Gill, R. C. (2008) 'Empowerment/agency: Figuring female sexual agency in contemporary advertising', *Feminism and Psychology*, 18(1), 35–60.

13 Tozer, J. and Horne, M. (2011) 'Cocktail parties in stretch limos, catwalk shows and fake tattoos – the disturbing sexualization of little girls revealed', *Daily Mail*, 26 February, pp40–41.

14 Witheridge, A. (2012) 'The toddler whose mother gives her a fake tan every month', *Daily Mail*, 16 June, pp32–33.

15 Squire, A. S. (2012) 'What is her mother thinking?', *Daily Mail*, 12 April, pp37–39.

16 Davies, B. and Bentley, P. (2012) 'So what does her mother have to say for herself?', *Daily Mail*, 5 September, pp22–23.

17 Davies, B. and Bentley, P. (2012) *op. cit.*

18 Lay, K. (2012) 'It was either this or football', *The Sunday Times Magazine*, 2 September, 22–27.

19 Wonderlich, A. L., Ackard, D. M. and Henderson, J. B. (2005) 'Childhood beauty pageant contestants: Associations with adult disordered eating and mental health', *Eating Disorders*, 13(3), 291–301.

20 Allen-Mills, T. (2012) 'US goes sweet on Honey Boo Boo', *The Sunday Times*, 26 August, p28.

21 Lamb, S. and Brown, L. M. (2006) *Packaging Girlhood: Rescuing Our Daughters from Marketers' Schemes*. New York, NY: St Martin's Press; Pollett, A. and Hurwitz, P. (2004) 'Stripp til you drop', *The Nation*, 12/19 January, pp20–21, 24–25.

22 Nelson, A. (2000) 'The pink dragon is female: Halloween costumes and gender markers', *Psychology of Women Quarterly*, 24, 137–144.

23 Peters, C. (2002) 'G-strings for seven year olds: What's a parent to do?', *Znet Commentary*, 2 November, www.zmag.org/sustainers/content/2002=11/02peters.cfm.

24 O'Connell, V. (2007) 'Fashion bullies attack – in middle school', *Wall Street Journal*, 25 October, pD1; Goodale, G. (2002) 'Erotica runs rampant', *The Christian Science Monitor*, September, http://www.csmonitor.com/2002.0201/p13s01-altv; Deeley, K. (2007) 'I'm single, I'm sexy and I'm only 13', *The Times*, 28 July, www.timesonline.co.uk.

25 Pollet, A. and Hurwitz, P. (2004) *op. cit.*

26 Thomas, C. (2012) 'Should you really dress little girls in leopard-skin bikinis, Liz?', *Daily Mail*, 12 September, p9.

27 Steele, V. (1996) *Fetish: Fashion, Sex and Power*. Oxford, UK: Oxford University Press.

28 Steele, V. (1996) *ibid*; Kleinhans, C. (2004) 'Virtual child porn: The law and the semiotics of the image', *Journal of Visual Culture*, 3(1), 17–34.

29 Rush, E. and La Nauze, A. (2006) *Corporate Paedophilia; Sexualization of Children in the Media*, October. Canberra, Australia: Australia Institute, Discussion Paper 93.

30 Rush, E. and La Nauze, A. (2006) *ibid*.

31 Media Awareness Network (2007) 'Media stereotyping: Media and girls', www.media-awareness.ca/english/issues/stereotyping/women_and_girls/women_girls.

32 Rush, E. and La Nauze, A. (2006) *op. cit.*

33 Rush, E. and La Nauze, A. (2006) *op. cit.*

34 Brown, J. D., Halpern, C. T. and L'Engle, K. L. (2003) 'Mass media as a sexual super peer for early maturing girls', *Journal of Adolescent Health*, 36(5), 420–427.
35 Varney, W. (1994) 'Children's make-up: masking the contradictions', *Journal of Australian Political Economy*, 1(1), 21–35.
36 Chaplin, H. (1999) 'Smell my Candie's', *American Demographics*, August, 21, 64–65.
37 Dalton, P. (2005) 'What's wrong with this outfit Mom?', *The Washington Post*, 20 November, pB01, www.washingtonpost.com, accessed 18 April 2006; Levin, D. E. (2005) 'So sexy, so soon: The sexualization of childhood', in S. Olfman (Ed.) *Childhood Lost: How American Culture Is Failing Our Kids*, pp137–153. Westport, CT: Praeger Press. Bloom, A. (2004) 'Sex and the 6-year-old girl', *O, The Oprah Magazine*, September, pp209–210; Brooks, G. (2006) 'No escaping sexualization of young girls', *Los Angeles Times*, 25 August, www.commondreams.org/view06.0825–33.
38 Buckingham, D., Willetts, R., Bragg, S. and Russell, R. (2010) *Sexualized Goods Aimed at Children: A Report to the Scottish Parliament Equal Opportunities Committee*. Edinburgh, UK: Scottish Parliament equal Opportunities Committee, http://www.scottish.parliament.uk/s3/committees/equal/reports-10/eor10–02, accessed 14 December 2012.
39 Kaiser, S., Chandler, J. and Hammidi, T. (2001) 'Minding appearances in female academic culture', in A. Guy, E. Green and M. Bannin (Eds.) *Through the Wardrobe*, pp117–136. Oxford, UK: Berg.
40 Tiggeman, M. and Lacey, C. (2009) 'Shopping for clothes: Body satisfaction, appearance investment, and functions of clothing among female shoppers', *Body Image*, 6, 285–291.
41 Cook, D. T. and Kaiser, S. B. (2004) 'Betwixt and be tween: Age ambiguity and the sexualization of the female consuming subject', *Journal of Consumer Culture*, 4, 203–227; see also Haynes, M. (2005) 'Bawdy T-shirts set off "girlcott" by teens', *The Piitsburgh Post-Gazette*. 3 November, www.post-gazette.com/pg/05307/599884, accessed 26 August 2006; Levy, A. (2005) *Female Chauvinist Pigs: Women and the Rise of Raunch Culture*. New York, NY: Free Press.
42 George, L. (2007) 'Eight-year-olds in fishnets, padded "bralettes" and thing panties: Welcome to the junior miss version of raunch culture', *Maclean's*, January, 119, 37–40.
43 Merskin, D. (2004) 'Reviving Lolita? A media literacy examination of sexual portrayals of girls in fashion advertising', *American Behavioural Scientist*, 48, 119–128.
44 Goodin, S. M., Van Denburg, A., Murnen, S. K. and Smolak, L. (2011) '"Putting on" sexiness; A content analysis of the presence of sexualizing characteristics in girls' clothing', *Sex Roles*, 65, 1–12.
45 Jeffreys, S. (2005) *Beauty and Misogyny: Harmful Cultural Practices in the West*. London, UK: Routledge.
46 Starr, C. R. and Ferguson, G. M. (2012) 'Sexy dolls, sexy grade-schoolers? Media and maternal influences on young girls' self-sexualization', *Sex Roles*, 67, 463–476.
47 Satrapa, A., Melhado, M. B., Curado-Coelho, M. M., Otta, E., Taubemblatt, R. and Fayetti Siqueria, W. (1992) 'Influence of style of dress on formation of first impressions', *Perceptual and Motor Skills*, 74, 159–162.
48 Cassidy, L. and Hurrell, R. M. (1995) 'The influence of victim's attire on adolescents' judgments of date rape', *Adolescence*, 30, 319–323; Johnson, K. K. P. (1995) 'Attributions about date rape: Impact of clothing, sex, money spent, date type, and perceived similarity', *Family and Consumer Sciences Research Journal*, 23, 292–311.
49 Hebl, M. R., King, E. G. and Lin, J. (2004) 'The swimsuit becomes us all: Ethnicity, gender and vulnerability to self-objectification', *Personality and Social Psychology Bulletin*, 30, 1322–1331.
50 Entwistle, J. (2000) *The Fashioned Body: Fashion, Dress and Modern Social Theory*. Malden, MA: Blackwell.
51 Cahoon, D. D. and Edmonds, E. M. (1989) 'Male–female estimates of opposite-sex first impressions concerning females' clothing styles', *Bulletin of the Psychonomic Society*, 27, 280–281.

52 Lukavsky, J., Butlet, S. and Harden, A. J. (1995) 'Perceptions of an instructor: Dress and students' characteristics', *Perceptual and Motor Skills*, 81(1), 231–240.
53 Gurung, R. A. R. and Vespia, K. M. (2007) 'Looking good, teaching well? Linking, liking, looks and learning', *Teaching of Psychology*, 34, 5–10.
54 Kwon, Y. and Farber, A. (1992) 'Attitudes toward appropriate clothing in perception of occupational attributes', *Perceptual and Motor Skills*, 74(1), 163–168.
55 Koukounoas, E. and Letch, N. M. (2001) 'Psychological correlates of perception of sexual intent in women', *Journal of Social Psychology*, 141, 443–456.
56 Glick, P., Larsen, S., Johnson, C. and Branstiter, H. (2005) 'Evaluations of sexy women in low- and high-status jobs', *Psychology of Women Quarterly*, 29, 389–395.
57 Cassidy, L. and Hurrell, R. M. (1995) *op. cit*; Vali, D. and Rizzo, N. (1991) 'Apparel as one factor in sex crimes against young females: Professional opinions of U.S. psychiatrists', *International Journal of Offender Therapy and Comparative Criminology*, 35, 167–181.
58 Gurung, R. A. R. and Chrouser, C. J. (2007) 'Predicting objectification: Do provocative clothing and observer characteristics matter?', *Sex Roles*, 57, 91–99.
59 Buckingham, D., Willetts, R., Bragg, S. and Russell, R. (2010) *op. cit.*
60 Boden, S., Pole, C., Pilcher, J. and Edwards, T. (2005) 'New consumers: Children, fashion and consumption', *Sociology Review*, 15(1), 28–32.

3

CHILDREN'S PRODUCTS AND SEXUALIZATION

The children's and teenagers' product markets are huge. The worldwide retail sales of children's toys were estimated to be worth US$80.2 billion in 2009.[1] In most of the leading toy markets around the world, such as Australia, Sweden, the United Kingdom and France and, to a lesser extent, Germany and Japan, toy sales increased steadily between 2006 and 2011. While sales stagnated during this time in the US, it has remained the world's largest market by far for toy sales.[2]

In the last chapter we looked at products targeted at children that were linked to clothing fashions. We now turn our attention to products that form part of the play and entertainment lives of young people. We are talking here about products such as toys and games that children play with. Today, many games are electronic and played on computers. In this chapter, therefore, we will examine the presence of sexualized content in non-clothes products that can be bought for children and adolescents, including computer games that are played with on television sets, fixed and mobile computers, tablets, mobile telephones and custom-made computer game consoles. Although the primary purpose of these products is entertainment, some of the play products that are aimed at children – such as make-up kits – are, like clothing fashions, also linked to the outward appearances children can take on. Hence, in terms of the behaviours they practise at play, how significant is sexualization as an aspect and outcome of involvement with these commodities?

Culture of consumption

The sociology of children and consumption helps to set the context for the study of the production, distribution and use of sexualized goods, linking the sexualization of children's goods (such as toys and fashion) to the broader commercialization of childhood. The commercial invention of child markets (the toddler, 'tween', teenager) has its roots in the first half of the 20th century; but as the importance of brands grew in the last quarter of that century, so children have emerged as legitimate targets for an increasingly diverse range of commodities designed for their consumption.[3]

Research on children and consumption has highlighted a variety of empirical foci and methodological approaches. However, some writers have identified an overall slant towards the 'production of culture', meaning relatively more attention has been directed at the production and circulation of goods (e.g. toys) than at users (e.g. children and parents).[4] This trend within the research is also linked to debates about the difficulties associated with measuring the effects of marketing on consumers which is used to determine the way in which commercial commodities' markets have changed.[5]

Previous debates about children as consumers have focused on two distinct positions – the exploited child and the empowered child. The concept of the exploited child has embraced concerns about children being cultivated and recruited by marketers and, as in the current context, about children becoming targets of sexual predators.[6] The notion of the empowered child has accepted the idea that children are 'getting older younger' and that even pre-school children are active consumers in their own right.[7] Yet, for some critics, this perspective has gone too far the other way in its reaction to the 'exploited child' position. It remains as important as it perhaps ever was to acknowledge that children both learn about consumerism and negotiate their positions as consumers within the contexts of their families.

Research by UK marketing data analyst Mintel into the 'kids getting older younger' (KGOY) phenomenon was linked to the falling age at which children lose interest in traditional toys and move to computer consoles, iPods and so on. The findings of this investigation revealed that toys (as a general category) fall in popularity for children ten years and older. Channels of distribution were dominated by relatively few suppliers, with half the market being claimed by Argos (the number one UK toy retailer), Woolworths and Toys 'R' Us. In addition, the major supermarkets, especially Asda and Tesco, were gaining stronger market share.[8]

An earlier Mintel report on the KGOY assumption concluded that 'children become interested in their appearance at an ever earlier age'; but this needs substantiating through longitudinal data. Here it was found that 38 per cent of seven- to 10-year-olds reportedly liked keeping up with the latest fashions; 29 per cent felt it was important to be trendy – but these results were stratified by class (keeping up with fashion and trendiness were more important to children from economically more downmarket households) and gender (girls were more likely than boys to keep up with fashion). Furthermore, 98 per cent of seven- to 10-year-olds said they shopped for clothes with parents, and 67 per cent say they chose clothes with some parental input.[9]

In addition, Mintel linked the KGOY phenomenon to the fading distinction between adult and children fashion. The blurring of products for younger children/older children/young adult/adult markets is reflected both in the products and channels of distribution. Young adult fashion was found to be increasingly scaled down for children's markets and some retailers' lines were less differentiated for 4- to 14-year-olds.[10] Other researchers have suggested a 'trickle down' dynamic of increasingly sexualized adult feminine conventions being passed on and projected to young girls, but acknowledged that this works in league with the 'trickle up' of youthful fashions to older women.[11]

As with fashion, sexualization is, in part, a function of targeting children with toiletry goods that are frequently associated with adult sexuality and attractiveness (e.g. perfume/cologne, cosmetics, grooming products). Research has found that amongst 7- to 10-year-olds, 14 per cent of boys and 45 per cent of girls claimed to use body spray. Girls in this age range also exhibited an increased use of lipstick.

Parental views of make-up use by young children were stratified by class, with working-class mothers 'considerably more tolerant than middle class mothers – to the point of trying to encourage them to wear it, and/or to teach them to wear it properly'.[12] American research found that more than one in two 13- to 17-year-olds claimed to use personal hygiene products such as deodorant or antiperspirant (84 per cent), whitening toothpastes (55 per cent), lip balm/moisturizer (54 per cent), and perfume or cologne (52 per cent) to improve their physical appearance and to feel better about themselves.[13]

Sexualization in the retail environment

The main illustrations of sexualized approaches in the retail environment include the use of sexualized marketing messages and the sale of goods for children that are defined by adult themes. Scholars who have observed the children's product marketplace believe that child products – both appearance and play related – engage youngsters in activities that do not just encourage fantasy escapism, but also invite role-playing of a kind that represents a powerful socializing force.[14]

In this context, sex is widely used to define and sell products targeted at children and teenagers. We have seen that girls' clothing lines embrace adult fashion styles with an emphasis on the female form and feminine sexuality. With toys and games, themes of sexualization surface again by drawing girls' attention to sexiness as a defining attribute of being female in the ways that they are invited to play with dolls. For boys and girls, sexual themes that show men and women treated differently underline gender stereotypes that, in turn, can have sexualizing effects on both sexes.

The accusation here is that children are being sexualized by inappropriate toys. Much of the focus of attention has centred on products aimed at girls. One principal culprit are popular brands of dolls that display mature female characteristics and that girls can dress up in provocative clothing that emphasize the dolls' sexual attributes. Critics' claims that the styles of play encouraged by these toys bring sexuality to the forefront before the girls at whom they are targeted are psychologically ready to engage with such issues. Messages of sexuality are also allegedly promulgated by merchandise targeted at young girls with *Playboy* branding. Although such merchandise contains no overt sexual imagery, the use of *Playboy* logos and branding are deemed to represent an extension of a sexual adult-oriented brand.[15]

There have been concerns raised about the techniques used by marketers with children and adolescents that present cultural and social scripts in support of brand promotions that are too mature for them to handle psychologically.[16] This issue has become especially acute in the context of computer video games that draw young players into fantasy worlds of growing complexity. While much concern has focused on the violently themed nature of video games,[17] there has also been increased attention devoted to the presence of sexualized content in them.[18]

A number of sexually themed online games have emerged specifically for girls to play. These include *Beach Catfight* in which players engage in a virtual fight on screen. There is also *Classroom*, which involves sexually themed narratives involving a teacher. Teenage girls have indicated being put under growing pressure by peer groups to engage in sexual intercourse.[19] The virtual world has created a sexually themed environment in which children and teenagers are encouraged to display sexual behaviour.

A UK Home Office review into sexualization concluded that the use of sexualized imagery in advertising has increased over time. In addition, there has been an upward trend in the use of sexualized images of children.[20] There has also been an increase in the prevalence of sexually themed content in magazines targeted at children and teenagers. This is a topic that will be revisited later in Chapter 4.

Children's products and the importance of play

The kinds of children's products we will examine in this chapter can be differentiated from those linked to clothing fashions. The fashion industry has targeted children with commodities that are utilized in the context of how children present themselves to the world in terms of their outer appearance. In this chapter we are concerned more with products children use at play. Play represents an important aspect of children's early development. Play activities enable children to develop their physical, mental and social skills, all of which are essential to their day-to-day functioning as children and will equip them eventually to cope with the challenges life will throw at them as adults.[21]

Play enables children to practise a range of cognitive, affective and interpersonal processes. These processes include problem-solving and abstract thought, creativity through divergent thinking and fantasy, knowing how to express and control emotions and interpret and respond to the emotions of others, and being able to interact socially with others and engage with other people in mutually beneficial ways. Different kinds of play activities will enable children to practise these skills and rehearse them across different settings. Toys and games can provide activities through which these various skills can be learned and practised. Pretend play is known to influence specific cognitive abilities such as problem-solving, flexible thinking and the development of internalized scripts that guide choices in terms of how to behave in different social settings.[22] Fantasy play behaviour can be particularly important in relation to the development of these cognitive skills.[23] The process here can be two-way, with higher cognitive skills also enabling even more creative fantasizing on the part of children.[24] Play can enhance many different cognitive abilities, but creativity enhancement has emerged as the cognitive function affected most profoundly.[25]

Imaginative play can also help pre-school children to develop strategies very early on for alleviating the fear they experience in scary situations.[26] Play can help children to establish internal reflective practices through which they can make assessments about themselves and others. Although this learning initially takes place through early experiences with parents, imaginative play allows them to test out ideas about themselves to find out how robust these are when put to the test in different situations.[27] There is evidence that children who engage more actively and more frequently in make-believe play during their early years display greater adjustment and ability to cope at school and in wider social settings as they get older.[28]

Whether the outcomes of make-believe play are constructive can vary, however, with the nature of that play and the themes that characterize it. Aggressiveness is one theme that can enter children's play, being more commonplace among boys than girls. The outcome of this style of play can depend, in turn, on whether aggression is integrated in a coherent or incoherent fashion with the play narratives that children act out. Incoherent use of aggression in play in early life has been linked to the development of behavioural problems later on.[29] One reason for this is that children who engage in productive fantasy play develop abilities to make more informed judgements about their own emotional states and those of others and these skills can influence the way in which they behave around others.[30]

Sexual themes have also been found to represent a defining characteristic of children's play. Children's toys and games represent part of this play scenario and in many instances are sex-typed. In other words, there are toys that are aimed at girls and others that are designed for boys as primary target markets. Girls and boys can display different interests in toys from an early age, whereby some toys have greater visual appeal to one gender than to the other.[31] These gender differences in toy preferences can begin to appear from as early as 18 months of age.[32] Even before consciously articulated differences have emerged in terms of gender awareness, infants display gender-defined differences in their toy preferences.[33] To some extent also, these differential toy preferences of children are reinforced by the reactions of parents, older siblings and others with whom they interact socially who may display gender stereotyped responses to the toy choices of girls and boys, ensuring some degree of conformity with cultural norms in terms of behaviours that are deemed most appropriate for each gender.[34] Fathers are often more active than mothers in reinforcing gender-appropriate play.[35]

Gender stereotyping with toys extends to the specific attributes that are used to describe products deemed to be girls' toys versus boys' toys. Toys classed as more appropriate for girls have tended to be described as attractive and nurturing, whereas boys' toys are described more often as being competitive and constructive and even as aggressive.[36] The nature of play behaviours differs between girls and boys when playing with conventionally gender-appropriate toys. Hence, girls were observed to play with dolls in a caring, nurturing fashion with behaviours such as feeding, putting to sleep or attending to their appearance being manifested, while boys tended to the functional features of toys that were more mechanical in nature (e.g. motor vehicles, trains, other mechanical constructions).[37]

Elsewhere, among children aged between two to four years, girls showed a greater preference for toys classed as gender neutral (e.g. bears, crayons, doctor's kit and puzzles) than for any other toys, whereas boys tended to play mostly with toys classed as conventionally 'masculine' (e.g. car, camera, tow truck) in a free-play setting. Girls spent more of their time playing with dolls than did the boys, but both genders exhibited more complex forms of play with these feminine toys than with any others.[38]

More usually, girls and boys – from a very early age – display preferences to play with toys conventionally regarded as appropriate for their own gender. One study of children aged one, three and five years observed play behaviour in a setting in which youngsters were given access to a range of toys. These included feminine toys such as a female doll with a feeding bottle, Barbie and Ken dolls, and a beauty set with brushes, a comb, a mirror, hair-slide, bracelet and necklace. Masculine toys included a bus, a garage with four cars, a construction toy, and two fighting figures (X-men). Boys and girls across these age groups tended to play mostly with those toys classed as appropriate to their gender. The one exception was with the X-men dolls, which boys tended to ignore but girls played with. From the age of three, girls were particularly interested in the beauty set and Barbie and Ken dolls that enabled them to practise dressing up things (dolls or themselves).[39]

What has become apparent from general observations of children at play is that from a very early age they display gender-stereotyped patterns of play behaviour that, in turn, trigger specific toy preferences. Among the toys consistently preferred by girls, even from when they are infants, are those that enable them to engage in appearance-related activities. Girls as young as three enjoy playing with beauty sets where they can engage in personal makeovers and seem naturally to orient towards dolls which they can also dress up. Whether these play patterns can be regarded as evidence that sexualized play is a natural aspect of children's behaviour is not proven here. What these findings do show, however, is that consistent gender-typed toy preferences occur from an early age, perhaps with some parental and other social environmental encouragement, and in the case of girls, play that involves dressing up themselves or dolls emerges quite naturally. The important question in the context of the ongoing concerns about the sexualization of childhood is whether some toy products provide further and inappropriate levels of encouragement to adopt forms of fantasy play with stronger sexual themes than would occur through the natural play choices of children.

Dolls

Dolls are extremely popular toys and form an important part of the play activity of young children. There is nothing intrinsically bad about the kinds of pretend play in which children can engage while playing with dolls. Some brands of dolls, however, have embraced sexual themes in terms of the way in which they are presented to children and the ways they are promoted. One very successful brand, Bratz dolls, represents teenage figures that can be dressed in a range of different types of clothing. Female Bratz dolls have often been marketed wearing bikinis in which womanly body shapes are revealed. Other clothing has tended to be characterized by revealing styles, with short skirts and low-cut tops, fishnet stockings and so on.

Bratz is not the only successful brand that has adopted sexualization attributes. Troll dolls that were big in the 1960s were largely non-sexual in their appearance and overall image. Latterly they have been reinvented as Trollz and five female dolls with different names that are borrowed from precious stones (Sapphire, Amethyst, Onyx, Ruby and Topaz) are sold with a revealing wardrobe of short skirts, bare midriffs, glamour hairstyles, and belly gems. Although marketed at four- to eight-year-olds, these dolls emphasize sexuality.[40]

The influence of dolls on the way in which girls perceive their own bodies has been seen to occur from the age of five. The use of dolls as role models, however, seems to be age restricted. This does not mean that their effects on the way young girls perceive themselves disappear with age, but rather that once such ideas are fully internalized, girls no longer need to play with or see the dolls themselves to be reminded of the way they look in comparison. The messages transmitted by these children's products with their focus on a narrowly defined concept of female sexuality are believed by some academics to condition a restricted view of the self.

Girls develop self-identities that centre on physical appearance and sexual attractiveness that stay with them into later years when they begin to mature into women. Such identities can, in turn, influence the range of aspirations they believe to be appropriate or feasible for them.[41] Meanwhile, toys targeted at boys frequently promote an exaggerated masculinity that might be regarded as the norm. Any exposure that boys might have to hyper-sexualized girls' toys might, in turn, shape their ideas about girls and eventually about women, and influence both the ways in which they evaluate girls/women and, ultimately, behave towards them.[42]

As a result of this social conditioning through sexualized toy play, girls and young women can become fixated on transforming what they regard as inadequacies in themselves such as their breast size, hair colour and style, skin tone and facial appearance, adopting norms or ideals of attractiveness created by popular culture. The sexualization of children's products in this way presents children with a ready-made set of norms and targets for themselves for the future. Even more significantly, some of these products introduce children to sexual themes at ages that their parents are not ready to address.[43]

One critical cultural moment when this phenomenon entered the marketplace was 1959, when Mattel launched its Barbie doll. Barbie was originally intended to be seen as a teenage girl or young woman with an attractive figure and pretty face accompanied by supporting merchandise from which children could dress her in different ways and create different social settings for her. As a doll she represented a product for which the dominant target market was pre-teen. Yet, Barbie herself was not a pre-teen. It was palpable from her appearance that she was a physically mature young woman with obvious sexual attributes. The sexuality of Barbie was further emphasized through the types of clothing accessories that could be bought for her. These often further accentuated her sexual attractiveness. One recurrent concern about Barbie was that she drew attention to sexual themes and also to materialistic themes among a target age group that had not yet entered puberty or usually had their own disposable money. In effect, according to some social commentators, Barbie encouraged teenage thinking among pre-teenage girls.[44]

There is a further historical note of interest that serves further to position Barbie in terms of the origins of her sexualized image. The inspiration for Barbie for the founder of Mattel Toys, Ruth Handler, was a popular German doll called 'Lilli' that she saw on a trip to Europe with her daughter in the late 1950s. Lilli had been modelled on a cartoon prostitute character and was sold in bars and tobacco shops to adult male consumers who were apparently attracted to her skin-tight attire which could be removed.[45]

Helga Dittmar, Emma Halliwell and Suzanne Ive of the University of Sussex in the UK investigated the impact of exposure to Barbie dolls upon the body self-perceptions of girls aged between five and eight.[46] Barbie was regarded as a potentially significant influence on pre-teenage girls' self-images because this doll has dominated the marketplace worldwide for decades and also because of her distinctive body shape. Assessments of Barbie alongside the average body shapes of women, in general, and of women with serious misgivings about their bodies who are driven to adopt extreme dieting as a consequence showed that Barbie's waist would be significantly smaller than even the average for anorexic patients.[47] The potential importance of this disclosure has been underlined by research showing that toys such as Barbie dolls represent part of a cultural iconic mix to which young children refer in their fantasy lives and as part of developing a personal identity.[48] Barbie can serve as a benchmark for an ideal body shape that young girls then internalize for future reference.[49]

This internalization of a body identity based on Barbie seems to occur within a particular developmental window between the ages of five and seven. When 10- to 14-year-old American girls were invited to think back over their past experiences with Barbie, they disclosed that Barbie was the ideal role model at first before subsequently being rejected.[50]

Dittmar and her colleagues conducted a study with girls aged five to eight years from East Sussex in southern England. These girls were drawn from the first three year groups in six schools. They were allocated to three conditions in which they looked through a picture book that featured Barbie, or Emme (an alternative doll with a US size 16 figure), or no doll at all. A researcher read the story from each picture out loud as the children read through it. After working through the picture book it was taken away and the girls completed a short test in which they evaluated their own body image and indicated the type of body they would like to have now and when they are grown up.

Comparisons between the three groups indicated that the girls who looked through the Barbie picture book exhibited lower body self-esteem and greater dissatisfaction with their body than did girls in the other two groups. The Emme picture book produced no such effects compared with the condition in which girls saw a picture book that did not feature any kind of female doll character. Further analyses revealed that the Barbie effect occurred among the youngest age groups of girls aged between five and seven years. The Barbie effect did not occur among girls from the oldest year group aged seven to eight years. The oldest group, however,exhibited an Emme effect in which those who saw the picture book that featured the larger body size doll were more likely to say they wished to be thin when grown up. Dittmar concluded that Barbie did represent an aspirational role model for young girls, but that once the message of 'thinness' had been learned, they no longer needed to play with Barbie for it to be reinforced.

The sexualization of some products aimed at children or enthusiastically adopted by them derives from other media outputs from which they have spun off. The popular television series *America's Next Top Model*, and the British equivalent in the UK, have a fan base that consists not just of young women, but also of girls in their teens and even younger. In the series, ordinary young women enter a competition in which they get the opportunity to become professional models. The ultimate objective for the winners is eventually to join the ranks of the supermodels and enjoy a jet-setting lifestyle and become fabulously rich. A video game product has spun off from the show that has been rated as suitable for children as young as three. The game promotes the idea of modelling to players and presents a set of ideals for what a supermodel should look like that includes a need both to maintain a slender body shape but also to be sexually attractive. The sexy and thin combination has been regarded as particularly troublesome because of the messages it sends out to young girls not just about the importance of having a sexy appearance but also by determining what kind of body shape is ideal in this context. Such messages can create a climate of what one observer of this phenomenon has termed 'normative discontent' that begins to emerge among pre-teenage girls.[51]

Computer and video games

Electronic games that can be played on remote consoles, TV screens and internet-linked computers by single players, by pairs or teams of players or by massive numbers of players located in many different parts of the world have emerged as a widespread form of play and entertainment for children and teenagers. Although it is the case that most players are adults, there are significant numbers of players aged under-18. Initial computer game playing occurred offline using devices that plugged into TV sets and self-contained games played on consoles with their own screens. This type of game playing remains highly popular, but playing electronic games that are streamed over the internet has also grown immensely.

By the early 2000s it was estimated that nearly 80 per cent of children and teenagers in the US played video games. Many would play virtually every day.[52] In the UK, more than half of children and teenagers aged between 5 and 15 years (57 per cent) reportedly played computer games, with boys tending to outnumber girls throughout all ages. Children play computer and video games via a television set (73 per cent saying this in 2012), on a handheld games console (61 per cent) and on a computer, laptop or notebook (40 per cent). In 2012, children aged 5 to 15 years in the UK reported that they played computer or video games for 8.7 hours per week. Amongst those aged 12 to 15 years, this figure rose to 11 hours per week.[53]

Video games have been a source of concern for their violent content for many years, but from early on there was also controversy about the sexual content of some of these games. This concern was brought to a head by the release of a game called *Custer's Revenge* by Atari in 1982. The main character was General George Custer and the purpose of the game was for the player to guide him across the screen while dodging arrows until he reached the other side where he then engaged in sexual intercourse with a naked Native American girl in captivity.[54] Since then, other globally popular video games have featured sub-plots involving sexual activity between the characters. In the context of this book, the question is whether these games could be instrumental in cultivating sexualized beliefs, attitudes and behaviours among young people who play them.

Sexualized content in video games

To establish whether video games could be potential sources of influence in terms of the sexualization of children and adolescents, we first need to know whether they have content of relevance. A number of studies of video games have reported a gender divide in the characters that populate these virtual environments. Male characters have tended to outnumber female characters.[55] Even when female characters were present, they tended to be less likely to appear in lead roles or in roles that permitted sophisticated levels of play.[56] What is more significant is the highly sexualized nature of the female characters and the prevalence of explicit sexual imagery and narratives in these games.

Many games have been found to have highly sexualized content.[57] Although some major video game manufacturers, such as Nintendo, have adopted family friendly policies and restricted sexual content in their games, not everyone in the industry has followed suit.[58] As well as sexual themes in games that have been distributed in the mainstream market, on the fringes a number of adult-oriented games have emerged from the pornography industry. These adult video games have been classified for age-limited consumption, but have nonetheless been developed to play on mainstream home consoles.

As computer games technology has evolved since they first emerged in the 1970s, so games themselves have become increasingly realistic. Their narrative complexities and production formats have grown ever closer in sophistication and texture to those found in movies and television programmes. These developments mean that, potentially, their ability to draw users in psychologically has also advanced. Such advances have an upside and downside. There is little doubt that regular players expect these developments and welcome them if they render standard games more enjoyable. At the same time, where these techniques are used with games that contain sexual themes with the result that the sexual content becomes more graphically portrayed, there is understandable concern about the impact they might have upon young players.[59]

Sexualization has been manifest in video games in the broader context of the objectification of female characters. Female characters were more often depicted in a sexually objectified way.[60] The way in which female characters in these games were dressed reinforced gender-role stereotypes. Women characters displayed shapely bodies and were scantily clothed so as to show off their bodies and draw attention to their sexual attractiveness.[61] With male characters, an emphasis was placed on their muscularity and their physical potency.[62]

One study of video games rated as suitable for teenage players found that more than one in four contained sexual themes. There was also a stronger tendency for female characters featured in these games to be depicted partially nude or involved in sexual behaviours.[63] Further research noted not only an emergence of sexual themes in computer games, but also the relative absence of strong female characters. An overwhelming majority of male characters in these games were aggressive and most of the female characters were depicted in a highly sexualized fashion – often scantily clad.[64] The sexual objectification of female characters in video games has become apparent from studies of the games themselves, the package covers of the games and from reviews of the games in specialist magazines.[65]

One study examined review and analysis articles about video games that appeared in specialist magazines published in association with the dominant game platforms Xbox, PlayStation and Nintendo to provide an assessment of the representations of female and male characters. All video game characters in a sample of 300 taken from 49 games were evaluated on a number of traits, including attractiveness, sexiness and the type of clothing they wore. There were five times as many male characters as female characters in this sample. One in two of the male characters were playable compared with only one in four of female characters. Playability here meant that the player could manipulate the behaviour of the characters on screen. Other characters were not under the player's control and occupied largely support roles. Proportionately more of the male characters than of the female characters had abilities and weapons. Male characters were, as expected, more muscular and powerful than were the female characters. Female characters were rated as significantly more attractive and 'sexy' than the male characters, although there was limited evidence that the clothing worn by female characters emphasized their sexuality.[66]

Some sexually themed computer games display violence against women. This is a theme to which we return later in my analysis of pornography. Some computer games have now adopted pornographic undertones. Sexually violent themes can be found in games in which female characters are stalked and sexually attacked by male characters – all under the control of the player, unlike in a movie.[67] Under controlled exposure conditions, researchers have found that video games that have sex-stereotyped characters were found to produce short-term effects in the form of increased tolerance for sexual harassment of women by men. Playing games with these portrayals did not produce short-term changes in male players' beliefs that women really enjoyed being raped (also known as rape myth acceptance). When longer-term effects of playing video games with sexual stereotypes were examined, it emerged that those who played these kinds of games most often exhibited greater tolerance of real-life incidents of sexual harassment and greater rape myth acceptance.[68]

Impact of video games

The possibility that computer and video games might play a part in the sexualization of children stems from observations that young people often look upon fictional media characters as role models. Over time, video games have acquired greater production quality and more sophisticated narratives that make them more psychologically engaging. The physically interactive nature of these games has always meant that they involve players differently from the narratives of television programmes and movies. Their relatively crude production qualities, however, meant that they lacked the realism of fictional dramas on television or movies made for the cinema. As computer technologies have evolved and production budgets have grown, video games have become more engaging in terms of their characterizations. This has meant that video game characters might serve more effectively now as role models for young players in terms of how they behave and how they appear.[69]

The potential of video games to influence players has been demonstrated in respect of their violent themes. Playing games with violent content has been found to generate aggressive thoughts in players, can enhance aggressive mood states, and may also encourage them to demonstrate more aggressive behavioural tendencies under controlled laboratory conditions.[70] There have been further signs that as video games become more realistic, their effects could transfer from the laboratory to the outside world.[71]

Despite the popularity of video games among males, there are also many female players. This fact, combined with the varied effects other media have been observed to have on girls and women in terms of their gender identity, body self-esteem and sexual values and behaviours, has led researchers to devote increased attention to whether video games can have similar effects.

Sexual content has been a feature of video games from the early days of this product attaining mass market status. The nature of this content can vary widely, however, from relatively innocuous depictions to highly explicit portrayals. The realism of the sex has grown as the computer graphics have become more life-like. The nature of the sex also varies with the way in which it is integrated with a surrounding narrative and with the settings in which it can occur. Sometimes, sex is used as an extension of the personalities of on-screen characters or to establish the nature of the relationship between male and female characters. In some instances, the sex may be used to demonstrate male dominance or simply to objectify the female characters. In more adult-oriented games, sexual depictions enable players to explore sexual fantasies. There are educational games that have been developed which enable parents and their children to talk about sexual relations in an environment that may be less embarrassing for both of them.

There is ample evidence from other media, and especially from movies and television, that gender depictions and representations of sexualization can shape media consumers' sex-related attitudes, beliefs and behaviours. These media can act as socialization agents for children in these contexts.[72] There is fairly limited evidence so far about similar effects of playing with video games.

One investigation of female and male players' reactions following their use of a video game that depicted gender-stereotyped portrayals and violence mixed with sex found that male players subsequently exhibited more stereotyped beliefs about women.[73] Other researchers found that male players of video games that depicted females in highly sexualized ways later focused on the physical sexual attributes of female characters in the games when questioned about them.[74]

Research has begun to emerge that has demonstrated the power of video games to shape sexist attitudes towards women and to encourage men to believe that sexual harassment of women is socially acceptable behaviour. Both men and women have been found to exhibit some susceptibility to these effects, meaning that men's perceptions of women and women's perceptions of their own gender can take on a less positive psychological tone.[75]

Yao, Mahood and Linz of the University of California, Santa Barbara, explored how male college students' thoughts about women and their sexuality could be influenced by playing a video game that depicted female characters in a sexually objectified manner. They used an adult game called *Leisure Suit Larry: Magna cum Laude*[TM] in which the lead male character is a socially inadequate college student who enters a televised dating show. Along the way, Larry must interact with various female characters in different situations that included drinking games and wet T-shirt contests. The players controlled this character and were required as part of the training in playing this game to complete exercises that included further interactions with a female character. The game contained animated nudity and photographs of sexily dressed human female models.[76]

A number of measures were used by the researchers to assess players' reactions. A lexical decision task was used in which participants' reactions times were assessed to words that provided sexually objectifying or non-objectifying descriptions of women and to sexual words. A further scale was used to measure the propensity of participants to say whether they would be likely to take advantage of women if placed in a number of sexually exploitative scenarios. These tests were administered to participants after they had played with a video game for 25 minutes. One game (*Leisure Suit Larry*) depicted sexually objectifying scenarios featuring female characters. A second game depicted situations in which male players had to engage in socially and emotionally positive interactions with female characters. A third game involved no interactions with humanoid characters or relationship scenarios.

The findings showed that participants who had played with the sexually explicit game exhibited significantly faster reaction times to sexual words than did participants in the other two game-playing conditions. Male game players who played with the *Leisure Suit Larry* game were far quicker to recognize words that described women as sex objects than were players in the other conditions. Perhaps more seriously, the young males who had played the sexually explicit game also subsequently displayed stronger tendencies to engage in situations involving sexual harassment of women.

This study indicated that even a relatively short bout of playing with a sexually explicit video game in which female characters were sexually objectified primed sexualized thoughts and socially problematic attitudes towards women among young adult male game players. One explanation for the findings was that exposure to sexually exploitative narratives and fictitious scenarios that show women in a highly sexualized fashion can generate stereotyped beliefs about women and produce behavioural scripts that are based on distorted perceptions of how women like to be treated. In effect, video games provide a source of social scripts that can be internalized by players and later called upon to guide their conduct in real-life social situations in which those scripts are perceived to be relevant. This social information processing explanation had previously been examined in relation to the potential effects of violent scenarios in interactive and non-interactive media.[77]

It is also worth noting that the findings observed here occurred in relation to one specific video game and were measured shortly after the game had been played. The researchers themselves observed that further tests are needed to find out whether such effects can be replicated with other games that contain sexual themes and whether they can persist over time.

Longer-term effects of playing video games on sexual beliefs have been found. Other findings have shown, for instance, that men who played video games with sexist themes subsequently displayed higher levels of sexism in their own beliefs. In a survey of relationships between video game playing and sexist beliefs about women, college-age men who reported regular game playing exhibited beliefs about women that were far more sexist than those displayed by men from within their own age group who did not play video games. There was no evidence of a relationship between video game playing and sexist attitudes or beliefs among young adult women.[78]

Summary and conclusions

This chapter has considered the premise that sexual attributes and themes have come increasingly to characterize products that have been produced for and targeted at children. The focus here was placed on products other than clothing-related fashions which were examined in Chapter 2. Here, we were concerned with the nature of products such as toys and games – in other words, products that form part of children's play. The significance of the observation that such products are often sexualized stems from the attention they then draw to sexual themes in relation to the way in which children play.

The sexualization of play is important insofar as play represents a critical aspect of children's early development in that it is through play activities that they learn about how to interact with others, how to evaluate them and how to present themselves. Observations of children at play have found that from a very early age, children exhibit toy preferences that match conventional gender stereotypes. In other words, girls tend to choose mostly those toys regarded culturally as most appropriate for their gender, and boys display toy preferences in a similar fashion.

Girls' choices tend to include toys that involve appearance-related play, such as applying beauty sets to themselves or dressing up dolls. During these activities, there are naturally occurring styles of play that might be classed as sexualized. If these behaviours are simply a natural extension of normal psychological development, then they ought not to be a cause for concern. When toys invite more attention to sexualized themes than would naturally occur, however, then we need to ask whether these attributes are appropriate when they occur among children at a very early stage of development. If the activities that occupy such a prominent part of children's early lives are coloured by sexual intonations, there might arise from this phenomenon a legitimate concern that young people are being encouraged to think in sexual ways about themselves and others before they have reached a stage of development where they achieve sexual maturity.

There are popular children's toys that draw attention to sexual themes through the display, often overtly, of sexual attributes. We saw in Chapter 2, in relation to children's clothes, that fashion trends directed towards the youngest consumers have been characterized by an emphasis on adult themes. In other words, even very young children, and especially pre-teenage girls, have been encouraged to dress like grown-ups. The sale of bras with sexually suggestive names such as 'Little Miss Naughty' for girls who have not yet developed breasts is a prime example of this trend. The toy market has joined the fashion market and provided further reinforcement of sex through fashion play with products such as Bratz dolls. Despite earlier concerns about the Barbie brand, compared with Bratz, Barbie appears sexually conservative. Bratz dolls are more overtly sexualized, with associated clothing and cosmetic accessory products that enable girls to dress the dolls in sexually alluring ways for different social occasions.

Computer and video games have attained widespread popularity among children, and most children play versions of these games from the age of five. By the time they reach their teens, children in the UK, for instance, have been found to play with the games at least 11 hours a week. Many of these games now have sexualized themes. These themes are manifest through the way in which female characters are represented, as well as through the kinds of behaviours that are displayed. There are sexually explicit video games produced by the pornography industry, but these tend to be on the fringes of the mainstream games market. Nevertheless, there are explicitly sexually themed games that draw attention to the sexual attributes of female characters that have become a part of mainstream markets. Although these games would not be classed as 'porn', they are often characterized by sexist scenarios that have been found to shape the perceptions that young male players develop about girls and women.

As will become clear as we work through the different mediated platforms on which sexualized themes are presented, the sexualization of childhood appears across a range of media. Sexualization messages in one medium can also be reinforced by their presence in another medium. In addition, we must not forget that the messages can be interpreted in different ways by different children and mediated sexual themes can undergo dramatic renegotiation among young consumers, with local socio-cultural factors – often linked to their social cliques – playing an important part.[79] The sexualized themes identified in relation to children's products have been reinforced by magazines aimed at children. These publications advertise children's fashions and play-related products and discuss these commodities in feature content in the context of advice on personal appearance and real relationships with other children, especially the opposite sex. In the next chapter we turn our attention to magazines as a source of sexualization content to which children are regularly exposed.

Notes

1 Toy Industry Association (2009) *Toy Markets in the World: Summary Charts Annual 2009*, NPD Group, http://www.toyassociation.org/AM/PDFs/Trends/ToyMarkets10, accessed 12 January 2013.
2 Euromonitor International (2012) 'Has toy spending peaked in the US?', 26 October, http://www.blog.euromonitor.com/toys-and-games, accessed 12 January 2013.
3 Cook, D. (2004) *The Commodification of Childhood*. Durham, NC: Duke University Press; Cook, D. T. and Kaiser, S. B. (2004) 'Betwixt and between: Age ambiguity and the sexualization of the female consuming subject', *Journal of Consumer Culture*, 4, 203–227.
4 Martens, L., Southerton, D. and Scott, S. (2004) 'Bringing children (and parents) into the sociology of consumption', *Journal of Consumer Culture* 4(2): 155–182.
5 Best, J. (1998) 'Too much fun: Toys as social problems and the interpretation of culture', *Symbolic Interaction* 21(2): 197–212.
6 Cook, D. (2005) 'The dichotomous child in and of commercial culture', *Childhood* 12(2): 155–159.
7 Pole, C. (2007) 'Researching children and fashion: an embodied ethnography', *Childhood* 14(1): 67–84.
8 Mintel (2008b) *Toy Retailing – UK*, December, http://academic.mintel.com.ezproxy.lib.le.ac.uk/sinatra/oxygen_academic/search_results/showand/display/id=298582.
9 Mintel (2006) *Marketing to Children Aged 7–10*, UK, January, http://academic.mintel.com.ezproxy.lib.le.ac.uk/sinatra/oxygen_academic/search_results/showand/display/id=173640.
10 Mintel (2008a) *Childrenswear Retailing – UK*, January, http://academic.mintel.com.ezproxy.lib.le.ac.uk/sinatra/oxygen_academic/search_results/showand/display/id=280568.
11 Cook, D. and Kaiser, S. (2004) *op. cit.*
12 Mintel (2006) *op. cit.*
13 Marketing Charts (2008) 'Teens' self-image shaped by friends, family, TV', 26 March, http://www.marketingcharts.com/television/teens-sel-image-shaped-by-friends-family-TV, accessed 28 January 2010.
14 Bachen, C. M. and Iilouz, E. (1996) 'Imaging romance: Young people's cultural models of romance and love', *Critical Studies in Mass Communication*, 13, 279–308; Sutton-Smith, B. (1986) *Toys as Culture*. New York, NY: Gardner Press.
15 Maddox, D. (2008) 'Girls aged 5 sexualized by toys like Bratz dolls, MSPs told', *News.scotsman.com*, 3 December, http://www.news.scotsman.com/latenews/Girls-aged-5-sexualized, accessed 23 March 2009.
16 Bachen, C. M. and Iilouz, E. (1996) *op. cit.*

17 Anderson, C. A. (2002) 'Violent video games and aggressive thoughts, feelings, and behaviours', in S. L. Calvert and R. R. Cocking, (Eds.) *Children in the Digital Age: Influences of Electronic Media on Development*. London, UK: Praeger, pp101–116; Anderson, C. A. and Bushman, B. J. (2001) 'Effects of violent video games on aggressive behaviour, aggressive cognition, aggressive affect, physiological arousal and prosocial behaviour: A meta-analytic review of the scientific literature', *Psychological Science*, 12, 353–359.

18 Stermer, S. P. and Burkley, M. (2012) 'Xbox or sexbox? An examination of sexualized content in video games', *Social and Personality Psychology Compass*, 6/7, 525–535.

19 Braithwaite, B. (2007) *Sex in Video Games*. Boston, MA: Charles River Media.

20 Papadopoulos, L. (2010) *Sexualization of Young People*. London, UK: Home Office.

21 Russ, S. W. (2004) *Play in Child Development and Psychotherapy: Toward Empirically Supported Practice*. Mahwah, NJ: Lawrence Erlbaum Associates.

22 Singer, D. G. and Singer, J. L. (1990) *The House of Make-Believe: Children's Play and the Developing Imagination*. Cambridge, MA: Harvard University Press.

23 Singer, J. J. and Singer, D. L. (1976) 'Imaginative play and pretending in early childhood: Some experimental approaches', in A. Davids (Ed.) *Child Personality and Psychopathology*, vol 3, pp69–112. New York, NY: Wiley; Sylva, K., Bruner, J. and Genova, P. (1976) 'The role of play in the problem solving of children 3–5 years old', in J. Bruner, A. Jolly and K. Sylva (Eds.) *Play*. New York, NY: Basic Books.

24 Sherrod, L. and Singer, J. (1979) 'The development of make-believe play', in J. Goldstein (Ed.) *Sports, Games and Play*, pp1–28. Hillsdale, NJ: Lawrence Erlbaum Associates.

25 Fisher, E. (1992) 'The impact of play on development: A meta-analysis', *Play and Culture*, 5, 159–181.

26 Golumb, C. and Galasso, L. (1995) 'Make believe and reality: Explorations of the imaginary realm', *Developmental Psychology*, 31, 800–810.

27 Morrison, D. (1988) 'The child's first ways of knowing', in D. Morrison (Ed.) *Organizing Early Experience: Imagination and Cognition in Childhood*, pp3–14. Amityville, NY: Baywood.

28 Singer and Singer (1990) *op. cit.*

29 Von Klitzing, K., Kelsey, K., Emde, R., Robinson, J. and Schmitz, S. (2000) 'Gender-specific characteristics of 5-year-olds' play narratives and associations with behaviour ratings', *Journal of the American Academy of Child and Adolescent Psychiatry*, 39, 1017–1023.

30 Seja, A. L. and Russ, S. W. (1999) 'Children's fantasy play and emotional understanding', *Journal of Clinical Child Psychology*, 28, 269–277; Niec, L. N. and Russ, S. W. (2002) 'Children's internal representations, empathy and fantasy play: A validity study of the SCORS-Q', *Psychological Assessment*, 14, 331–338.

31 Alexander, G. M., Wilcox, T. and Woods, R. (2009) 'Sex differences in infants' visual interest in toys', *Archives of Sexual Behaviour*, 38, 427–433.

32 Cakdera, Y. M., Huston, A. C. and O'Brien, M. (1989) 'Social interactions and play patterns of parents and toddlers with feminine, masculine and neutral toys', *Child Development*, 60, 70–76; Mayes, L. C., Carter, A. S. and Stubbe, D. (1993) 'Individual differences in exploratory behaviour in the second year of life', *Infant Behavior and Development*, 16, 269–284.

33 Alexander, G. M. and Saenz, J. (2012) 'Early androgens, activity levels and toy choices of children in the second year of life', *Hormones and Behaviour*, 62, 500–504.

34 Servin, A., Bohlin, G. and Berlin, L. (1999) 'Sex differences in 1-, 3-, and 5-year-olds toy-choice in a structured play session', *Scandinavian Journal of Psychology*, 40, 43–48.

35 Berenbaum, S. A., Martin, C. L., Hanish, L. D., Briggs, P. T. and Fabes, R. A. (2008) 'Sex differences in children's play', in J. Becker, K. Berkley, N. Geary, E. Hampson, J. Herman and E. A. Young (Eds.) *Sex Differences in the Brain from Genes to Behavior*, pp275–290. New York, NY: Oxford University Press.

36 Miller, C. L. (1987) 'Qualitative differences among gender-stereotyped toys: Implications for cognitive and social development in girls and boys', *Sex Roles*, 16, 473–487.

37 Caldera, Y. M. and Sciaraffa, M. A. (1998) 'Parent–toddler play with feminine toys: Are all dolls the same?', *Sex Roles*, 39, 657–668.

38 Cherney, I. D., Kelly-Vance, L., Glover, G., Ruane, A. and Ryalls, B. O. (2003) 'The effects of stereotyped toys and gender on play assessment in children aged 18 to 47 months', *Educational Psychology*, 23(1), 95–106.

39 Servin, A., Bohlin, G. and Berlin, L. (1999) *op. cit.*

40 Brown, I. M. and Lamb, S. (2005) 'Selling an ideal of lipstick and lace', *The Boston Globe*, 21 December; La Ferla, R. (2003) 'Underdressed and hot: Dolls moms don't love', *The New York Times*, 26 October, Section 9, p1, www.nytimes.com/2–3/10/26/fashion.

41 Coy, M. (2009) 'Milkshakes, lady lumps and growing up to want boobies: How the sexualization of popular culture limits girls' horizons', *Child Abuse Review*, 18, 372–383.

42 Levin, D. and Kilbourne, J. (2008) *So Sexy So Soon: The New Sexualized Childhood and What Parents Can Do to Protect Their Kids*. New York, NY: Ballantine Books.

43 Cook, D. T. and Kaiser, S. B. (2004) 'Betwixt and between: Age ambiguity and the sexualization of the female consuming subject', *Journal of Consumer Culture*, 4, 203–227.

44 Hymowitz, K. (2000) *Ready or Not: What Happens When We Treat Children as Small Adults*. San Francisco, CA: Encounter Books.

45 Hymowitz, K. (2002) 'Thank Barbie for Britney', 3 May, www.old.nationalreview.com/comment/comment-hymowitz2050302.asp, accessed 30 July 2013.

46 Bordo, S. (1997) *Twilight Zones: The Hidden Life of Cultural Images from Plato to O. J.* Berkeley, CA: University of California Press.

47 Norton, K. L., Olds, T. S., Olive, S. and Dank, S. (1996) 'Ken and Barbie at life size', *Sex Roles*, 34, 287–294.

48 Gleason, T. R., Sebanc, A. M. and Hartup, W. W. (2000) 'Imaginary companions of preschool children', *Developmental Psychology*, 36, 419–428.

49 Bussey, K. and Bandura, A. (1999) 'Social cognitive theory of gender development and differentiation', *Psychological Review*, 106, 676–713.

50 Kuther, T. L. and McDonald, E. (2004) 'Early adolescents: experiences with and views of Barbie', *Adolescence*, 39, 39–51.

51 McRobbie, A. (2007) 'Illegible rage: Reflections on young women's post feminist disorders', Gender Institute, Sociology and ESRC New Feminist Series, 25 January, http://www.lse.ac.uk/collections/LSEPublicLecturesAndEvents/pdf/20070125_McRobbie.pdf.

52 Gentle, D. A. and Walsh, D. A. (2002) 'A normative study of family media habits', *Journal of Applied Developmental Psychology*, 23, 157–178.

53 Ofcom (2012) *Children and Parents: Media Use and Attitudes Report*, 23 October, London, UK: Office of Communications.

54 Braithwaite, B. (2007) *op. cit.*

55 Beasley, B. and Standley, T. C. (2002) 'Shirts vs skins: Clothing as an indicator of gender stereotype in video games', *Mass Communication and Society*, 5, 279–293; Scharrer, E. (2004) 'Virtual violence: Gender and aggression in video game advertisements', *Mass Communication and Society*, 7, 393–412.

56 Ivory, J. (2006) 'Still a man's game: Gender representation in online reviews of video games', *Mass Communication and Society*, 9, 103–114.

57 Dietz, T. L. (1998) 'An examination of violence and gender role portrayals in video games: Implications for gender socialisation and aggressive behaviour', *Sex Roles*, 38, 425–442; Dill, K. E., Gentile, D. A., Rachter, W. A. and Dill, J.C. (2005) 'Violence, sex, race and age in popular video games: A content analysis', in E. Cole and J. Henderson Daniel (Eds) *Featuring Females: Feminist Analyses of Media*, pp115–130. Washington, DC: American Psychological Association.

58 Sheff, D. (1993) *Game Over; How Nintendo Zapped an American Industry, Captured Your Dollars and Enslaved Your Children.* New York, NY: Random House.

59 Martinez, M. and Manolovitz, T. (2009) 'Incest, sexual violence and rape in video games', www.inter-disciplinary.net/wp-content/uploads/2009/06/incest-sexual-violence-and-rape-in-vieo-games.

60 Dietz, T. L. (1998) 'An examination of violence and gender role portrayals in video games: Implications for gender socialisation and aggressive behaviour', *Sex Roles*, 38, 425–442.

61 Beasley, B. and Standley, T. C. (2002) *op. cit.*

62 Scharrer, E. (2004) *op. cit.*

63 Haninger, K. and Thompson, K. M. (2004) 'Content and ratings of teen-rated videos games', *Journal of the American Medical Association*, 291, 856–865.

64 Burgess, M. C. R., Stermer, S. P. and Burgess, S. R. (2007) 'Sex lies, and video games: The portrayal of male and female characters on video game covers', *Sex Roles*, 57, 419–433; Dill, K. and Thill, K. P. (2007) 'Video game characters and the socialisation of gender roles: Young people's perceptions mirror sexist media depictions', *Sex Roles*, 57, 851–864.

65 Dill, K. E. and Thill, K. P. (2007) *op. cit.*

66 Miller, M. K. and Summers, A. (2007) 'Gender differences in video game characters' roles, appearances and attire as portrayed in video game magazines', *Sex Roles*, 57, 733–742.

67 Martinez, M. and Manolovitz, T. (2009) *op. cit.*

68 Dill, K. E., Brown, B. P. and Collins, M. A. (2008) 'Effects of exposure to sex-stereotyped video game characters on tolerance of sexual harassment', *Journal of Experimental Social Psychology*, 44(5), 1402–1408.

69 McDonald, D. G. and Kim, H. (2001) 'When I die, I fell small: Electronic game characters and the social self', *Journal of Broadcasting and Electronic Media*, 45, 241–259.

70 Anderson, C. A. and Dill, K. E. (2000) 'Video games and aggressive thoughts, feelings, and behaviour in the laboratory and life', *Journal of Personality and Social psychology*, 78, 772–790; Anderson, C. A., Camagey, N. L., Flanagan, M., Benjamin, A. J., Eubanks, J. and Valentine, J. C. (2004) 'Violent video games: Specific effects of violent content on aggressive thoughts and behaviour', *Advances in Experimental Social Psychology*, 36, 199–249; Deselms, J. L. and Altman, J. D. (2003) 'Immediate and prolonged effects of video game violence', *Journal of Applied Social Psychology*, 33(8), 1553–1563.

71 Eastin, M. S. and Griffiths, R. P. (2006) 'Beyond the shooter game: Examining presence and hostile outcomes among male game players', *Communication Research*, 33, 448–466; Scharrer, E. (2004) 'Virtual violence: Gender and aggression in video game advertisements', *Mass Communication and Society*, 7, 393–412.

72 Gunter, B. (2002) *Media Sex: What Are the Issues?* Mahwah, NJ: Lawrence Erlbaum Associates; Ward, L. M. (2002) 'Does television exposure affect emerging adults' attitudes and assumptions about sexual relationships? Correlational and experimental confirmation', *Journal of Youth and Adolescence*, 31, 1–15.

73 Brenick, A., Henning, A., Killen, M., O'Connor, A. and Collins, M. (2007) 'Social evaluations of stereotypic images in video games: Unfair, legitimate or "just entertainment"?', *Youth and Society*, 38, 295–419.

74 Dill, K. E. and Thill, K. P. (2007) *op. cit.*

75 Dill, K. E., Brown, B. P. and Collins, M. A. (2008) 'Effects of exposure to sex-stereotyped video game characters on tolerance of sexual harassment', *Journal of Experimental Social Psychology*, 44, 1402–1408.

76 Yao, M. Z., Mahood, C. and Linz, D. (2010) 'Sexual priming, gender stereotyping and likelihood to sexually harass: Examining the cognitive effects if playing a sexually explicit video game', *Sex Roles*, 62(1), 77–88.

77 Huesman, L. R. (1998) 'The role of social information processing and cognitive schema in the acquisition and maintenance of habitual aggressive behaviour', in R. G. Geen (Ed.) *Human Aggression: Theories, Research and Implications for Social Policy*, pp73–109. San Diego, CA: Academic Press.

78 Stermer, S. P. and Burkley, M. (2012) *op. cit.*
79 Clark, J. (2013) 'Passive, heterosexual and female: Constructing appropriate childhoods in the "Sexualization of Childhood" debate', *Sociological Research Online*, 18(2), 13, www.socresonline.org.uk/18/2/13, accessed 29 October 2013; Wouters, C. (2010) 'Sexualization: have sexualization processes changed direction?', *Sexualities*, 13(6), 723–741.

4

MAGAZINES AND SEXUALIZATION

Offering one of the greatest potentials for exposure to sexualized content of all mass media are magazines targeted at young people. Teen magazines, in particular, abound with sexual images and themes. These occur in advertising and in feature content. We look at advertising separately elsewhere. Here, our attention will rest on the article content of magazines. These publications contain fictional stories with romantic and sexual themes, reports about celebrities that often focus on their romantic and sex lives, and a lot of 'factual' advice about relationships. These publications have long been thought to have influences on children and teenagers in terms of their values, beliefs, attitudes and behaviour. Most attention has been paid to the potentially harmful effects of exposure to this material, and this has given rise to the widespread impression that media effects are predominantly harmful in nature.

Policy-makers have been quick to jump to conclusions that not only is sexualization of contemporary culture widespread, but also that it represents a primary agent of social influence in children's lives and a source of bad influence. Sexual content in magazines has been accused of encouraging premature interest in sex, under-age sexual activity, promiscuity, unwanted pregnancies and the spread among young people of sexually transmitted diseases, as well as distorted beliefs among young males about female sexuality that can contribute to sexually deviant behaviour. Such content is believed to encourage children to engage in behaviours that emphasize sexual attributes before they have reached an age when this is appropriate and, in consequence, can put them at risk of unwanted sexual attention.[1]

It is easy for policy-makers to make bold statements about the prevalence of sexualizing content in magazines to which children are exposed, but such statements are often triggered by specific incidents rather than based on systematic and comprehensive audits of representative samples of magazines. High-profile incidents include the December 2010 French edition of *Vogue* magazine that featured a fashion spread with pre-teenage girls in sexualized poses, with one picture on the front cover. The clothes being promoted were designed for children, but their style and the way in which they were modelled were distinctly adult like. Child models were pictured in heavy make-up, wearing high heels and displaying a sultry demeanour that belied their true age.

There is little doubt that the opportunities for children and teenagers to be exposed to sexualized content through magazines are plentiful. The pre-teen and teen magazine markets expanded dramatically during the last decade of the 20th century and continued to provide a diversity of brands for adolescent readers to choose from into the 21st century.[2] Not only that, but teenagers have reported widespread and regular readership of magazines that are dominated by themes that deal with appearance and relationships, and sex. Teenagers have reported reading magazines every day, although average daily reading time often amount to only a few minutes for many of them.[3] While exposure to magazines can be a regular occurrence, what is it exactly that they are exposed to? How worried should we be?

The potential for sexualization effects of magazines on children and teenagers stems not simply from the highly sexualized content that they frequently depict, but also from the fact that young people turn to these publications for information about sex and sexual relationships. Even as young adults, women have been found to turn to magazines to understand more about how to become more sexually attractive and sexually skilled, as well as how to protect their sexual health. Magazines are sources to which young people with their newly emergent sexualities turn to find out about different ways of expressing their sexuality.[4]

The importance of magazines to female sexual socialization begins, however, before they become young adults. In the absence of effective sex education from parents or schools, adolescents have turned to the mass media, and in particular magazines targeted at their age group instead.[5] Although same-gender friends were also important sounding boards for advice and feedback about girls' sexual experiences, these conversations about romance, relationships and being sexually active were also informed by the advice columns and features of teen magazines.[6]

Much of the evidence about sexualization in magazines has focused on the representation of women. Some research has also turned our attention towards whether men are sexualized in print media. Hence, in examining what we know about magazines and sexualization, a lot of the evidence so far is based on the analysis of images of women (and, to a lesser extent, of men). This research identifies patterns in the ways in which women and men are treated by popular print publications that are widely read every week or every month, but it does not provide direct evidence about how readers might be influenced by these publications.

Much less research has tried to investigate more directly whether magazines have sexualization effects on readers, and especially on young readers whose ideas about gender and sex are still under development. In reviewing the evidence, studies of sexualization content in magazines can be differentiated in terms of the specific magazine genres they have examined. This is an important distinction to make because genres are distinguished primarily by the reader markets they target.

Sexualized content has been found in magazines aimed at general readers, teenagers, so-called lads' mags that are aimed at young adult males, sports magazines, and adult magazines that contain the most explicit sexual content.

Magazines aimed at women continue with the themes that have often been introduced in teen magazines. Emphasis is placed on matters of appearance – not simply to feel good about oneself through adopting the right hairstyle, make-up and clothing, and sculpting the right physical body through diet, exercise or cosmetic surgery, but, as importantly, to be well regarded by others.[7] Adolescent girls would appropriate stories about sexual relations presented in teen magazines into their own repertoire of sexual scripts and experience if they identified with them and the actors involved.[8]

One of the most popular culture and lifestyle magazines in the United States is *Rolling Stone*. Its primary focus has been music, but it has also established a reputation for coverage of the wider world of entertainment, as well as of current events and political issues. A longitudinal analysis of over 1000 covers of *Rolling Stone* over four decades from 1967 to 2009 found that sexualized images of both men and women had increased over time.[9] This increase was statistically significant in the case of women but not for men. Women were likely to be more frequently sexualized than were men. Furthermore, women were sexualized to a more extreme degree than were men.

This extreme sexual treatment or 'hypersexualization' of women was characterized by well-known female figures appearing naked on the front cover of the magazine or dressed in a sexually provocative fashion. Other characteristics of extreme sexualization were when the featured women posed with their legs apart, their breasts pushed up, their pants pulled down and when in some cases they were shown simulating sex acts.

Non-sexualized images of women fell progressively and sometimes dramatically from decade to decade, from 58 per cent in the 1970s, to 49 per cent (1980s), 22 per cent (1990s) and then to 17 per cent (2000s). More poignantly, while there was just one hyper-sexualized image of a woman on the cover of *Rolling Stone* in the 1960s (11 per cent of all images of women at that time), by the 2000s, this figure had reached 61 per cent of all front cover images of women.

Pre-teen magazines

There are many magazines targeted at pre-teenage girls. Many of the leading brands originated in the US but are published all around the world. One such publication, *Barbie Magazine*, linked to the ubiquitous girls' toy, has been labelled as the child equivalent of a woman's feature magazine.[10] Other publications include *Disney Girl* and *Total Girl* that provide features on celebrities, the worlds of entertainment and fashion, and deal with themes including romantic relationships and sexual attractiveness. In terms of format and thematic content, magazines targeted at girls aged between 6 and 13 years have tended to be similar to those targeted at the older teens' market. These similarities have been brought acutely into focus when pre-teen and teen publications feature the same celebrities on their front covers.[11]

Sexualized content has been detected as a prevalent feature in magazines targeted at pre-teenage girls. One analysis carried out in Australia took three leading girls' magazines designed for 5- to 12-year-olds. In two of these publications, the researchers judged about half the content to be sexualized. This sexualized material cuts across feature articles and advertising in these magazines. The use of child models to sell products in advertisements, especially in commercial messages that were targeted at adults, was regarded as problematic. In addition, feature articles written for girls under 12 not only discussed grown-up male celebrities in terms of their careers and their lives but also evaluated their attractiveness.

Female celebrities from the worlds of music, film and television were held up as role models not simply in terms of their careers but their appearance. Some female celebrities, such as Paris Hilton, might be regarded as more problematic not only because their fame is not borne out of any special talent, but also because they have attracted notoriety for being featured in sexually explicit videos of themselves posted on the internet.

Perhaps the most explicit sexual content in these magazines occurred in articles that discussed boys and male adult celebrities. Young readers were invited to think about male celebrities in terms of which ones represented their ideal 'crushes' or 'dream date'. One important question raised by this content, that has yet to be empirically tested, is whether encouraging girls to think about adult male celebrities in this way also makes them more susceptible as they reach their initial dating years to respond differently to inappropriate sexual advances from men whom they meet in their own lives.[12] As we will see later when examining the effects of sexualized content in other mass media, evidence has emerged that exposure to sexual portrayals during pre-teenage and teenage years has been linked to earlier onset of sexual activity and earlier loss of virginity.[13]

Teen magazines

Not surprisingly, magazines targeted at teenagers deal with themes known to be of interest to them. As they enter adulthood and become physically mature, teenagers become more interested in matters that are uppermost in their minds – namely, their personal identity, whether others like them and relationships with others. Identity is frequently defined primarily in terms of physical attractiveness, and relationships in this context commonly mean sexual ones. Hence, teen magazines discuss these issues and provide advice on appearance and being attractive to others.

Girls' magazines pay a lot of attention to fashion trends but primarily in the context of advising girls and young women on how to dress to impress boys and men. The language used in these features is often sexualized in nature, and for girls, in particular, the advice given centres on ways of looking to get your man. These narratives are often accompanied with highly sexualized images of women who exude sex through their body language and the way they are dressed. Teen magazines define what it means to be a woman largely in terms of sexual identity and attractiveness.[14]

Extensive coverage of sexual matters has characterized teen magazines for many years. This market is not homogeneous, with some publications being aimed mainly at the younger end of the teenage range (12 to 18 years) and others targeted at the older end (18+). Coverage of sexual issues has tended to be more explicit in those magazines (e.g. *Glamour*, *Mademoiselle*) that seek to reach women in their late teens or early twenties. Sex is just as prevalent in magazines for the younger teenage range (e.g. *Seventeen*, *YM*), and the themes covered tended to engage directly with sexual matters, although they often presumed that at least some readers were not yet sexually active.[15]

Across this genre, however, some changes were noted over time in the types of sexual themes on which advice was given. In the mid-1970s, the focus was placed on broad issues such as sexual trends, infidelity, pregnancy and abortion, sexually transmitted diseases, as well as more detailed performance-related issues such as dating behaviour, handling problematic relationships, ending a relationship and dealing with a break-up. By the mid-1980s, the issues of a decade earlier were still covered, but there was more open advice about sexual performance and the nature of male and female sexuality. By the mid-1990s, themes such as being a virgin and whether this made a difference to a guy, taboo sexual relations, sexual orientation, sexual addiction and sexual abuse, and methods for enhancing male and female sexual performance became more prominent.[16]

What has been an even more disturbing trend for some critics of teen magazines' sexualization of childhood is that children and young teenagers depicted in these publications are treated similarly to fully adult young women. The photography draws the readers' attention to sexual attributes in articles that advise this still developing age group on how to make themselves more attractive objects of male desire through the use of cosmetics, hair styling and the way in which they dress.[17]

Magazines targeted at adolescent girls and young women cover a diverse range of sex-related topics that include sexual techniques, sexual orientation, safe sex practices, and establishing and maintaining relationships.[18] Many observations of teen magazines aimed at girls were found to construct an image of female sexuality based on the need to look physically attractive and to be sexually desirable and available to boys or men.[19] Success in life for a woman was defined in terms of making the most of her appearance, having good fashion sense, being socially adept and finding the right man to be with.[20]

Evidence has emerged, however, that magazines aimed at teenage girls and young adult women can give conflicting messages about sex. While encouraging girls to make themselves look sexy in an objectified way, they would then emphasize the importance of sex as part of a committed relationship in which 'looks' is not everything. Girls might at one point be told to experiment with their sexuality, but then cautioned to avoid rushing into sexual relationships.[21] It was important for girls to behave like ladies, but also to know how to flirt with a man whom they found attractive. They should project a quality of innocence but also not be afraid to make it known to a man that they found him attractive.[22] Girls were advised by teen magazines to know how to satisfy a man's sexual needs but not then to feel pressured into having sex.[23]

Before jumping to conclusions either about the prevalence of problematic messages and images or their impact upon young people, it is important to examine the research evidence. To what extent are youngsters likely to be exposed to this content? Even if they are exposed to it, do they absorb its messages and change their self-impressions, interest in sex and behavioural practices?

Children can be exposed to sexual references in the media but do not always understand or identify with them. Even if they do notice this material, its lack of immediate relevance to their lives may lead them to largely ignore it. Alternatively, if messages about sex in the media contradict social standards they have learned from parents or at school, they may adopt a highly critical stance dismissing such depictions as crude, rude, offensive and unacceptable.[24] Pre-teenage girls have been found to articulate and adhere to their own standards in relation to exposure to sexualized magazine content and acceptance of it.[25]

Teenage girls' sexual development occurs at its own pace and is not automatically accelerated by the media. While turning to teenagers' magazines such as *More* and *Sugar* as a source of social learning about sex, the sexual advice or reported sexual experiences of girls that appear in these publications are compared with other information sources and personal life experiences. If anything is learned about sexual relations from these magazines, the information they provide is not accepted invariably at face value. Instead, its relevance to girls' own lives is determined through discussions with their peers and what they had already learned from more direct sexual experiences.[26]

Early onset of sexual interest and activity has been attributed by the medical profession to progressively earlier biological developments in children. This trend is linked to children becoming bigger generation by generation, and specifically to an increase in body mass index among pre-teens. Hence, physiological factors are driving sexual maturity patterns and it is these factors that are raising earlier awareness of sexuality.[27]

The teen magazines targeted at girls are dominated by relationship themes and associated messages encouraging girls to enhance their sexual attractiveness. Key messages here focus on the social importance of being sexually desirable and the need to get the attention of men. In many ways, therefore, these publications actively encourage girls to present and promote themselves as objects of desire and to highlight this feature as an all-important goal in life. Despite the plethora of advice about relationships, much more coverage is devoted to creating an outward appearance that is designed to gain the attention of men. Both teens' and women's magazines have repeatedly been found to focus significantly on telling and showing their readers how to make themselves look sexually desirable.[28] In magazines targeted at teen girls, such as *YM*, *Teen*, *Seventeen*, *Glamour* and *Mademoiselle*, the advice routinely provided encouraged girls and young women to define themselves as sexual objects whose identity could only be complete once they had attracted a man.[29] Girls and young women are continuously encouraged by these magazines to take good care of their appearance and to think carefully about what they wear so as to appear sexually attractive to men.[30]

Teenage girls are told they must look sexy for boys. This objective is reinforced both in articles and in accompanying photographs. It almost becomes a lifestyle choice because sexual attractiveness is attained through all aspects of your being. This means that girls must continually think about their hairstyle, the make-up they wear, and their fashion sense as expressed through their clothes and through their overall physical 'look'. This 'look' also embraces their body shape that must adhere to an idealized norm of beauty that may be attainable only through special diet and exercise plans.[31] At a time when teenage girls are most self-conscious about their appearance, these publications do not simply provide advice but also exert social pressure to seek perfection in terms of their make-up, hair style, skin texture and body shape, and, of course, to buy a range of beauty products advertised in the magazines.[32]

At the same time as placing teenage girls under pressure to project a stereotyped sexual image to boys/men, teen magazines also portrayed adolescent boys in an unflattering light as emotionally insecure, easily manipulated and disposable. Girls needed both to attract boys and then to change them. The techniques involved in attracting boys, however, also conditioned still further the beliefs and values about female sexuality that girls needed to change to convert boys into loving, loyal romantic partners.[33]

Women athletes and sexualization

The ideal body shape might be attainable only through exercise and diet, but even those women who engage in extreme forms of exercise as serious sports competitors find themselves treated as sexual objects before accomplished sportswomen. Although success in sport might be seen as empowering for women and provides an opportunity for them to be evaluated in terms of their physical prowess and abilities, media images of female athletes have nevertheless still focused on sexualized aspects of their appearance.[34]

Sexualization abounds in the way in which women in sport are treated and this style of coverage characterizes many sports magazines. Male athletes can be treated as sexual objects of desire as well, but this type of coverage is more usually reserved for female athletes.[35] Some female athletes have played along with this trend. A number of internationally famous female athletes have appeared in editions of *Playboy*, including German ice skater Katerina Witt and the American swimmer Amanda Beard. So, too, have a number of women professional wrestlers such as Candice Michelle, Chyna and Sable. Other famous sportswomen such as golfer Natalie Gulbis, beach volleyball player Misty May and race car driver Danica Patrick have appeared in photo shoots in revealing swimwear in men's magazines such as *FHM* and *Maxim*.

In general, women sports stars have been found to receive much less media coverage than their male counterparts. This trend has been observed over all major sports media across the second half of the 20th century.[36] Even during major sports events such as the Olympic Games, when greater parity in amount of coverage might be expected, a gender divide in sports coverage has still occurred.[37] This pattern of male dominance in sports coverage begins even with young sports performers. Media coverage of school and college sports events in the US has exhibited gender bias in the relative amounts of coverage given to young female and male sports performers.[38]

It is not so much the quantity of coverage that is important in the context of the cultivation of sexualization effects, but the nature of that coverage that counts. It has been argued that because high performance in sports was traditionally associated with males and required a level of competitiveness that called upon conventionally male attributes of physical strength and aggression, the media tried to redress the balance by referring also to the more feminine qualities of leading sports women so as to remind everyone that success in sports for women did not mean denial of their femininity.[39] Sports commentators and sports writers have been found to provide further reminders of the feminine qualities of high-performing female athletes through their frequent references to qualities such as physical attractiveness and sexuality more often than they ever would make such references in the case of equivalent male sports performers.[40] While male athletes would be discussed in the media almost solely in terms of their athletic prowess, equally successful female athletes from the same sports would be examined in terms of their hairstyle, application of cosmetics and fashion sense. Discussion of physical attributes for male athletes was usually restricted to how these supported their sports performance, but for female athletes their physicality often adopted a sexual tone.[41]

Another study of appearances made by female athletes in editions of *Sports Illustrated* and *Sports Illustrated for Women* during 1997 to 1999 found that just one in ten of the photographs that appeared in these magazines depicted women. One in 20 of those photographs were sexually suggestive in nature. In contrast, less than 1 per cent of photographs of male athletes were classified as being sexualized. Most pictures of male athletes showed them in sports action shots compared with just one in three pictures of female athletes.[42]

Research into the way in which the US women's soccer team were treated by the media, including magazines, found frequent subtle sexualization of these athletes by pictures focusing more on their appearance than their performance, explicit sexual references towards members of the team, and focus also on their personal lives rather than their professionalism as competitors.[43] The tendency for sports media to present contradictory messages about female athletes that confound their sports performance as serious and dedicated competitors and their sexual attractiveness as women was found in newspaper coverage of the 1999 Women's World Soccer Championship.[44]

A study of coverage of women rock climbers featured in 114 issues of *Climbing* magazine that were published between 1991 and 2004 revealed that they were generally under-represented compared with male climbers. When female climbers were pictured, they were usually shown in the context of climbing as male climbers would be. In feature articles about female climbers, however, there was a tendency to balance the special attributes of successful women climbers in a male-dominated sport with narratives that referred to their feminine qualities and traditional roles as girlfriends, wives, mothers and homemakers, and to highlight their physical attractiveness.[45]

Lads' magazines

There are numerous magazines targeted specifically at men that are characterized by abundant images of sexually attractive young women. These men's 'lifestyle' magazines include publications such as *FHM*, *Loaded*, *Maxim* and *Stuff* and contain features that focus on men's interests, but are permeated by pictures and articles about attractive female celebrities from the worlds of entertainment, fashion, film, music and sport. Other weeklies, such as *Nuts and Zoo* in the UK, feature images of both female celebrities and glamour models, but even more so ordinary girls frequently pictured nude or topless. The themes are generally much more sexualized than even the men's monthlies. Specific themes are featured that focus on female body parts such as the biggest boobs or best bum. Young women are therefore sexually objectified in the most direct and explicit fashion with photographic emphasis placed on specific aspects of the female body.

This market emerged during the 1990s and expanded dramatically in the new century. By 2005, for instance, *Maxim* attracted at least 2.5 million US readers and *Nuts* and *Zoo* reached half a million UK readers every week.

These magazines have been the source of controversy. Mainstream retailers in the UK have tended to treat them similarly to adult sex magazines in placing them on higher shelves and sometimes even concealing their front-page images of scantily clad young women. In the US, in May 2003, Wal-Mart stopped selling *FHM*, *Maxim* and *Stuff* magazines allegedly because of complaints from customers about explicit and sexualized images of women on their front covers.[46] In the UK, the potential impact of lads' magazines upon the attitudes that young men held about sex and about young women was widely debated by policy-makers and social commentators. There was evidence, though, that these magazines could also represent a valuable source of sexual information for young people embarrassed to seek advice about sex from other sources such as their parents or teachers.[47] Research among British sixth-form students found, however, that girls aged 17 and 18 were angered and offended by the way in which women were depicted in magazines such as *Nuts* and *Zoo*.[48]

Lads' magazines are characterized by a strong focus on female sexuality. These publications are not technically classified as pornography, but they do contain regular and large quantities of sexually explicit material. They abound with images that depict women in highly sexualized poses. Women are objectified and presented, often explicitly, as sex objects. Frequently, the women in question are shown wearing few or no clothes.[49] One report found that a magazine such as *Nuts* would contain, on average, around 70 images of women and that in at least one third of these the women had their breasts exposed.[50]

One analysis of lad's magazines *Maxim* and *Stuff* in the US found that they used images of young women to construct male-oriented perspectives on female sexuality. The images of women and accompanying texts in these magazines frequently dealt with sexual themes and provided highly objectified descriptions of female sexuality. They also placed emphasis on the importance to male self-esteem and wider social regard of being sexually successful with women and provided tips on how to find women and get them to submit to male sexual demands. Much less attention is devoted to sexual activity as part of a loving and committed relationship. More often, emotional commitment is treated as irrelevant to sex and accumulating many sexual conquests is seen as being better in social status terms than commitment to long-term and monogamous relationships.[51]

An analysis by Dana Menard and Peggy Kleinplatz of the School of Psychology, University of Ottawa, found that magazines that targeted both young men and young women were preoccupied with articles about sex that focused on methods for achieving 'great sex'. Regardless of the gender of the target market, great sex tended to revolve around making the right technical and social preparations that would maximize sexual gratification from a male perspective.[52]

Elsewhere, it has been noted that lads' magazines present depictions of women that reflect many of the values and beliefs about female sexuality found in pornographic media. Women are presented as available for male sexual gratification, and young men are encouraged to adopt an assertive and even aggressive stance towards sexual dominance of women.[53]

Laramie Taylor of the Department of Communication, University of Michigan, examined three lads' magazines on sale in the US, *Maxim*, *Stuff* and *FHM* (*For Him Magazine*). A sample of 91 articles was compiled from 53 issues of these publications that dealt with sexual behaviour or relationship themes. The articles tended also to be illustrated with images of women who were described in terms of their sex appeal. The topics covered by these articles were classified in terms of whether they dealt with themes such as improving one's sex life, finding out what women like sexually, the keys to sexual satisfaction, unorthodox sexual behaviours or positions, unorthodox sexual locations, and drugs, alcohol and sex. The articles were also coded for the different kinds of relationship that might exist between sexual partners, ranging from sex with strangers through sex with known partners without emotional attachment, to sex in more committed relationships. Accompanying images were coded in terms of whether they illustrated any of the foregoing themes from the narrative content. The images were also classified in terms of their sexual explicitness that was grounded in the level of nudity depicted and also whether male–female partners were shown engaging in sexual activity.

The most common primary topics dealt with what women like sexually, unorthodox sexual behaviour and positions, and ways of improving one's sex life. Sexual health issues, in contrast, were rarely featured as primary themes. Unorthodox sexual locations and using drugs and alcohol in sexual contexts were prevalent secondary themes. Despite concerns about the role played by sexualized media in promoting a dehumanized or objectified form of sexuality, in terms of relationship contexts, the most prominent theme was sex as part of a committed relationship. An emphasis was regularly placed on improving sexual performance as part of enhancing one's sex life with a partner with whom a commitment had been made. Where the relationship context did not take the form of a long-term commitment, a strong focus was placed on how to behave in new relationships to enhance their potential for longevity. Much of the image content linked to these articles contained attractive women, but nudity and sexual explicitness were rare.

Taylor concluded that lads' magazines drew a lot of attention to sexual issues, raising their salience and therefore possibly their perceived importance in the lives of young men. A regular focus on ways of improving one's sex life might have cultivated an impression among each magazine's male readers that their own sex life was probably inadequate because sexual improvement was something they always needed to strive for. Sexual improvement often meant being better at physical sexual acts by learning new sexual techniques or by trying sex in different locations. Despite the prominence of articles dealing with what women want, these were not mostly characterized by sexual altruism but more by the need to give women what they want so that they give even more in return in terms of better sexual gratification for their man. The solutions here tended to be physical rather than emotional in nature and as such maintained a highly sexualized impression of women as sex objects to be mechanically manipulated to make them perform better for men.[54]

Effects of print media images of women

There has been extensive research on the way in which women are represented in magazines, but rather less direct study of how female or male readers might be influenced by this content. There are several theories that have been invoked to offer potential explanations of the kinds of effects that might occur upon exposure to sexualized images or descriptions of women. Social learning theory would propose that children and teenagers could acquire gender stereotypes from this content that distorted general perceptions of what women and men are like and what they are capable of achieving in life.

Objectification theory focuses on the propensity of media and the world of consumerism to sexually objectify the female body. Hence, women are shown as sexual objects and magazine readers are encouraged to evaluate women at this level. Such media representations can influence the way in which women perceive themselves as well as how they are evaluated by men.

Cultivation theory has posited that media representations often distort social reality and that repeated exposure to them can result in a warped view of the world. This can take the form of believing that certain types of events (e.g. crime, divorce) occur more frequently than they do and that certain social groups are best suited to specific social roles (e.g. men as doctors and women as nurses).[55]

As we have seen already in this chapter, a number of magazine genres have been found to depict stereotyped impressions of female (and male) sexuality that could have potential effects on the sexual self-identities and 'other' identities of their readers. Adult pornographic magazines depict highly explicit sexualized images of women and convey messages about the sexual dominance of men and submissiveness of women. Such publications, however, tend to have limited circulations and access to them is usually restricted. Perhaps of greater social concern are popular magazines that are characterized by highly sexualized themes and content. These range from general magazines and sports magazines that often depict women in sexualized ways to genres such as lads' magazines that for some observers represent a form of 'borderline pornography'.[56] These magazines not only contain abundant images of nude and topless young women in explicitly sexualized poses, but also feature content that underlines the sexual objectification of women through the type of sexual advice it provides to young men. Sometimes, this content goes beyond encouraging men to adopt tactics that maximize their sexual success with women to messages that appear to endorse sexual coercion.[57]

Sports magazines

One early interventionist analysis of how young men and women perceived print media coverage of male and female athletes assigned college students to conditions in which they read different fictitious newspaper profiles about the same Olympic athlete.[58] In one version, the profile emphasized the athlete's attractiveness and in the other version it focused on their sporting abilities. Some students read profiles about a male athlete and others read profiles about a female athlete. Afterwards, the students were invited to complete a test in which they evaluated the athlete they had just read about. The scale comprised 'feminine' attributes (e.g. affectionate, compassionate, gentle, tender), attributes that measured whether the athlete was seen as a respectable individuals and good role model, as well as attributes measuring their athletic abilities and aggression.

Female athletes were perceived as more attractive when depicted in terms of their attractiveness than in terms of their athletic prowess. This effect did not occur in the case of ratings of male athletes. Regardless of gender, when the athlete was described in terms of their attractiveness, they were seen as less aggressive, less heroic and less talented. These findings indicated that gender biases in the way that female and male athletes are presented in the media could therefore affect the way they are perceived by people who read about them. The outcome could be disadvantageous for athletes whose sporting successes are underplayed in the presence of focus on the way they look.

Elizabeth Daniels and Heidi Wartens of the University of Oregon investigated the ways in which teenage boys in the United States reacted to images of female athletes and models.[59] The boys who took part in this study were aged between 12 and 17 years. They were assigned at random to different conditions in which they viewed a series of images that depicted accomplished female athletes playing their sports, or images of well-known female athletes in sexually attractive poses, or images of female models in sexually appealing poses. The images were selected from popular magazines that included *Glamour, Marie Claire, Sports Illustrated* and *Sports Illustrated for Women*. The female athletes were all identified verbally by name and their sport. The sexualized models were give fictitious names and had their occupation listed simply as 'model'. In the pictures of sexualized athletes, the sports-women who were featured wore swimsuits (either one-piece or bikinis).

The teenage participants viewed five images in all. They were invited to write a short passage after exposure to each image in which they described the women in the picture and how the photograph made them feel. These verbal accounts were then analysed by the researchers and with particular focus given to references to the depicted women's appearance and sexual attractiveness, as well as their athleticism. The sexualized images both of athletes and models generated significantly more references to appearance and sexiness than did the images of female athletes playing their sports. References to body weight were most likely to occur in relation to the pictures of models, but featured rarely in response to the pictures of the female athletes (including sexualized images of athletes). Boys were likely to make more references to female athletes' physical prowess after seeing pictures of these athletes in action than after seeing them in sexualized poses, but the difference here was only marginally significant. Hence, even sexualized images of well-known athletes could trigger teenage boys to describe how good these women were at playing their sport.

In general, the findings showed that while teenage boys were ready to recognize the physical abilities of high-performing female athletes, when these athletes were depicted in a sexualized pose, they were described in more sexually objectified ways by young male admirers. There was clear evidence here that female athletes' sports abilities were rendered less prominent or front of mind among teenage boys after the boys had seen the athletes in sexualized pictures. This outcome was much less likely to occur in response to images of female athletes playing their sport.

Magazines targeted at men

As we have seen already, there have been widespread concerns about the potential effects of lads' and men's magazines. Men's magazines refer to those titles that publish explicit sexual content and typically feature multiple nude photographic images of young women. Those publications that derive from the best-known 'brands' such *Playboy* and *Penthouse* are generally classed as pornography. The women depicted in these magazines are sexualized not only because they are shown with little or no clothing, but also through their postures and facial expressions. Lads' magazines represent a relatively recent genre that has been targeted at the young adult male market. Technically not classed as porn, these publications nevertheless depict scantily clad young women in highly sexualized poses.

Interest in the effects of these magazines has centred on whether they produce a certain kind of social learning about sex and cultivate specific sets of beliefs about women and about male and female sexuality. Sexualized messages about women are presented not only visually, but also through the feature content of these magazines. Effects research has tried to establish the impact of these magazines on men's perceptions of women and on men's perceptions of themselves. Debates about these magazines have been polarized and a number of commentators and researchers have claimed that these magazines provide harmless entertainment and might even represent valuable information sources on sexual matters and sources of empowerment for women.[60]

In terms of the effects of men's and lads' magazines, three broad types of evidence have emerged. The first evidence type comprises self-attributed effects whereby young men have been asked to comment in their own words on whether they feel they have been influenced by reading men's or lads' magazines. The second type of evidence has explored relationships between reported use of these magazines and sex-related perceptions, attitudes and beliefs. The third type of evidence has derived from experimental methodologies in which changes in sex-related perceptions, attitudes and beliefs are measured subsequent to controlled exposure to sexualized magazine content.

Self-attribution data have derived from in-depth interviews with men. When asked to talk about their experiences with *Playboy* magazines, young American men stated that they felt the sexual advice they had received from this publication was problematic, particularly in terms of the ways in which men ought to express themselves sexually. Nonetheless, some men admitted that they had internalized some of this advice and that it had shaped their own sexual identity to some degree.[61]

Laramie Taylor compared the effects of reading lads' magazines and pornographic magazines on the sex-related attitudes and beliefs of male university students.[62] The aim of this study was to find out whether the sexualized content published in these magazines could shape the sexual beliefs male readers held about themselves. The self-schema has been defined as a collection of beliefs that a person has internalized about their identity as a sexual being.[63] Taylor reasoned that men's magazines were often characterized by messages about sexual coercion, with males as dominant sexual partners and females as submissive receptacles of male sexual desire. Lads' magazines would often present a diluted version of this sexual proposition. There was an expectation, therefore, that young men who read these magazines on a regular basis might absorb some of these messages and that their self-perceptions as sexual beings might be influenced accordingly. Although female sexual pleasure was always frequently put in the foreground in these publications, this was not treated as an end in itself but as a means to delivering greater sexual gratification for men. Hence, these magazines were not only thought to shape men's perceptions of themselves but also their attitudes towards women in sexual contexts.

In an initial study, Taylor recruited a small sample of male undergraduate students aged 18 to 24 years and asked them questions about their readership of a number of named lads' and men's magazines and about their sexual attitudes and expectations. They were given a list of 20 intimate behaviours and asked about the extent to which they would normally expect to engage in each of these activities with a romantic partner. These behaviours included passionate kissing and erotic massage and, more unusually perhaps, sexual bondage and group sex. Further scales were administered to measure the men's opinions about women and rape and about sexual permissiveness.

In subsequent analyses, Taylor found that those young men who reportedly read lads' magazines and men's magazines more often expected a more varied sex life with their sexual partners. While these men were not more inclined to support or accept ideas about male sexual dominance over women, they were more likely to accept intimate sexual activity divorced from emotional or romantic commitment.

In a second study, a further sample of male undergraduates aged 18 to 25 years was recruited and indicated their frequency of readership for each of a list of 25 lads' and men's magazines. They then completed further tests designed to measure their sexual attitudes, descriptions of themselves in terms of whether they felt they were romantic, loving, passionate, aggressive, domineering, exciting and so on. Further questions measured their sexual orientation (heterosexual, homosexual or bisexual), numbers of sexual partners they had had, their current relationship status and level of recent sexual activity.

Subsequent analyses revealed that those young men who had reported more frequent reading of lads' magazines regarded themselves as more aggressive and powerful rather than romantic and loving in their sexual relations. These young men also held more permissive sexual attitudes. Those men who reported more frequent exposure to men's magazines held more permissive sexual attitudes, but their readership of these publications made no difference to how they perceived themselves. Having more permissive sexual attitudes was, in turn, related to having had more sexual partners. Those men who regarded themselves as more dominant sexual partners reported a greater number of recent sexual partners. Further, more complex statistical analyses revealed that readership of lads' magazines and men's magazines predicted a more sexually permissive outlook even when the potential effects on sexual attitudes of number of sexual partners and recent sexual experiences were cancelled out. Reading of the more pornographic men's magazines appeared to play no part in the way in which these young men defined themselves in sexual terms. It is possible, therefore, that these men identified more with the content of lads' magazines than with the more extreme sexual messages projected by men's magazines.

Other research has emerged to show that reading lads' magazines might change the way in which they perceive themselves, especially in regard to their evaluations of their body shape. Although reported readership of magazines that presented sexually objectifying images did not influence women in this way, with male readers it increased the extent to which they became sensitive about their own bodies.[64] In a further extension of this research, it became clear that the triggering of anxieties about their body shape among young men in their late teens and early 20s did not occur in response to viewing pictures of well-muscled male fashion models but followed exposure to lads' magazine images of sexually attractive young women. Exposure to pictures of sexually objectified young women led young men to question their own physical desirability and, in turn, affected their confidence in romantic relationships.[65]

Lads' magazines have been investigated in the context of the influence they may have over the perceptions and ideas young men develop about women. In one British study, a sample of 90 young men were presented with a series of derogatory statements about women that they were told had either been made by convicted rapists or extracted from articles in lads' magazines. The men in the study were then asked to indicate the extent to which they agreed with it. In an initial test, it emerged that these young men were more inclined to identify with a statement if they thought it had been taken from a lads' magazine than if they believed it was something that had been said by a convicted rapist. In a further study, a small sample of 40 young men and young women were presented with the same quotes and were asked to judge whether they thought they had been made by convicted rapists or had been taken from lads' magazines. They were unable to do this with any consistency and were as likely to say that the quotes had come from magazines as from rapists. One conclusion reached from this investigation was that lads' magazines frame ideas about female sexuality that are not inconsistent with the extreme sexual attitudes held by men found guilty of sexual aggression.[66]

Moving beyond the perception that lads' magazines might convey sexually extreme messages about women, a follow-on concern is that the contents of these magazines might prompt readers to believe that sexual coercion against women is socially acceptable. If this climate of opinion becomes established there is a further risk that it could encourage more men to engage in sexual harassment of women and even for women themselves to become more accepting of this behaviour. As we have seen earlier in this book, one of the problematic outcomes of a sexualized world is that through the sexual objectification of both genders, but especially of women, and through the liberalizing of sexual promiscuity and the dehumanizing of sexual relationships, a social climate could occur that gives licence to those who would perpetrate sexual crimes.

So far, the research evidence about whether lads' magazines can cultivate these kinds of sexual schema among men and women has been inconclusive. The evidence in relation to men's magazines is less equivocal. Sexually explicit media have been found to attract the attention of young men who have reportedly behaved in a sexually harassing way.[67] There is further evidence that exposure to magazine advertisements with sexual and sexist themes can increase acceptance of sexually problematic and criminal behaviour both among male and female readers.[68]

Other developments

Despite the concern about women as victims of objectification through the use of sexualized images of the female body in magazines, there have been two further developments that have not often been placed in the foreground and yet represent important factors that need to be addressed. There has been a traditional concern about the way in which women have been depicted in magazines as objects dressed purely to satisfy male desires and fantasies. Yet, a new generation of young women has emerged, led by young female celebrities often found in the fashion and music businesses, who proactively seek to display themselves in a highly sexualized fashion. They dress and behave in sexually provocative ways and offer themselves as sex objects to admiring male and female audiences. Rather than defining themselves as the weaker and dependent sex, however, these young women use their own sexuality as a signal of their independence and power and their freedom to choose how they present themselves to the world.[69] These images appear in magazines that can be readily consumed by girls who have not yet reached puberty. Furthermore, these celebrity icons may be featured in publications that are targeted specifically at the pre-teen girls' market.[70]

A second important development concerns the representation of the male body. A trend in the use of a more sexualized masculine body image has been noted in men's magazines. Images are used that objectify the male body by using techniques such as depicting males without clothes and showing specific parts of the body with heads and faces hidden, effectively dehumanizing the models that are featured. Such images emphasize the physical body and tend usually to present idealized body shapes defined by smooth, unblemished skin and well-toned muscularity.[71] Hence, the body is presented as the most important factor by which men should be judged and the removal of the face enhances the focus on physicality as the primary determinant of attractiveness and status.

Summary and conclusions

There is a wide range of magazines targeted at children, teenagers and young adults that contain frequent sexual themes. Concerns about these publications arise from the prevalence of sexual content and the degree of detail in which sexual matters are discussed. Some magazines openly invite readers to contribute their own thoughts, feelings and experiences concerning sex. In some instances, the sexual themes are linked to stories about celebrities. In others, they derive from apparently true stories involving ordinary people and even the magazine's own readers.

These publications are popular and extensively consumed. Their potential influences stem from the salience of sex as a subject matter which constantly raises the subject to the top of readers' minds, the values that are promulgated concerning sexual relationships, and the more technical details in the case of some publications concerning sexual techniques. Among those publications targeted at young adults and to which teenagers may often be exposed, sexually objectified images of young women abound. These include both female celebrities and images of ordinary young women who have submitted photographs of themselves in various states of undress.

How worried should we be about these publications? There is fairly limited research that has tried to measure the effects of exposure to magazines with sexualized content. Readership of magazines aimed at young men that are characterized by multiple sexually objectified images of young women – usually aged from their late teens to mid-20s – has been found to exhibit a relationship to some ideas that young male readers have about their sex lives, but does not seem to create sexual monsters who expect women to fall at their feet or believe that one-sided sexual dominance over women is accepted. There are signs, however, that these publications can contribute towards a climate of sexually promiscuous opinion and accompanying behavioural expectations.

Notes

1 Egan, D. R. and Hawkes, G. L. (2012) 'Sexuality, youth and the perils of endangered innocence: How history can help us get past the panic', *Gender and Education*, 24(3), 269–284.

2 La Nauze, A. and Rush, E. (2006a) 'Corporate paedophilia: Sexualization of children in Australia', The Australia Institute Discussion Paper No. 90, October; La Nauze, A. and Rush, E. (2006b) 'Letting children be children: Stopping the sexualization of children in Australia', The Australia Institute, Discussion Paper No. 93, December.

3 Roberts, D., Foehr, U. and Rideout, V. (2005, March) *Generation M: Media in the lives of 8–18 year olds*. Menlo Park, CA: Kaiser Family Foundation.

4 Bielay, G. and Herold, E. S. (1995) 'Popular magazines as a source of sexual information for university women', *Canadian Journal of Human Sexuality*, 4, 247–261; Treise, D. and Gotthoffer, A. (2002) 'Stuff you couldn't ask your parents: Teens talking about using magazines for sex information', in J. D. Brown, J. R. Steele and K. Walsh-Childers (Eds.) *Sexual Teens, Sexual Media: Investigating Media's Influence on Adolescent Sexuality*, pp173–189. Mahwah, NJ: Lawrence Erlbaum Associates.

5 Fine, M. (1988) 'Sexuality, schooling and adolescent females: The missing discourse of desire', *Harvard Educational Review*, 58(1), 28–53; Moore, S. and Rosenthal, D. (1993) *Sexuality in Adolescence*. New York, NY: Routledge.

6 Thompson, S. (1995) *Going All the Way: Teenage Girls' Tales of Sex, Romance, and Pregnancy*. New York, NY: Wang & Hill.

7 McMahon, K. (1990) 'The *Cosmopolitan* ideology and the management of desire', *Journal of Sex Research*, 27, 381–396.

8 Finders, M. J. (1997) *Just Girls: Hidden Literacies and Life in Junior High*. New York, NY: Teachers College Press.

9 Hatton, E. and Trautner, M. N. (2011) 'Equal opportunity objectification: The sexualization of men and women on the cover of *Rolling Stone*', *Sexuality & Culture*, 15, 256–278.

10 Sanders, F., Gwynne, E. and Gaskill, D. (1998) '*Barbie* magazine: The first 12 months', in D. Gaskill and F. Sanders (Eds.) *Challenge the Body Culture Conference Proceedings, Brisbane 1997*, Publications and Printing Unit. Queensland, Australia: Queensland University of Technology, pp111–114.

11 Rush, E. and La Nauze, A. (2006, October) *Corporate Paedophilia: The Sexualization of Children in Australia*, The Australia Institute, Canberra, Discussion Paper No 90, http://www.tai.org.au, accessed 10 December 2012.

12 Rush, E. and La Nauze, A. (2006a) *ibid.*

13 Brown, J. D., L'Engle, K. L., Pardun, C. J., Guo, G., Kenneavy, K. and Jackson, C. (2006) 'Sexy media matter: Exposure to sexual content in music, movies, television and magazines predicts black and white adolescents' sexual behaviour', *Pediatrics*, 117, 1018–1027.

14 Duffy, M. and Gotcher, M. J. (1996) 'Crucial advice on how to get the guy: The rhetorical vision of power and seduction in the teen magazine *YM*', *Journal of Communication Inquiry*, 20(1), 32–48; Evans, E. D., Rutberg, J., Sather, C. and Turner, C. (1991) 'Content analysis of contemporary teen magazines for adolescent females', *Youth and Society*, 23(1), 99–120.

15 Garner, A., Sterk, H. M. and Adams, S. (1998) 'Narrative analysis of sexual etiquette in teenage magazines', *Journal of Communication*, 38, 59–78.

16 Garner, A., Sterk, H. M. and Adams, S. (1998) *ibid.*

17 Duffy, M. and Gotcher, M. J. (1996) *op. cit.*
18 McMahon, K. (1990) *ibid.*
19 McRobbie, A. (1991) *Feminism and Youth Culture: from Jackie to Just Seventeen.* Boston, MA: Unwin Hyman; Peirce, K. (1990) 'A feminist theoretical perspective on the socialisation of teenage girls through *Seventeen*', *Sex Roles*, 29, 59–68.
20 Duffy, M. and Gotcher, M. J. (1996) 'Crucial advice on how to get the guy: The rhetorical vision of power and seduction in the teen magazine *YM*', *Journal of Communication Inquiry*, 20, 32–48;
21 Carpenter, L. M. (1998) 'From girls into women: Scripts for sexuality and romance in *Seventeen* magazine, 1974–94', *Journal of Sex Research*, 35, 158–168; Durham, M. (1998) 'Dilemmas of desire: Representations of adolescent sexuality in two teen magazines', *Youth and Society*, 29, 369–389; Duffy, M. and Gotcher, M. J. (1996) *ibid*; Garner, A., Sterk, H. M. and Adams, S. (1998) *op. cit.*
22 Wood, A. (1974) 'Relating', *Seventeen*, April, 33, 58, 62.
23 Durbin, K. (1974a) 'The intelligent woman's guide to sex', *Mademoiselle*, April, 80, 94; Durbin, K. (1974b) 'The intelligent woman's guide to sex', *Mademoiselle*, October, 80, 70; Soria, S. S. (1984) 'Sexual involvement: The experts answer your questions', *Teen*, April, 28: 9–12.
24 Buckingham, D., Willetts, R., Bragg, S. and Russell, R. (2010) *Sexualized Goods Aimed at Children: A Report to the Scottish Parliament Equal Opportunities Committee.* Edinburgh, UK: Scottish Parliament equal Opportunities Committee, http://www.scottish.parliament.uk/s3/committees/equal/reports-10/eor10–02, accessed 14 December 2012.
25 Kehily, M. J. (2012) 'Contextualising the sexualization of girls debate: Innocence, experience and young female sexuality', *Gender and Education*, 24(3), 255–268.
26 Kehily, M. J. (1999) 'More Sugar? Teenage magazines, gender displays and sexual learning', *European Journal of Cultural Studies*, 2(1), 65–89.
27 *The Obstetrician and Gynacologist* (2012) 'Girls who start puberty very early are more likely to have psychological problems', *The Obstetrician and Gynacologist*, 27 April.
28 Carpenter, L. M. (1998) *op. cit*; Durham, M. (1998) 'Dilemmas of desire: Representations of adolescent sexuality in two teen magazines', *Youth & Society*, 29, 569–589; Garner, A., Sterk, H. M. and Adams, S. (1998) *op. cit.*
29 Garner, A., Sterk, H. M. and Adams, S. (1998) *op. cit.*
30 Duffy, M. and Gotcher, J. M. (1996) 'Crucial advice on how to get the guy: The rhetorical vision of power and seduction in teen magazines – *YM*', *Journal of Communication Inquiry*, 20, 32–48.
31 McMahon, K. (1990) 'The *Cosmopolitan* ideology and the management of desire', *Journal of Sex Research*, 27, 381–396.
32 Labre, M. P. and Walsh-Childers, K. (2003) 'Advice? Beauty messages in web sites of teen magazines', *Mass Communication & Society*, 6, 379–396.
33 Firminger, K. B. (2006) 'Is he boyfriend material? Representation of males in teenage girls' magazines', *Men and Maculinities*, 8(3), 298–308.
34 Knight, J. and Giuliano, T. A. (2001) 'He's a Laker; she's a 'Looker': The consequences of gender-stereotyped portrayals of male and female athletes by the print media', *Sex Roles*, 45, 217–229; Heywood, L. and Dworkin, S. L. (2003) *Built to Win: The Female Athlete as Cultural Icon.* Minneapolis, MN: University of Minneapolis Press.
35 Kane, M. J. (1996) 'Media coverage of the post-Title-IX female athlete: A feminist's analysis of sport, gender and power', *Duke Journal of Gender Law and Public Policy*, 3, 95–127.
36 Duncan, M. C. and Hasbrook, C. A. (1988) 'Denial of power in televised women's sports', *Sociology of Sport Journal*, 5, 1–21; Lumpkin, A. and Williams, L. D. (1991) 'An analysis of *Sports Illustrated* feature articles, 1954–87', *Sociology of Sport Journal*, 8, 1–15.
37 Eastman, S. T. and Billings, A. C. (1999) 'Gender parity in the Olympics: Hyping women athletes, favouring men athletes', *Journal of Sport and Social Issues*, 23, 140–170.
38 Sagas, M., Cunningham, G. B., Wigley, B. J. and Ashley, F. B. (2000) 'Internet coverage of university softball and baseball websites: The inequity continues', *Sociology of*

Sport Journal, 17(2), 198–212; Woodcock, A. T. (1995) 'Media coverage of boys' and girls' high school ice hockey in Minnesota', *Melpomene Journal*, 14, 27–29.

39 Kane, M. J. (1996) 'Media coverage of the post TitleXI female athlete', *Duke Journal of Gender Law and Policy*, 3, 95–127.

40 Birrell, S. and Theberge, N. (1994) 'Ideological control of women in sport', in D. M. Costa and R. S. Guthrie (Eds.) *Women and Sport: Interdisciplinary Perspectives*. Champaign, IL: Human Kinetics; Duncan, M. C. (1990) 'Sport photographs and sexual difference: Images of women and men in the 1984 and 1988 Olympic Games', *Sociology of Sport Journal*, 7, 22–43.

41 Boutilier, M. A. and SanGiovanni, L. (1983) *The Sporting Woman*. Champaign, IL: Human Kinetics; Messner, M. (1988) 'Sports and male domination: The female athlete as contested ideological terrain', *Sport Sociology Journal*, 5, 197–211.

42 Fink, J. S. and Kensicki, L. J. (2002) 'An imperceptible difference: Visual and textual constructions of femininity in *Sports Illustrated* and *Sports Illustrated for Women*', *Mass Communication & Society*, 5, 317–339.

43 Shugart, H. A. (2003) 'She shoots, she scores: Mediated constructions of contemporary female athletes in coverage of the 1999 US women's soccer team', *Western Journal of Communication*, 67, 1–31.

44 Christopherson, N., Janning, M. and McDonnell, E. D. (2002) 'Two kicks forward, one kick back: A content analysis of media discourses on the 1999 Women World Cup Soccer Championship', *Sociology of Sport Journal*, 19, 170–188.

45 Vodden-McKay, S. and Schelkl, B. L. A. (2010) 'Climbing high or falling flat? Representations of female rock climbers in *Climbing* magazine (1991–2004)', *Journal of Research on Women and Gender*, 3.

46 Carr, D. and Hays, C. L. (2003) '3 racy men's magazines are banned by Wal-Mart', *New York Times*, 6 May, C1.

47 OFSTED (2007) *Time for Change? Personal, Social and Health Education*. London, UK: OFSTED.

48 Jakubowicz, L. M. and McClelland, K. (2008) *The Top-Shelf Campaign: Findings and Report*. Unpublished report.

49 Aubrey, J. S. and Taylor, L. D. (2009) 'The role of lad magazines in priming men's chronic and temporary appearance-related schemata: An investigation of longitudinal and experimental findings', *Human Communication Research*, 35, 28–58; Krassas, N. R., Blauwkamp, J. M. and Wesselink, P. (2003) '"Master your Johnston": Sexual rhetoric in *Maxim* and *Stuff* magazines', *Sexuality and Culture*, 7, 98–119; Taylor, L. D. (2005) 'All for him: Articles about sex in American lad magazines', *Sex Roles*, 52, 153–163.

50 Turner, J. (2005) 'Dirty young men', *The Guardian*, 22 October, http://www.guardian.co.uk/theguardian/2005.oct/22/weekend7.weekend3, accessed 24 July 2008.

51 Krassas, N. R., Blauwkamp, J. M. and Wesselink, P. (2003), *op. cit.*

52 Menard, A. D. and Kleinplatz, P. J. (2008) 'Twenty-one moves guaranteed to make his thighs go up in flames: Depictions of "great sex" in popular magazines', *Sexuality & Culture*, 12(1), 1–20.

53 Taylor, L. D. (2006) 'College men, their magazines and sex', *Sex Roles*, 55, 693–702.

54 Taylor, L. D. (2005) 'All for him: Articles about sex in American lad magazines', *Sex Roles*, 52(3/4), 153–163.

55 Gunter, B. (1995) *Television and Gender Stereotyping*. London, UK: John Libbey.

56 Krassas, N. R., Blauwkamp, J. M. and Wesselink, P. (2003), *op. cit.*

57 Matacin, M. L. and Burger, J. M. (1987) 'A content analysis of sexual themes in *Playboy* cartoons', *Sex Roles*, 17(3/4), 179–186; Coy, M. and Horvath, M. A. H. (2010) '"Lads' mags": Young men's attitudes towards women and acceptance of myths about sexual; aggression', *Feminism and Psychology*, 20(2), 1–7.

58 Knight, J. L. and Guilianao, T. A. (2001) *op cit.*

59 Daniels, E. A. and Wartens, H. (2011) 'Athlete or sex symbol: What boys think of media representations of female athletes', *Sex Roles*, 65, 566–579.

60 Benwell, B. (2004) 'Ironic discourse: Evasive masculinity in British men's lifestyle magazines', *Men and Masculinities*, 7(1), 3–21; Tinckenell, E., Chambers, D., Van Loon, J. and Hudson, N. (2003) 'Begging for it: New femininities, social agency and moral discourse in contemporary teenage and men's magazines', *Feminist Media Studies*, 3(1), 47–63.

61 Beggan, J. K. and Allison, S. T. (2003) 'What sort of man reads *Playboy?* The self-reported influence of *Playboy* on the construction of masculinity', *Journal of Men's Studies*, 11(2), 189–206.

62 Taylor, L. (2006) 'College men, their magazines and sex', *Sex Roles*, 55, 693–702.

63 Anderson, B. L., Cyranowski, J. M. and Espindle, D. (1999) 'Men's sexual self-schema', *Journal of Personality and Social Psychology*, 76(4), 645–661.

64 Aubrey, J. S. (2006) 'Effects of sexually objectifying media on self-objectification and body surveillance in undergraduates: Results of a 2-year panel study', *Journal of Communication*, 56(2), 366–386.

65 Aubrey, J. S. and Taylor, L. D. (2009) 'The role of lad magazines in priming men's chronic and temporary appearance-related schemata: An investigation of longitudinal and experimental findings', *Human Communication Research*, 35(1), 28–58.

66 Hogarth, M. A. H., Hegarty, P., Tyler, S. and Mansfield, S. (2011) 'Lights on at the end of the party: Are lads' mags mainstreaming dangerous sexism?', *British Journal of Psychology*, 103(4), 454–471.

67 Brown, J. D. and L'Engle, K. L. (2009) 'X-rated sexual attitudes and behaviours associated with US early adolescents' exposure to sexually explicit media', *Communication Research*, 36(1), 129–151.

68 Lanis, K. and Covell, K. (1985) 'Images of women in advertisements: Effects on attitudes related to sexual aggression', *Sex Roles*, 32 (9/10), 639–649; Machia, M. and Lamb, S. (2009) 'Sexualized innocence: Effects of magazine ads portraying adult women as sexy little girls', *Journal of Media Psychology*, 21(1), 15–124.

69 Gill, R. (2007) *Gender and the Media*. Cambridge, UK: Polity Press; Gill, R. (2008) 'Empowerment/sexism; figuring female sexual agency in contemporary advertising', *Feminism and Psychology*, 18, 35–60.

70 Tankard Reist, M. (Ed.) (2010) *Getting Real: Challenging the Sexualization of Girls*. North Melbourne, Australia: Spinifex Press.

71 Rohlinger, D. A. (2002) 'Eroticizing men: Cultural influences on advertising and male objectification', *Sex Roles*, 46, 61–74.

5

TELEVISION AND SEXUALIZATION

There is ample evidence that sexual imagery in the traditional mass media that are popular with children and teenagers, particularly films and television, is widespread. In addition, there are plentiful opportunities for young people to witness this content. There is also evidence that these media present a non-normative representation of sexuality. Sexual attributes and scripts in television programmes and films made for showing in cinemas have often been found to present exaggerated impressions about sex, being sexy, and the significance of sex in everyday life. Sexual attractiveness is often packaged in a highly stereotyped way, particularly in relation to depictions of the physical human body. Sexual relations are also frequently dramatized in ways that present to young people a narrow repertoire of sexual scripts that could potentially lead to unrealistic expectations in their own lives.

Much of the empirical evidence has also revealed extensive gender stereotyping amongst the sexual imagery that the media present to young people. For a long time, television and movies were found to be guilty of generally restricting women's roles. Men occupied the most interesting leading parts, with women most often used as support acts. The numerical under-representation of women in television programmes and movies was compounded by perhaps an even more serious problem that when they were shown, women were generally stereotyped. Domestic roles were played up and roles showing women as successful in jobs and careers were rare. This pattern was certainly true from the 1950s through to the 1990s.[1]

Even when women were shown at work, their occupational roles were restricted and stereotyped (e.g. nurses rather than doctors) and they were less likely to be portrayed in positions of authority (machine operators rather than factory floor supervisors; secretaries rather than managers).[2] The pattern of gender stereotyping started to shift by the 1990s with a few examples appearing of women in lead roles who depicted abilities the equal of men's. Strong women, who often had special abilities superior to those of men and other women, appeared across a range of genres, although often in highly fictionalized and sometimes period settings (e.g. *Buffy The Vampire Slayer; Zena – Warrior Princess*). Despite the strength and independence of these female role models, these fictional characterizations also still focused on their womanly physical attributes that were frequently magnified by the revealing costumes they wore.[3]

Sexual attractiveness is placed more often as a core defining attribute of women than of men in the media, and especially in movies and on television. Over many years, female characters have been found to display affectionate behaviour on screen much more often than men do.[4] Yet, men were generally more likely to initiate sex on screen and this male dominance in taking control in sexual encounters increased over time on mainstream television.[5]

Many more media depictions of girls and women present them with unrealistic body shapes than is true of depictions of boys and men.[6] Both sexes tend to receive some degree of exaggerated treatment, however. Women are shown with slim waists but ample chests and hips, while men are shown with muscular physiques. Media depictions of body shape have been found to have the potential to influence girls' self-perceptions and general satisfaction with their own bodies.

Sex on television

Sex on television has been monitored over several decades using a methodology known as content analysis. This methodology attempts to quantify the attributes of television programmes in terms of the kinds of behaviours that are depicted, the types of people involved in those behaviours, the physical and social settings in which the behaviours occur, the causes of or motives underpinning specific behaviours, and the consequences of those actions for the people involved. The starting point must be to define the nature of the behaviour being examined. In the current context, therefore, researchers must begin by determining what types of behaviours on screen can be defined as sexual in nature. Sexual behaviour can take many forms that include kissing on the mouth, intimate touching and penetrative intercourse. It can occur between different types of partners distinguished in terms of gender, age, ethnicity, marital status and other relationship status. It can occur in different social contexts ranging from sex as part of a marital relationship, sex between partners who are being unfaithful to others, sex that is paid for, non-consensual sex, and so on. Televised or filmed depictions of sex can also vary in how explicit they are. Scenes can range from talk about sexual relations to highly realistic simulated sexual activity. In some erotic films shown on limited video releases or encrypted television channels, the sex on camera is not simulated.

There have been concerns voiced about the amount of sex shown on television and in cinema films (that there is too much of it) and also about the way in which it is shown. Sexual depictions on mainstream television have become more explicit over the decades. Scenes of full frontal nudity – especially that of female characters – can be found on contemporary television in the 21st century that would never have been broadcast 30 or even 20 years earlier. In some major US television series such as *Boardwalk Empire*, *Game of Thrones* and *Spartacus*, most episodes depicted female and male nudity and graphic sexual simulations. The use of sex also became commonplace in Hollywood movies designed for mainstream cinema release and often shown on television. In contrast to this trend, however, anecdotal evidence has also emerged that Hollywood executives had moved away from sex as an audience teaser and pleaser, with indications emerging that audiences preferred action and special effects over steaminess. Moreover, some widely marketed films with strong sexual themes, such as *The Paper Boy* (starring Nicole Kidman) and *The Sessions* (with Helen Hunt) failed at the box office.[7]

From the perspective of the sexualization of children and adolescents, the important questions do not simply concern whether it is appropriate to show scenes of nudity and realistic simulated sex because of the embarrassment they might cause for parents, but also whether these drama representations are cultivating the wrong kinds of sexual scripts for young people to learn from. Are these scenes teaching young people to regard casual sex as the norm? Do these scenes justify marital infidelity? Can they encourage high-risk sexual practices? Do they also teach the wrong lessons about female and male sexuality? Do mediated depictions of female sexuality encourage boys to develop more callous attitudes towards women?

Researchers have found that women on television are far more likely to be dressed in a sexually provocative way.[8] Sexual comments are more likely to be addressed to women than men.[9] On American peak-time television, women were judged frequently to have been sexually objectified and had comments of a sexual nature directed at them.[10] In her review of evidence for the British government, the psychologist Linda Papadopoulos cited research from the United States that reported a significant increase in the depiction of violence against women on television between 2004 and 2010. Depictions of violence against teenage girls rose by more than three times the rate of violence against women, in general. The violence often had seriously damaging or fatal consequences for the female victims and in most cases these incidents were clearly shown on screen rather than being reported or implied (pp40–41).[11]

The effects of television on sex-related attitudes, beliefs, values and behaviours can take a number of forms. Television can influence viewers' conceptions of everyday social reality by depicting distorted representations of society. Human sexuality can be shown in stereotyped ways that place emphasis on specific types of sexual relationships. Thus, if television drama series or comedies present images of young people engaging in sexually promiscuous lifestyles, regular viewers of these programmes might come to believe that sexual liberalism is rife among their peers in real life. Such effects may be especially likely to occur when viewers attach a high level of credibility to television's representations of social reality.[12]

It is important to begin by establishing how much sex television usually depicts and of what kinds. Only then can the potential social learning lessons or potential cultivation effects of the medium be determined. Much of the research evidence has derived from the US. This work has some relevance to other parts of the world given that American television programmes dominate global media markets. The earliest major studies dedicated to auditing sex on television emerged in the 1970s. Some of the authors of these initial studies produced follow-up investigations in the 1980s and 1990s, or else new authors constructed replication studies that embraced many aspects of the methodologies of the early studies.

Sex was found to be present in peak-time and daytime television dramas and in situation comedies on US network television in the 1970s, but explicit portrayals tended not to occur. Television characters kissed, touched and embraced, but more intimate sexual acts were inferred or reported upon within the storyline and not generally seen. Some shows contained controversial sexual themes of marital infidelity, rape and prostitution, but these were known to viewers only through verbal references and not from overt depictions.[13]

The tendency for more explicit sexual themes to be talked about rather than physically enacted and visibly shown persisted on US network television into the 1990s. Nevertheless, sex was observed as a prevalent theme in major drama series and serials, and sexual activity of some kind occurred in virtually all episodes of major drama shows.[14]

One major programme genre that was both highly popular with television audiences and featured sexual themes as a cornerstone of much of the storytelling was the serialized drama or 'soap opera'. These programmes were shown throughout the day and attracted loyal followings as they played out convoluted and continuing plotlines with resident characters day after day or week after week. These shows were found to contain more sex than other genres. The sex was not explicitly shown, but the themes were often controversial and dealt with marital infidelities, high-risk sexual practices and relationship merry-go-rounds in which characters frequently switched sexual partners.[15]

Researchers recorded marked increases in the amount of sexual content in soap operas across the 1980s and 1990s.[16] Perhaps more important in terms of the social lessons that might be taught by these programmes was the observation that sex between unmarried partners and promiscuity in sexual relationships had become the norm.[17] Despite the growing prevalence of sexual themes in programmes that were popular with young people as well as adult audiences, there was no evidence that sex had become visibly more graphic. Controversial sexual themes were more often featured in soap operas but were talked about rather than physically portrayed.[18]

From the mid-1990s, sex continued to increase in prevalence on US network television, but portrayals continued to be largely restricted to kissing and caressing. Depictions of sexual intercourse were still rare. One important change was that there was more talk about sex.[19] More detailed analyses were reported that used more refined measures of physical sexual activity and talk about sexual activity, but which also maintained core measures from earlier research. From the mid-1970s to the mid-1990s there were significant increases in the proportions of situation comedies and dramas that contained depictions of sexual behaviour and talk about sex. This increase in the presence of sexual content was especially pronounced for drama series and serials.[20] In one study, a composite week of television programmes was compiled by sampling programmes from different time slots over a period of several months. In a final sample of over 900 programmes, nearly four in ten (39 per cent) contained at least one scene that was characterized by a sexual theme. On average each programme contained a little over three such scenes per hour.[21]

The largest and most comprehensive content analysis research on the sexual content on television was sponsored by the Kaiser Family Foundation in the US. The project was led by Professor Dale Kunkel who with his colleagues at the University of California, Santa Barbara, conducted four studies in 1999, 2001, 2003 and 2005. They documented the frequency with which sex occurred across different television programme genres, the nature of the sexual depictions, and the social contexts in which sex occurred. They were also especially interested in whether themes of sexual risk and responsibility were present.

Across these studies, Kunkel and his colleagues analysed over 4700 television programmes over 4000 hours of television output. The first two reports compiled programmes from the ten most watched American television channels, and the final two reports also included a further sub-sample of the 20 most watched television series for 12- to 17-year-olds. A substantial increase was observed in the proportions of programmes that featured sexual content between the 1997–1998 television season (56 per cent) and 2004–2005 (70 per cent). Over this time, the average frequency per hour of scenes with sexual themes also increased from 3.0 to 4.6.

Kunkel and his co-workers found that the percentage of programmes that included sexual content increased significantly from 56 per cent in the 1997–1998 television season to 64 per cent in 2001–2002 to 70 per cent in 2004–2005. Likewise, the study reported a significant increase in the number of scenes within each programme that contained sexual content, from 3.2 scenes per hour in 1997–1998 to 4.4 scenes per hour in 2001–2002 to 5.0 scenes per hour in 2004–2005. The increase in sexual content was accounted for mainly by the more frequent depiction of scenes of flirting, kissing and caressing, while depictions of sexual intercourse did not alter greatly in frequency. There were signs, however, that verbal references to sexual intercourse increased over time.[22]

What is more important in terms of the sexualization of young people is not just how much sex occurs on television, but the way in which it is shown. We need to know whether the way sex is built into fictional storylines can potentially impart messages to viewers about risks associated with certain kinds of sexual conduct and the need therefore to behave responsibly. Engaging in high-risk sexual behaviour including casual sexual encounters or relations with professional sex workers without taking relevant precautions can result in the contraction of sexually transmitted diseases or unwanted pregnancies. The Kaiser Foundation's research found that references to sexual risks or to precautions were rare. Very few scenes contained these references and this pattern remained largely unchanged across the television seasons that were monitored.[23]

Potential sexual scripts

Research has shown that sexual remarks and references are commonplace on television. Numerous sexual messages on television included sexually objectifying comments. There has long been concern about the role played by television as a socialization agent. In the context of the medium's depiction of sexual content, the sex does not have to be explicit to have socialization effects. In fact, most sex on television is subtle rather than graphic. In addition, a lot of televised sex is spoken about rather than shown at all. What is significant from a social learning perspective is whether television presents sexual scripts that children and teenagers can encode and internalize for later use. Such scripts could be powerful whether the sex is shown or merely verbally described or reported on. Even where the televised sexual content comprises talk about sex, we need to know whether socially appropriate and constructive actions are being described. In other words, does sex on television teach good or bad lessons about sexual behaviour, attitudes towards sex and the nature of interpersonal relationships underpinned by sex?

Sexual themes have been found to characterize a number of fictional sub-genres of television, including drama series, serialized dramas and situation comedies. The dialogue between fictional characters has often been found to touch on sexual relations and other sexual matters. Formal research into the contents of television programmes has indicated that women are frequently treated as sexual objects and their value to the drama is often determined by their sexual attractiveness. An emphasis is placed here on women's physical appearance. Sex was central to the social (and self-) definition of fictional female characters, and they were as likely as male characters to be active instigators of sexual relations. It was fairly rare for women to be shown as passive recipients of sexual attention. They acted both as assertive sex seekers and also as sex limit setters. In other words, female television characters were generally not unconditionally promiscuous or sexual pushovers. While there was a prevalent recreational attitude towards sex, there was also a clear tendency for many fictional female characters to seek to retain their virtue in sexual relations.[24]

One sexually themed script that has been identified is the way in which marital relations are depicted. Despite the depiction of sexually active married partners, most sexual activity and sexual talk in fictional television programmes has tended to occur between characters who are not married to each other. A predominant message that is projected here, therefore, is that sex outside marriage is the norm. In today's society this observation is also true of everyday reality. Although moral judgements were drawn about television's preoccupation with extra-marital sex in the 1970s and 1980s, they would be regarded as largely irrelevant today.[25]

Of more relevance has been the propensity of television drama producers to depict intimate sexual relations as occurring even among partners who have only recently met, do not really know each other, and who do not plan to forge a long-term emotional commitment to each other. In addition, there is a preponderance of sexual depictions that occur between characters who although not married to each other are married to other people.[26] Such portrayals project the social script that marital infidelity is the norm and its frequent occurrence in high-profile televised drama may also somehow lend some justification to it, especially among young viewers.

Other evidence did emerge that revealed sexual activity on television being depicted as part of an established marital or romantic relationship.[27] Furthermore, in programmes that were specifically targeted at the teenage audience, sexual behaviours tended to occur mostly between characters who were not married, but who were in an established relationship. Not only that, but romantic and sexual partners tended to remain faithful to each other in the great majority of cases.[28] These findings indicated a turn towards more sexually responsible themes on television. Reinforcing these findings, further evidence emerged that popular American soap operas had displayed increasingly positive attitudes towards sex inside marriage while frowning upon sex outside it.[29]

In spite of this apparent rise in marital fidelity themes, less negative social and sexual scripts were noted to be on the increase during the 1990s. In particular, the numbers of unwanted pregnancies increased, as did references to characters with sexually transmitted diseases. The unwanted pregnancies, however, were as likely to occur among characters who were married as among those who were not. Thus, the scripts emerging from these storylines did not invariably represent morality tales about casual sex outside marriage, but also about the difficult lifestyle decisions married partners sometimes faced when becoming pregnant.[30]

A further sexual theme that has invoked great debate and considerable social concern is coercive sexual intercourse. Depictions of characters being sexually harassed or forced to have sex can give rise to strong emotional reactions in audiences. Some viewers might understandably experience distress upon witnessing such scenes, especially if they identify with them. Another concern is that if these depictions occur often enough, some viewers may become desensitized to them in a way that subsequently shapes their wider perceptions about female and male sexuality. Systematic analyses of television programming have generally found that depictions of rape or other forms of sexual harassment have formed part of the repertoire of sexual activities featured in screen drama, but have been rarely visibly depicted. Nonetheless, the presence of violent sexual conduct has been indicated through inferential signals in the drama narrative and by direct verbal references to it.[31]

Sexually aggressive themes have been featured even in comedic television scenarios. Many television situation comedies have set the action in workplace locations in which men and women are depicted as co-workers. The storylines have often featured sexual jokes targeted at women and varying forms of sexual harassment that are often played down or treated are light-hearted in comedy contexts. Some researchers have argued, however, that these portrayals might be guilty of over-trivialization of a serious social problem.[32]

Much of the research on how young people respond to sexual content on television has adopted quantitative perspectives in which their opinions about sexual images are measured in numerical terms and related through statistical analysis to other factors that characterize their personal identities and social background. This approach when used in the context of controlled interventionist studies or experiments can test causal hypotheses. It may not be sensitive, however, to the ways in which young people negotiate meanings about sex and their own sexual identities from the different mediated and non-mediated experiences upon which they draw in this context.

A British study adopted a different approach by inviting pre-teenage children aged 6 and 7 years and 10 to 11 years to take part in open-ended interviews and discussions about the sexual contents of various types of television programme.[33] Many of these children were aware of sexual content in programmes and the older children had begun to watch programmes that were produced for more adult audiences. These children were able to converse about sexual content in soap operas and situation comedies, and girls disclosed some interesting television dating shows. There were clear developmental differences in the way that sexual content on television was discussed and in the extent to which the children were able to offer opinions about how appropriate this content was for different types of programme.

Using a similar qualitative research approach with teenagers in the US, there was confirmation that young people respond to sexual content in the media in ways that are framed by the stage of development they have reached. They call upon their life experiences in reaching judgements about the representation of sex in the media and these experiences are informed not only by the mass media such as television but also by their families and friends.[34]

In the first part of this chapter, we have looked at empirical evidence concerning the way in which sexual themes have been shown on television. The reason for doing this is to establish whether television has presented sexualized content that could impart to young viewers ideas about sexuality characteristics of men and women, sexual values, sexual behaviour and sexual relationships. This evidence alone cannot indicate whether viewers are influenced by sexual content on television.

To find out whether this happens and in what ways television's effects are manifest requires a different perspective in which audiences' history of exposure and reactions to televised sex are measured. Estimating the effects of any mass medium on its audience can be challenging because establishing the existence and the direction of causal relationships between media exposure and psychological changes in members of the audience is not always straightforward. This observation is especially true when research is conducted with audiences that already have a history of media consumption and the factors which shaped that pattern of media behaviour are unknown. Finding, for example, that a certain level of consumption of movies and television programmes that contain sexual portrayals is related to young people's sexual behaviour patterns might show that these two sets of behaviour appear to have a connection, but it does not demonstrate which one causes the other. From the evidence reviewed below, this point will become increasingly apparent.

Effects of TV sex on teenagers' self-perceptions

As they mature, teenagers become more interested in sex. They are also more aware of their own sexuality. A growing preoccupation with sexual matters can also mean that their attention is primed in relation to sexual content in the media. The critical question here is whether they are significantly influenced in their own attitudes towards sex and their own sexual activities by exposure to media sex content.

Evidence on representations has indicated a tendency to depict young women in roles that are sexualized and where their preoccupation is with their physical appearance.[35] While the thin ideal has been dominant, it has more recently been partly supplanted by a shapely sexual appeal. Young men are sexualized in terms of having a tall, strong, muscular physique and where such attributes are linked to power and control. For women, having a sexy body is the key to success socially and even professionally.[36]

The gender and sex-related stereotyping of the media can affect boys as well as girls. As part of their natural development, boys become increasingly occupied by their physique and behaviour as they enter their teenage years. They reach a stage in development where girls are temporarily rejected in favour of male bonding. During this phase, boys begin to establish a masculine identity that is defined significantly in terms of the display of specific overt behaviours.[37] While boys may have played happily with girls during their pre-teen years, as they enter adolescence, this is discouraged by their own gender peer group as social pressures are applied to engage exclusively in masculine pursuits usually linked to specific sports.

Evidence has emerged that television programmes in which objectified images of women and men appear might influence the way in which young men and women perceive themselves. As we saw earlier in this book, objectification theory was developed to explain the potential effects of mediated representations of the human body, which frequently treat it as an object. This phenomenon is an integral aspect of the sexualization of females and males through representations that emphasize the sexual attributes of each gender and objectify them rather than treating them as defining elements of what it means to be human. Where this objectification tendency is internalized by us, we begin to see ourselves in objectifying terms.[38]

When the media repeatedly depict objectified representations of women and men, they can socialize us into adopting these conceptions of ourselves. Television has been shown to present a distorted view of the world through which regular viewers of its content can be influenced in terms of the perceptions they develop of everyday reality.[39] In a similar way, we can become 'cultivated' to accept objectified impressions of each gender and therefore of ourselves that have been repeatedly promulgated by the media. Research has emerged that supports this idea. Adolescent girls were found to adopt a more objectified conception of themselves following exposure to video clips that featured women athletes. White Americans were especially susceptible to this influence when shown images of lean female athletes, whereas black American girls responded similarly to images of non-lean female athletes.[40]

In another investigation of this phenomenon, American university students were followed over a period of two years. As we reported earlier, this study examined magazine exposure as well as television exposure. In this chapter, we are most interested in the television exposure effects. Those who reported greater amounts of exposure over time to television programmes that objectified men and women in a sexual way displayed stronger and more frequent tendencies to monitor their own appearance and body shape. This finding occurred for both young women and young men. Young women, however, were also influenced in this respect by their families and friends whose impact upon self-monitoring was as profound as that of television. These non-media pressures to aspire to an idealized body shape deemed as sexually attractive were not so apparent among young men.[41] This behaviour is controlled tightly, with social penalties for non-conformity being severe. Inappropriate consorting with girls or any hint of non-masculine conduct can trigger name-calling, insults, bullying and social alienation.[42]

Effects of televised depictions of sex have been associated with broader ideas about self than those involving objectification of the self. Young people can make comparisons between the sexuality of people seen on screen and their own sexuality. This exercise can lead to unfavourable comparisons being made. One early investigation found that where television depictions were regarded as true to life, young people were more likely to see them as legitimate and relevant points of comparison for evaluating their own lives. Such comparison-making occurred amongst teenagers and college students in respect of their own sex lives and often led them to feel dissatisfied.[43] Another study from the same period found that heavy television viewing teenagers also held the most negative attitudes about remaining a virgin. This research was unable to demonstrate whether television had imparted specific messages about early onset of sexual activity to teenagers. Nonetheless, relationships between television viewing and sexual attitudes emerged consistently and raised questions about the socializing role the medium might play in the sexualization of young people.

This issue was taken up 30 years later by Jennifer Aubrey of the University of Missouri who studied whether female university undergraduates' sexual self-concepts could be influenced by their exposure to television representations of sex. In this research, the small sample of 149 undergraduates reported on their frequencies of watching soap operas, music videos, prime-time situation comedies and prime-time dramas. In each case, the genres were further represented in terms of named programmes (or music networks) and respondents indicated their viewing frequencies to these broadcasts. They then answered questions or responded to attitude scales about their sex lives, their sexual self-confidence, motivation, anxiety and self-consciousness. They were also asked about their virginity status, relationship status, general self-esteem and religiosity.

Aubrey hypothesized that television could influence how young women felt about themselves as sexual beings because many of its programmes contained sexual scripts that they could learn from that involved female characters. The nature of these sexual scripts, however, could vary from one type of programme to another. Many serious drama serials (or soap operas) and series contained storylines that depicted failures in sexual relationships or conflicts that could occur that derived from these relationships. Comedy shows could present a more light-hearted look at sex, but sometimes with serious undertones nonetheless. Music videos could present sexually suggestive content permeated with gender stereotypes characterized by the sexual dominance of men and sexual submissiveness of women.

Data were collected at two points in time, one year apart. When the data were analysed, therefore, much of the focus was placed on changes in sexual self-concepts from time one to time two and whether any such changes were related to television viewing habits. Aubrey examined how reported viewing of each pro-gramme genre was related to self-concept changes. Heavier soap opera viewing was related to a decrease in sexual self-concept. A similar relationship existed between television drama viewing and sexual self-concept. In addition, there was further evidence that those young women who already had a poor self-concept turned to watch television drama more often. Viewing of situation comedies and music videos was unrelated to sexual self-concept.

Effects on young people's attitudes about sex

Sexualization messages on television can, according to some experts, go beyond shaping how young people perceive themselves when entering stages of their development in which their self-identity is starting to emerge and influence their attitudes towards others. This effect can be a cause of considerable concern if it results in girls and women being treated as sex objects. The scientific evidence for these kinds of influences derives from two primary sources. The first of these comprised sur-veys of young people in which their reported television viewing habits have been statistically related with the attitudes they hold about other people and sex. The aim here has been to find out whether holding sexualized attitudes about girls and women, in particular, exhibit a systematic relationship to the amount of exposure to television programmes that depict girls or women in highly sexualized ways.

The second approach used to investigate the question of whether television can cultivate sexualization among young people has been to conduct controlled experiments. This methodology allows researchers to examine cause–effect links between television viewing and social attitudes. This is achieved by presenting different matched groups of people with specific televised sequences that show girls or women in different (sexualized and non-sexualized) ways.

One major review of research evidence concerning use of the mass media and sexual attitudes and behaviours of young people found limited evidence for media effects.[44] This review covered research on this subject that had been published between 1983 and 2004. It emerged that only a small proportion of the empirical studies published had attempted directly to measure media effects and those that had were blighted by methodological limitations, which meant they were ill equipped to test causal relations between media consumption and sex attitudes and behaviour. Although a lot of studies focused on the effects of television, the relative absence of comprehensive data tracking the representation of sex in large and comparable samples of televised broadcast output meant that there was often little current data about the sexual nature of television that could be used to help interpret audience effects findings.

Research evidence did emerge during the 1980s, 1990s and 2000s that greater reported exposure to television genres known to feature sexual themes was corre-lated with a number of sex-related attitudes and beliefs. More frequent reported viewing of soap operas, for example, was associated with holding more liberal attitudes about sex.[45]

Viewing television programmes that depict sexual themes, often with disproportionate representation of certain kinds of sexual relationships, has been found to be
correlated with perceptions of social reality than depart from the actual frequencies
of specific types of behaviour. American university students who said they often
watched soap operas gave high estimates of the percentages of marriages that end in
divorce and of births of illegitimate children.[46]

One early investigation of this theme was conducted in the US among university
students. A survey was carried out in which these teenage and young adult respondents reported on their media habits, and their sexual attitudes and behaviours. Young
men and women who exhibited greater self-esteem tended to be more sexually
confident and more sexually active. For young women, another important factor
was their religious beliefs. The more religious they perceived themselves to be, the
less sexually active they were. Young adult females reported greater consumption
of television programmes characterized by sexually suggestive themes such as serialized dramas or 'soap operas'. General patterns of media consumption did not
predict sexual permissiveness, but greater consumption of music television was
linked to more open sexual attitudes.[47]

In another survey, heavy viewing of television, in general, and heavy viewing of
programmes with frequent sexual themes were strongly linked to American teenagers'
sexual attitudes, expectations and behaviour. For instance, greater exposure to sexual
content on television was strongly associated with endorsement of recreational
attitudes towards sex, greater expectations about being sexually active and the
perceptions that peers were more sexually active.[48]

Other research has indicated that greater viewing of televised soap operas was
correlated with stronger beliefs that relationships are doomed to fail.[49] An
experimental study in which teenage participants were shown sexual scenes from
well-known television soap operas found that exposure to this material was linked
to subsequent increases in their acceptance of marital infidelities.[50] More disturbing
evidence has emerged that viewing of televised soap operas is linked to greater
acceptance of sexual harassment scenarios involving women victims.[51]

In a controlled exposure study, clips from peak-time American network television
situation comedies and drama (*Friends*, *Seinfeld*, *Ally McBeal*) that depicted sexually
themed scenes were shown to female and male university undergraduates aged
between 18 and 22 years. Control participants watched clips from the same television series that were devoid of sexual references. Afterwards, all participants
completed questionnaires that asked them about their own sexual attitudes, beliefs
and experiences. Questions covered gender stereotypes and perceptions of their
peers' sexual experiences. The latter questions asked about such matters as how
many of their peers did they believe had had sex on a first date and how many had
had at least ten sexual partners. Further data were collected on self-reported media
consumption habits.[52]

Self-reported television viewing habits were found to correlate with a number of
beliefs about sexual relationships among female participants. In particular, those
young women who reported more viewing of television, whether for entertainment

or educational purposes, were more likely to agree that females are often treated as sex objects, males are sex driven and dating is a game. These relationships occurred also for male participants, but were statistically weaker.

Following the controlled viewing condition, female participants who viewed the sexually themed television scenes were more likely than those who did not to endorse the beliefs that women are treated as sex objects, males are sex driven and dating is a game. In contrast, the same effects were not observed among male participants. More frequent television viewing was also associated with beliefs that their peers were highly sexually active. The latter perception was once again especially pronounced among young women participants. Although many of these findings were based on correlations, the differences between students who saw either the sexually themed or non-sexually themed television clips indicated the potential of television to produce specific sexual views of the world, possibly reflecting the type of 'reality' represented in some mainstream television series.

In seeking explanations for these findings, the researcher hypothesized that young women viewers who watched these programmes for largely entertainment-oriented reasons uncritically absorbed the social 'lessons' they taught and internalized them as part of their wider world knowledge. The stronger 'effects' among female participants than among male participants could be explained by the fact that males endorsed specific sexual beliefs far more strongly than did females before exposure to the television clips and therefore displayed less variance in the degree to which these beliefs were endorsed.

Young people's sexual behaviour

Much of the research into the sexual content of television has measured its possible effects on players' sexual attitudes and beliefs. Is there any evidence that playing video games with sexual themes can influence players' sexual behaviour? Research on this question is sparse in part because of the logistical and ethical difficulties associated with constructing investigations that can measure cause–effect relations here. Such evidence as does exist on this question has derived mostly from surveys of young people in which they provide verbal reports of their video game playing and sexual habits.

As we have already seen in earlier chapters, the media can provide sources of social learning. Although much behavioural learning takes place by doing, a great deal also occurs more passively through observation. By witnessing the actions of others we can obtain examples of how to behave under different social circumstances. This learning process begins by storing away memories of behavioural actions and sequences of behaviour we have observed. We might also make a note of the particular circumstances under which specific behavioural actions occurred and also of the outcomes of those actions for the people who perpetrated them, as well as for anyone else present at the time.[53]

Television can provide an extremely rich source of social learning because its programmes are filled with characters engaging in actions and interactions across a wide range of social contexts. Viewers can observe how characters respond beha-viourally to the behaviours of others, what the consequences were for specific behaviours, and more generally how others in different social settings responded to the behaviour of a particular actor. Television programmes thus provide exam-ples of specific acts of behaviour, as well as more extended scripts comprising sequences of behaviour. All of these visibly displayed actions and action sequences can be encoded by viewers and committed to memory for future reference.

There are additional elements to these portrayals that are important in shaping their uptake by young people in the audience. Children and teenagers may be particularly sensitized to screen actions. This is because they are still passing through stages of their psychological development in which they are learning how to behave appropriately in different situations. On-screen behaviours are also frequently per-formed by role models that young members of the audience find attractive, with whom they identify or whom they would like to emulate. Hence, copying the behaviour of a popular television character, and especially one held in high regard by the individual's peer group, is often perceived to have considerable social capital.

While social learning, cultivation and self-objectification represent interesting and often useful theories to explain media effects, we must still unravel what it means when a research investigation indicates that a specified pattern of media consumption is statistically connected to a specified level of sexual activity. We cannot automatically assume that exposure to sexual content on television or in the movies has triggered the onset of sexual behaviour and that it has shaped the nature of that behaviour. One reason for saying this is important evidence that consumption of highly sexualized media content tends to change as children approach adulthood in their teen years. For instance, youngsters aged 12 may display less consumption of explicit sexual media and less interest in such content than those aged 14 or 15 years.

Furthermore, teenagers (and especially girls) who reach sexual maturity earlier tend to report more interest in viewing and reading about sex in the media and in listening to music with sexual themes. What is even more important is that early maturing teenage girls also place different meanings on sexual content in the media and often take from it a licence to engage in sexual intercourse themselves. Despite the risks that are associated with early sexual intercourse, early maturing girls also seem to be more sensitized than their peers who have not yet become sexually active to media messages about safe sex practices.[54]

The findings from television content analysis studies have catalogued dominant behaviour patterns in different programme genres and in so doing have identified the behavioural menus offered by television. These are behaviours that young people could potentially add to their own behavioural repertoires. Portrayals of sex can be especially relevant to young people entering adult maturity and becoming sexually active for the first time. In this context, a young person might learn about sexual techniques, about the social contexts in which sexual relationships occur, about how the opposite sex envisages sex and therefore how to behave towards them sexually to meet their usual expectations. Television's depictions of sexual behaviour might also inform young people about certain risks associated with sexual interactions with people whom they do not know very well. If television depicts sex as commonplace among young fictional characters, young viewers might generalize from these fictional representations to their own lives and feel pressured to become sexually active before they are ready.

The earliest studies of behavioural effects of watching sexual content on television found significant positive correlations between frequency of exposure to that content and having a greater number of sexual partners and becoming sexually active at an earlier age.[55] There is related evidence that teenagers who watched more sex on television felt that screen role models exerted more pressure on them to become sexually active. Television cultivated an impression that was generalized by young people to their own lives that everybody was having sex and that if they were not, they were somehow both missing out and not normal.[56]

The heavy reliance of research on the effects of televized sex on young people's sexual socialization on cross-sectional, self-report surveys has meant that there is little conclusive evidence of causality here. Tests of cause–effect relationships require the use of experimental methods that control media sex exposure conditions and utilize relevant and appropriate measures of sexual behaviour. There is experimental evidence from studies of music videos that are examined in the next chapter, but these all examined effects on sexual attitudes or behavioural intentions rather than on actual behaviour.[57]

Cross-sectional surveys obtain evidence only at one point in time. This means they can report links between variables that are based on correlation coefficients that indicate degrees of association between media exposure and sexual behaviour. One enhancement that researchers can introduce to survey methodology to strengthen its analysis of potential causal relationships between variables is to survey the same people more than once. This longitudinal approach means that if a target behaviour, such as the onset of sexual activity, occurs at one point in a young person's life, other evidence about them can be collected both before and after this change in their sexual status to find out whether its occurrence is closely associated with other factors in their lives, including the nature of their television viewing.

A longitudinal approach can also take multiple measurements about young people over time and track their development on a number of levels. This means that if their sexual status changes from one of inactivity to one that is fully active, comparisons can be made between those who have become sexually active and those who have remained sexually inactive in terms of a wide range of factors that go beyond their media exposure habits. Becoming sexually active at an earlier age, for example, might be linked to the type of family setting in which they live, the kinds of friends whose company they keep, whether they engage in other behaviours such as alcohol consumption, taking non-prescription drugs, or smoking. Statistical controls can be introduced by researchers that match sexually active and inactive teenagers on a range of these types of variables to find out which ones are most often significantly linked to onset of sexual behaviour.

Jane Brown and her colleagues at the University of North Carolina, Chapel Hill, used this type of longitudinal approach to investigate the significance of media consumption habits, including their television viewing, watching movies, music listening and magazine reading, as factors linked to the onset of sexual behaviour among adolescents who were studied over two years. These youngsters were aged between 12 and 14 years at the start of the research. Longitudinal data were collected from over 1000 participants over the duration of the study.

Brown and her co-workers established the sexual activity of these teenagers by asking them in each of two interviews whether they had ever had sex and how old they were when this first happened. The researchers tried to pin down the point at which sexual intercourse first occurred to the month when it happened. In addition to sexual activity defined in terms of full intercourse, participants were asked about pre-coital sexual behaviour such as kissing, intimate touching and oral sex. A further question was asked about sexual orientation.

Assessing the extent to which teenagers had been exposed to sexual content in the media, the researchers initially asked their participants in the first survey interview to identify television programmes, music videos and movies they had watched, and magazines they read. Those media that were most frequently used were then examined further by the research team for their sexual content. The most popular programmes, movies and videos were examined and content analysed for portrayals of sexual activity or references to such activity. Magazines were examined for verbal references to sexual topics and for photographic imagery defined as sexual in nature. By combining these data with each participant's reported media diets, a 'sexual media diet' could be defined and quantified for each medium.

In complex statistical analyses in which demographic characteristics of the teenagers were controlled, evidence emerged that those teens who reported the greatest sexual media diets at the first interview were more likely to report pre-coital sexual activity at the second interview. It was no surprise that those youngsters who were sexually active at the first interview were also the most likely to report being sexually active at the second interview. For those who were sexually active at the outset – in terms of pre-coital sexual experiences – having a diet of sexual media content further enhanced the degree of sexual activity only among white adolescents and not among black adolescents.

Turning to the onset of sexual intercourse, Brown and her colleagues reported that teenagers' sexual media diets predicted the likelihood that they would become sexually active. This finding was true for both black and white adolescents. Once statistical controls were introduced for parenting style and attitudes of parents towards sex and for the sexually permissive nature of the peer groups that young-sters associated with, their sexual media diet predicted onset of sexual intercourse only for white adolescents and not for black adolescents.

Hennessy et al. confirmed the findings of Brown and her colleagues that exposure to sexual content in different media was correlated with the onset of sexual behaviour among American adolescents, but the strength of this relationship was weaker among black teenagers than white teenagers and also declined as teenagers got older.[58]

Further longitudinal studies similar in design to the one just reviewed followed during the next few years. These yielded further evidence that exposure specifically to sexual content on television could predict the likelihood of sexual onset among teenagers. One longitudinal study of nearly 1800 American youngsters aged 12 to 17 years explored their reported television viewing habits and their personal sexual experiences. A range of other factors known to be linked to sexual activity among adolescents were also measured. The researchers tracked those teenagers who became sexually active during the year of the study and examined other factors measured at the outset, and then again during the second wave of the survey to find out which one differentiated them best from teenagers who had remained sexually inactive. The findings showed that those respondents who had engaged in sexual intercourse during the year of the study also reported the heaviest exposure to televised sexual content. Among African-American teenagers only, those who had seen more television programmes in which the risks of unsafe sexual practices had been presented were less likely to have become sexually active during the year.[59]

The same researchers reported further findings from the same population of adolescents after they had been monitored over three years. This research was published in two papers after the researchers re-analysed the original data to confirm initial relationships between reported viewing of sexual content on television and their own sexual experiences. On this occasion, the researchers focused their attention on teenage pregnancy. They measured pregnancy rates for the girls and responsibility for causing pregnancy amongst the boys. For both genders, their experiences of pregnancy were predicted significantly by the amount to which they had been exposed to sexual content on television.[60]

The studies reviewed above have been critiqued and in one case its data re-examined by others. This further examination of longitudinal research has thrown out questions about whether all the initially published findings can be accepted as they stand. Although correlation-based evidence has indicated that teenagers' self-reports of their exposure to sexual content in the media is related to the likelihood that they will become sexually active earlier, questions have been raised about whether other relevant factors known to underpin sexual behaviour had been effectively discounted or controlled. One particular review of this evidence suggested that the original findings of Jane Brown and her colleagues could have been distorted by the way in which they selected respondents for inclusion in their data analyses. It was suggested that some respondents were discounted too readily and that had they been included, the overall findings would have changed. While the onset of sexual activity of any kind was once again found to be related to how much teenagers were exposed to sexual content in the media they consumed, earlier onset of sexual intercourse was found no longer to be related to their media sex diet.[61]

Amy Bleakley and her colleagues reported a further study with a small sample of 16- to 18-year-olds that attempted to go further than other studies in exploring how sexual content in the media sits alongside other psychological and social factors that characterize teenagers in influencing the onset of their sexual behaviour. They adopted the integrative model of behavioural prediction as a framework to guide the design of their investigation. This model had been developed from earlier models of attitude and behaviour change, and posited that any change in an individual's behaviour can usually be explained as reasoned action that is underpinned by earlier changes in their perceptions of the world around them, as well as their beliefs about themselves and their social competence. Behaviour cannot be considered in a psychological vacuum in any analysis of behaviour change. Internal constructs such as beliefs and attitudes often need to adjust first to create an appropriate cognitive and emotional state for changes in behaviour to follow on.[62]

One aspect of this integrated theory is social-cognitive theory, which proposes that when we develop new behaviour patterns, the form these behaviours take has often been conditioned by a learning process that involves the observation of the behaviour of others. Individual behavioural acts might be memorized through this process, but more usually, we learn about sequences of behaviour, often referred to as behaviour 'scripts'. These ideas about patterns of behaviour are stored within our memories and can be retrieved when we experience relevant environmental settings that make these behaviours appropriate. Behaviour changes might also be underpinned by internal needs or urges that we develop which might also be reactions to environmental circumstances, or they might emerge as we pass through stages of physical development – for example, as we become sexually mature. Sexual maturity is not simply a matter of developing specific gender-defined physical characteristics, but can also be underpinned by hormonal changes in our bodies. Regardless of the urges that drive our behaviours, their manifestations are generally influenced by behaviour scripts we have learned in our social environment.

Bleakley and her colleagues analysed data from teenagers who had taken part in a much larger investigation of adolescent sexual development (Annenberg Sex and Media Study). The ASAMS was a five-year study that surveyed a panel of adolescents annually from 2005 in Philadelphia. The current study was based on data collected between 2005 and 2007. Respondents provided data about their media habits, which included their television viewing, movie watching, music artists they listened to (or whose videos they watched), video games they played and magazines they read. The media titles endorsed by respondents were separately coded in terms of whether they contained a lot of sexual content, some sexual content, a little or no sexual content. Each respondent's own self-reported media consumption profile could therefore be further classified in terms of the amount of sexual exposure it represented.

Further information was collected about whether respondents believed that their parents, siblings, friends and girl–boy friends thought they should have sexual intercourse and about their perceptions of the extent to which they felt that males and females in their own age group were sexually active. They were also asked about a number of barriers to having sexual intercourse and how much each of these applied in their case. They were further given a list of reasons why having sexual intercourse in the near future would be a good thing or a bad thing for themselves or for others. For instance, did they feel that having sexual intercourse would increase the feelings of intimacy between them and their partner? Did they think that becoming sexually active would raise their social standing with their friends? Did they think that their parents would respond badly if they found out?

What this study found was that although there was evidence that exposure to sexual content in the media they consumed was related to their sexual activity or intentions to become sexually active, this link was not necessarily a direct one as many previous studies had presumed. Instead, exposure to sexually themed media content was related to perceptions of normative pressure to have sex, although not with attitudes towards sex (i.e. whether having sex might be a good or bad thing to do for various reasons). Ultimately, having sex or holding firm intentions to have sex were underpinned first by positive attitudes towards it, second by the belief that everyone else was doing it and, hence, they were also under social pressure to do the same, and finally by having the opportunities to do it. Exposure to sex-permeated media content was related significantly only to beliefs about how normative adolescent sex was. Bleakley and her colleagues concluded that exposure to media sex did play a part in driving forward sexual activity, but did so by influencing young people's beliefs about how much social pressure there was for them to become sexual. Media sex did not directly drive sexual behaviour as implied by many earlier studies that had sought evidence for this relationship.

Further research was carried out using the Integrated Model of Behavioural Prediction that examined the earlier studies by looking in more detail at the nature of the sexual content adolescents consumed in terms of its explicitness and references made to sexual behaviour risks and safe sex.[63] Data were drawn from the same sample as the previous investigation. On this occasion, however, the researchers focused on exposure to sexual content on television only. An initial list of television programmes was drawn up based on industry audience ratings showing which ones were the most watched among young people in the age bracket covered by the survey. Measures were then obtained of exposure levels to these programmes among the survey sample. Three episodes of each of these programmes were recorded and a team of coders was trained to view and code each episode in terms of its sexual content. Sexual content was classified in terms of how explicit it was, whether it involved depictions of sexual behaviour to talk about sex, and whether any references were made to taking sexual precautions or risky sexual behaviour.

Overall reported exposure to sexual content on television did not predict the onset of sexual activity. Breaking down viewing habits by programme genres revealed that when each programme genre was examined separately, sexual content exposure in situation comedies was linked to increased likelihood of having had sex in the previous year, whereas viewing of televised dramas, cartoons and reality programmes was not. When all genres were entered in the same analysis, exposure to sexual content in situation comedies predicted increased likelihood and drama predicted decreased likelihood of the onset of sexual activity, while viewing of sexual content in cartoons and reality programmes did not. Situation comedy watching also predicted more positive attitudes about sex and stronger belief that sex was normative amongst their peer group. Exposure to drama programmes predicted less positive attitudes about sex and weaker belief in normative peer pressure to have sex. Elsewhere, analyses showed that both attitudes about sex and beliefs about peer pressure to have sex predicted increased likelihood of having sex.

This research therefore provided evidence that exposure to televised sex could work indirectly on the propensity to become sexually active earlier and could have more direct impact. The impact of televised sex, however, varied between programme genres and only certain genres had any effects at all. Where specific types of televised sex were related to the early onset of sexual behaviour among teenagers, this relationship was not consistent in direction. Viewing sex in televised comedy settings enhanced the probability of teens becoming sexually active, whereas viewing sex in televised drama had the opposite effect.

Explanations for these television sex effects on teenagers' sexual behaviour require deeper investigation of the sexual messages being transmitted in different types of programmes. In this study, the researchers speculated that sex in comedy may be regarded in a more light-hearted fashion by viewers and may, in effect, trivialize sex. This could, in turn, mean that teens are less inclined to take sex seriously and are willing to enter into sexual relations in a fairly casual way. Sexual depictions in televised dramas take on a more serious tone and may be integrated with storylines in which sexual relations end badly or result in unfortunate consequences for participants. In these settings, sex may be depicted as an activity that should not be entered into lightly. There are many important issues here that need to be more directly investigated.

Ross O'Hara and his co-workers, based at Dartmouth University in the US, found that children aged 12 to 14 years who watched movies with sexual themes and portrayals exhibited a tendency to start having sex earlier than other children. These children were also more likely to have more casual sexual partners and to engage in unsafe sexual practices.

Before surveying the children, O'Hara and his colleagues classified a sample of 684 top grossing movies released between 1998 and 2004 for their sexual content.[64] They coded these movies for the amount of running time they contained that was occupied by sexual activity. They also classified the nature of the sexual activity into different types of behaviour along a continuum from less to more intimate and explicit. They counted up the amount of sexual activity from passionate kissing to sexual intercourse. A majority of the films they examined, whether classified as suitable for child audiences or not, contained sexual activity.

In the survey of children, respondents were asked to say which films out of sets of 50 (randomly compiled from the larger movie sample) they had seen. The researchers were then able to aggregate over the sexual content identified in the chosen movies to produce an estimate of how much sexual material the children had been exposed to in their movie watching. Although this technique could not provide a precisely accurate measure of the children's overall exposure to sex in movies, it was sufficient to enable the researchers to differentiate between children with relatively high or low levels of potential exposure to movie sex.

The children were interviewed twice, six years apart. On the first occasion, the researchers focused on their movie watching, although also asked about early onset sexual behaviour. Six years later, when resurveyed, more questions were asked about their sexual habits and when they first became sexually active. Questions were asked about whether they were monogamous or had had multiple sexual partners and whether they engaged in safe-sex practices, such as wearing condoms, when having sexual intercourse.

The findings actually showed that watching movies with sexual content was related to sensation-seeking tendencies in adolescence and that this disposition, in turn, can lead to indulgence in many different kinds of adventurous and sometimes high-risk behaviour patterns, including a more varied sex life.

As we have seen, longitudinal research evidence has emerged, mainly from the US, that the television viewing habits of adolescents has been found to link to whether they are sexually active. In particular, those young people who mention programmes known to contain sexual content as being prominent and regular aspects of their viewing diets tend also to be the ones who are most likely to be sexually active, up to the point of having had sexual intercourse.

Research into adolescents' sexual behaviour has also shown that this activity can vary in terms of whether it takes place in or outside of a committed and established emotional and romantic relationship. This is an important point because of concerns about the spread of sexually transmitted diseases among adolescents and young adults and also about the prevalence of teenage pregnancies.[65] Although surveys of teen-age sexuality have reported that a majority claim to be sexually active only within a committed relationship, significant minorities have reported having only casual sex or to switching between commitment and playing the field.[66] The relative absence of attention to risks associated with casual and promiscuous sexual practices, and of messages about safe sex in sexual portrayal in mainstream television drama, opens up the possibility that this popular programming transmits messages that encourage careless or even reckless behaviour among impressionable adolescents.[67]

With these concerns in mind, research by Melina Bersamin of the Department of Child Development, California State University, and her colleagues not only examined relationships that developed over time between television viewing habits and sexual activity among American teenagers, but also determined whether those teens who were sexually active last had intercourse within a casual relationship or a committed one. Television viewing was differentiated in terms of overall reported exposure and viewing of cable television channels known to broadcast programmes with sexual content, including, in some instances, sexually explicit adult content. The data reported were collected from teenagers over a two-year period who were surveyed three times. Respondents were aged 12 to 16 years at the outset of this research.

Of those who were sexually active by the second wave of the survey, more than six in ten reported having last had oral sex or penetrative sex with someone as part of a committed relationship, while nearly four in ten said they had done so with someone they had just met or to whom they were not emotionally and exclusively committed. Turning to potential television influences, overall amount of viewing was greater in the second wave of this research amongst those teenagers who had not become sexually active. In contrast, greater amounts of reported viewing of music videos on television, premium cable television and of adult programming were reported by adolescents who had become fully sexually active since the first survey. Greater viewing of music videos and adult programmes occurred amongst the sexually active regardless of whether they were in a committed relationship or not. Greater viewing of premium cable television occurred amongst those adolescents who had last had sexual intercourse in a committed relationship but not among those who had had only casual sex.

These findings therefore went beyond earlier research in that it indicated that greater viewing of potentially sex-containing programmes was not invariably predictive of the onset of sexual activity amongst all sexually active adolescents. This evidence is important because, while it does not conclusively demonstrate causal relationships between television viewing habits and the onset of sexual activity among teenagers, it does indicate that if television has any influence in this context it may be important to examine more closely the types of programmes teenagers include in their viewing diets rather than focus only on the overall amount of viewing they do.

Selective exposure

Before we can accept research indicating that children are invariably changed by exposure to sexual content on television and in movies, we must be confident that patterns of exposure were the causal agent rather than an outcome of pre-existing sexual attitudes, beliefs, values and behaviour patterns. It is feasible, for instance, that once children have reached a stage of development at which sexual urges naturally emerge, they then develop a taste for sexual content in their media diets. There is research evidence that children and adolescents often seek out sexual material in the media.

The search for mediated sex has been found to shape young people's television viewing choices. Even pre-teenage children between 6 and 11 years were found to like television shows with sexual themes, most especially soap operas and dating shows.[68] As they enter adolescence, young people also display an ability to understand sexual innuendo, so even the subtle sexual themes of some situation comedies are not beyond their comprehension.[69]

The choice of sexual media content often depends upon the stage of development teenagers have reached. Girls forge emotional attachments with celebrity icons that acquire a sexual edge as they become sexually mature. At first, their celebrity fixations are often same gender ones, before later switching to male icons as their sexuality develops.[70] One of the reasons why teenagers seek out sexual content on television and in other media is that as they mature sexually, they seek to learn as much as they can about sexual relationships and sexual performance, and mediated sexual portrayals and scripts represent a valuable source of information.[71] Early sexual maturation amongst adolescent girls has been found to drive earlier interest in sexual media content. Girls who become sexually active at an earlier age are more likely than non-sexually active peers to view R-rated movies and to seek out more media content from television and other sources about dating and safe sex practices.[72] There is further evidence from among African-American adolescent girls that those who become pregnant show stronger interest in watching sexual content in movies and peak-time television drama series and serials.[73] The link between early sexual activity on the part of adolescent girls and contingent emergence of interest in sexual material has not, however, always been supported.[74]

Summary and conclusions

Television is a ubiquitous medium that is widely consumed by children. It has also been found to be a rich source of sexually themed content. This content may occur in mild forms throughout many different programmes, with some programmes offering more intense and explicit doses of sexual portrayals. Although the overall amount of sexual content on mainstream television has remained fairly stable over time, the overall growth in numbers of channels that can be received in most households has increased the opportunities for exposure. There is evidence also that sexual scenes in some televised dramas have become both more commonplace and much more explicit over time.

Television has been recognized for a long time as a medium that can have potentially powerful effects on audiences. These effects can be manifest at a number of psychological levels – in terms of how viewers think or feel about specific issues, and in terms of their behavioural intentions or actual behaviours. Television can be a source of information about sex for young people which they take away and utilize in positive ways. It has also raised concern because its sexual messages have been found more often to promote casual sexual practices over responsible ones. Furthermore, women are often depicted in sexually objectified ways across a range of programme genres. Prominent women on television also provide role models in terms of physical appearance that can be difficult for ordinary female viewers to emulate and can, for some young women, present unattainable targets of feminine beauty against which they draw unfavourable comparisons of themselves.

Over time, then, exposure to television has been linked to the development of lowered self-esteem and beliefs about the acceptability of specific sexual practices. Children nearing a stage of sexual maturity and reaching a point of sexual curiosity turn to television as an important information source on matters they may feel they cannot get from other sources, such as their parents. Relationships between level of sexual activity and exposure to sexual content on television therefore may not invariably represent evidence of an 'effect' of the medium. A role of influence played by television in relation to the sexualization of childhood cannot be completely explained away, however, by selective exposure.

Notes

1 Butler, M. and Paisley, W. (1980) *Women and the Mass Media*. New York, NY: Human Sciences Press; Head, H. (1954) 'Content analysis of television drama programs', *Quarterly of Film, Radio and Television*, 9, 175–194; Tedesco, N. (1974) 'Patterns in

prime time', *Journal of Communication*, 74, 119–124; Pribram, D. (1988) *Female Spectators: Looking at Film and Television.* New York, NY: Verso; Davis, D. M. (1990) 'Portrayals of women in prime-time network television: Some demographic characteristics', *Sex Roles*, 23, 325–332.

2   Manes, A. I. and Melnyk, P. (1974) 'Televised models of female achievement', *Journal of Applied Social Psychology*, 4, 365–374; Hodges, K. K., Brandt, D. A. and Kline, J. (1981) 'Competence, guilt, and victimization: Sex differences in ambition of causality in television dramas', *Sex Roles*, 7, 537–546.

3   Atkin, D. (1991) 'The evolution of television series addressing women, 1966–90', *Journal of Broadcasting and Electronic Media*, 35(4), 517–523.

4   Sprafkin, J. N. and Silverman, L. T. (1981) 'Update: Physically intimate and sexual behaviour on prime time television, 1978–79', *Journal of Communication*, 31(1), 34–40.

5   Sapolsky, B. S. and Tabarlet, J. G. (1991) 'Sex in prime time: 1979 vs 1989', *Journal of Broadcasting and Electronic Media*, 34, 505–516.

6   Cramer, P. and Steinwert, T. (1998) 'Thin is good, fat is bad: How early does it begin?', *Journal of Applied Developmental Psychology*, 19, 429–451.

7   Revoir, P. (2013) 'No sex please, it's a box office turn-off', *Daily Mail*, 25 March, 13.

8   Eaton, B. (1997) 'Prime-time stereotyping on the new television networks', *Journal of Mass Communication Quarterly*, 74, 859–872.

9   Ward, L. M. (2003) 'Understanding the role of entertainment media in the sexual socialization of American youth: A review of empirical research', *Developmental Review*, 23, 347–388.

10   Grauerholz, E. and King, A. (1997) 'Prime time sexual harassment', *Violence Against Women*, 3, 129.

11   Papadopoulos, L. (2010) *Sexualization of Young People.* London, UK: Home Office.

12   Wober, M. and Gunter, B. (1988) *Television and Social Control.* Aldershot, UK: Avebury.

13   Franzblau, S., Sprafkin, J. N. and Rubinstein, E. A. (1977) 'Sex on TV: A content analysis', *Journal of Communication*, 27(2), 164–170; Fernandez-Collado, C. F., Greenberg, B. S., Korzenny, F. and Atkin, C. K. (1978) 'Sexual intimacy and drug use in TV series', *Journal of Communication*, 28(3), 30–37; Sprafkin, J. N. and Silverman, L. T. (1981) 'Update: physically intimate and sexual behaviour on prime time television: 1978–79', *Journal of Communication*, 31(1), 34–40.

14   Greenberg, B. S., Stanley, C., Siemicki, M., Heeter, C., Soderman, A. and Linsangan, R. (1993) 'Sex content on soaps and prime-time television series most viewed by adolescents', in B. S. Greenberg, J. D. Brown and N. L. Buerkel-Rothfuss (Eds.) *Media, Sex and the Adolescent*, pp29–44. Cresskill, NJ: Hampton Press.

15   Greenberg, B. S., Abelman, R. and Neuendorf, K. (1981) 'Sex on the soap operas: Afternoon intimacy', *Journal of Communication*, 46, 153–160; Lowry, D. T., Love, G. and Kirby, M. (1981) 'Sex on the soap operas: Patterns of intimacy', *Journal of Communication*, 31, 90–96.

16   Greenberg, B. S., Stanley, C., Siemicki, M., Heeter, C., Soderman, A. and Linsangan, R. (1993) *op. cit*; Greenberg, B. S. and Busselle, R. W. (1996) 'Soap operas and sexual activity: A decade later', *Journal of Communication*, 46, 153–160; Lowry, D. T. and Towles, D. E. (1988) 'Prime-time TV portrayals of sex, contraception and venereal diseases', *Journalism Quarterly*, 66, 347–352.

17   Lowry, D. T. and Towles, D. E. (1988) *ibid.*

18   Greenberg, B. S., Brown, J. D. and Buerkel-Rothfuss, N. L. (1993) *Media, Sex and the Adolescent.* Cresskill, NJ: Hampton Press.

19   Kaiser Family Foundation (1996) *The Family House Focus Groups: Children's Responses to Sexual Content on TV*, December. Menlo Park, CA: Kaiser Family Foundation; Kunkel, D., Cope, K. M. and Colvin, C. (1996) *Sexual Messages on Family Hour Television: Content and Context.* Menlo Park, CA: Kaiser Family Foundation.

20   Kunkel, D., Cope, K. M. and Colvin, C. (1996) *ibid.*

21 Kunkel, D., Cope, K. M., Farinola, W. J., Biely, E., Roth, E. and Donnerstein, E. (1999) *Sex on TV: Content and Context.* Menlo Park, CA: Kaiser Family Foundation.

22 Kunkel, D., Cope-Farrar, K., Biely, E., Farinola, W. J. M., and Donnerstein, E. (2001) *Sex on TV2: A Biennial Report.* Menlo Park, CA: Kaiser Family Foundation; Kunkel, D., Biely, E., Eyal, K., Cope-Farrar, K., Donnerstein, E., and Fandrich, R. (2003) *Sex on TV 3: A Biennial Report.* Menlo Park, CA: Kaiser Family Foundation; Kunkel, D., Eyal, K., Finnerty, F., Biely, E., and Donnerstein, E. (2005) *Sex on TV 4.* Menlo Park, CA: Kaiser Family Foundation.

23 Kunkel, D., Eyal, K., Finnerty, F., Biely, E., and Donnerstein, E. (2005) *ibid*; Rideout, V. and Hamel, E. (2006) *The Media Family: Electronic Media in the Lives of Infants, Toddlers, Preschoolers and Their Parents,* May. Menlo Park, CA: Henry J Kaiser Family Foundation.

24 Ward, L. M. (1995) 'Talking about sex: Common themes about sexuality in the prime-time television programs children and adolescents view most', *Journal of Youth and Adolescence,* 24, 595–615.

25 Sapolsky, B. S. and Tabarlet, J. G. (1991) 'Sex in prime time television: 1979 vs 1989', *Journal of Broadcasting & Electronic Media,* 34, 505–516.

26 Greenberg, B. S. and D'Alessio, D. (1985) 'Quantity and quality of sex in soaps', *Journal of Broadcasting and Electronic Media,* 29, 309–321; Greenberg, B. S. and Woods, M. G. (1999) 'The soaps; Their sex, gratifications and outcomes', *Journal of Sex Research,* 36(3), 250–257.

27 Heintz-Knowles, K. E. (1996) *Sexual Activity on Daytime Soap Operas: A Content Analysis of Five Weeks of Television Programming.* Menlo Park, CA: Kaiser Family Foundation; Kunkel, D., Cope, K. M., Farinola, W. J., Biely, E., Roth, E. and Donnerstein, E. (1999) *op. cit.*

28 Cope, K. and Kunkel, D. (1999, May) *Sexual Messages in the Television Shows Most Frequently Viewed by Adolescents.* Paper presented at the annual conference of the International Communication Association, San Francisco.

29 Greenberg, B. S. and Busselle, R. W. (1996) *op. cit.*

30 Greenberg, B. S. and Woods, M. G. (1999) *op. cit.*

31 Lowry, D. T., Love, G. and Kirby, M. (1981) *op. cit*; Greenberg, B. S. and D'Alessio, D. (1985) *op. cit*; Greenberg, B. S. and Woods, M. G. (1999) *op. cit.*

32 Montemurro, B. (2003) 'Not a laughing matter: Sexual harassment as "material" on workplace-based situation comedies', *Sex Roles,* 48, 433–445.

33 Kelley, P., Buckingham, D. and Davies, H (1999) 'Talking dirty: Children, sexual knowledge and television', *Childhood,* 6(2), 221–242.

34 Steele, J. R. (1999) 'Teenage sexuality and media practice: Factoring in the influences of family, friends and school', *Journal of Sex Research,* 36(4), 331–341.

35 Lamb, S. and Brown, L. (2006) *Packaging Girlhood: Rescuing Our Daughters from Marketers' Schemes.* New York, NY: St Martin's Griffin; Borzekowski, D. L., Robinson, T., and Kellen, J. D. (2000) 'Does the camera add 10 pounds? Media use, perceived importance of appearance and weight concerns among teenage girls', *Journal of Adolescent Health,* 20, 36–41.

36 Coy, M. (2009) 'Milkshakes, lady lumps and growing up to want boobies: How the sexualization of popular culture limits girls' horizons', *Child Abuse Review,* 18, 372–382.

37 Seider, V. (2006) *Transforming Masculinities: Men, Culture, Bodies, Power, Sex and Love.* Oxford, UK: Routledge.

38 Frederickson, B.L. and Roberts, T. A. (1997) 'Objectification theory: Toward understanding women's lived experiences and mental health risks', *Psychology of Women Quarterly,* 21, 173–206.

39 Gerbner, G., Gross, L., Morgan, M. and Signorielli, N. (1994) 'Growing up with television: The cultivation perspective', in J. Bryant and D. Zillmann (Eds.) *Media Effects: Advances in Theory and Research,* pp17–42. Hillsdale, NJ: Lawrence Erlbaum Associates.

40 Harrison, K. and Frederickson, B. L. (2003) 'Women's sports media, self-objectification, and mental health in black and white adolescent females', *Journal of Communication*, 53, 216–232.

41 Aubrey, J. S. (2006) 'Effects of sexually objectifying media on self-objectification and body surveillance in undergraduates: Results of a 2-year panel study', *Journal of Communication*, 56, 366–386.

42 Nayak, A. and Kehly, M. J. (2008) *Gender, Youth and Culture: Young Masculinities and Femininities*. Hampshire, UK: Palgrave. Aubrey, J. S. (2006) *op. cit.*

43 Baran, S. J., (1976a) 'How TV and film portrayals affect sexual satisfaction in college students', *Journalism Quarterly*, 53, 468–473; Baran, S. J. (1976b) 'Sex on TV and adolescent sexual self-concept', *Journal of Broadcasting*, 20, 61–68.

44 Escobar-Chaves, S. L., Tortelero, S. R., Markham, C. M., Law, B. J., Eitel, P. and Thickston, P. (2005) 'Impact of the media on adolescent sexual attitudes and behaviour', *Pediatrics*, 116, 303–326.

45 Walsh-Childers, K. and Brown, J. D. (1993) 'Adolescents' acceptance of sex-role stereotypes and television viewing', in B. Greenberg, J. D. Brown and N. L. Buerkel-Rothfuss (Eds.) *Media, Sex and the Adolescent*, pp117–33. Cresskill, NJ: Hampton Press.

46 Buerkel-Rothfuss, N. L. and Strouse, J. S. (1993) 'Media exposure and perceptions of sexual behaviours: The cultivation hypothesis moves to the bedroom', in B. S. Greenberg, J.D. Brown and N. L. Buerkel-Rothfuss (Eds.) *Media, Sex and the Adolescent*, pp225–247. Cresskill, NJ: Hampton Press; Carveth, R. and Alexander, A. (1985) 'Soap opera viewing motivation and the cultivation process', *Journal of Broadcasting and Electronic Media*, 29, 259–273.

47 Strouse, J. S. and Buerkel-Rothfuss, N. I. (1987) 'Media exposure and the sexual attitudes and behaviours of college students', *Journal of Sex Education and Therapy*, 13, 43–51.

48 Ward, L. M. and Rivadeneyra, R. (1999) 'Contributions of entertainment television to adolescents' sexual attitudes and expectations: The role of viewing amount versus viewer involvement', *Journal of Sex Research*, 36, 237–249.

49 Haferkamp, C. J. (1999) 'Beliefs about relationships in relation to television viewing, soap opera viewing and self-monitoring', *Current Psychology*, 18, 193–204.

50 Bryant, J. and Rockwell, S. C. (1994) 'Effects of massive exposure to sexually oriented prime-time television programming on adolescents' moral judgment', in D. Zillmann, J. Bryant and A. C. Huston (Eds.) *Media, Children, and the Family: Social Scientific, Psychodynamic, and Clinical Perspectives*, pp183–195. Hillsdale, NJ: Lawrence Erlbaum Associates.

51 Strouse, J. S., Goodwin, M. P. and Roscoe, B. (1994) 'Correlates of attitudes towards sexual harassment among early adolescents', *Sex Roles*, 31, 559–577.

52 Ward, L. M. (2002) 'Does television exposure affect emerging adults' attitudes and assumptions about sexual relationships? Correlational and experimental confirmation', *Journal of Youth and Adolescence*, 31, 1–15.

53 Bandura, A. (1977) *Social Learning Theory*. Englewood Cliffs, NJ: Prentice-Hall; Bandura, A. (1986) *Social Foundations of Thought and Action: A Social Cognitive Perspective*. Englewood Cliffs, NJ: Prentice-Hall; Bandura, A. (2009) 'Social cognitive theory of mass communication', in J. Bryant and M. B. Oliver (Eds.) *Media Effects: Advances in Theory and Research*, 3rd ed., pp94–124. London: Routledge.

54 Brown, J. D., Halpern, C. T. and L'Engle, K. L. (2005) 'Mass media as a sexual super peer for early maturing girls', *Journal of Adolescent Health*, 36, 420–427.

55 Brown, J. D. and Newcomer, S. F. (1991) 'Television viewing and adolescents' sexual behaviour', *Journal of Homosexuality*, 21, 77–91; Strouse, J. S. and Buerkel-Rothfuss, N. L. (1987) 'Media exposure and the sexual attitudes and behaviors of college students', *Journal of Sex Education and Therapy*, 13, 43–51; Strouse, J. S., Buerkel-Rothfuss, N. L. and Long, E. C. (1995) 'Gender and family as moderators of the relationship between music video exposure and adolescent sexual permissiveness', *Adolescence*, 30, 505–521.

56 Durham, M. G. (1999) 'Girls, media and the negotiation of sexuality: A study of race, class and gender in adolescent peer groups', *Journalism and Mass Communication*

Quarterly, 76 (2), 193–216; Strasburger, V. and Wilson, B. (2002) (Eds.) *Children, Adolescents and the Media*. London: Sage.

57 Calfin, M. S., Carroll, J. L. and Schmidt, J. (1993) 'Viewing music-videotapes before taking a test of premarital sexual attitudes', *Psychological Reports*, 72, 475–481; Greeson, L. E. and Williams, R. A. (1986) 'Social implications of music videos for youth: An analysis of the content and effects of MTV', *Youth and Society*, 18, 177–189; Kalof, L. (1999) 'The effects of gender and music video imagery on sexual attitudes', *Journal of Social Psychology*, 139, 378–385.

58 Bleakley, A., Hennessy, M., Fishbein, M. and Jordan, A. (2008) 'It works both ways: The relationship between exposure to sexual content in the media and adolescent sexual behaviour', *Media Psychology*, 11, 443–461; Bleakley, A., Hennessy, M., Fishbein, M. and Jordan, A. (2009) 'How source of sexual information relates to adolescents' belief about sex', *American Journal of Health Behaviour*, 33, 37–48.

59 Collins, R. L., Elliott, M. N., Berry, S. H., Kanouse, D. E., Kunkel, D., Hunter, S. B. and Miu, A. (2004) 'Watching sex on television predicts adolescent initiation of sexual behavior', *Pediatrics*, 114, e280-e289.

60 Chandra, A., Martino, S. C., Collins, R. L. et al (2008) 'Does watching sex on television predict teen pregnancy? Findings from a national longitudinal survey of youth', *Pediatrics*, 122(5), 1047–1054. Collins, R. L., Martino, S. C., Elliott, M. N. and Miu, A. (2011) 'Relationships between adolescent sexual outcomes and exposure to sex in media: Robustness to propensity-based analysis', *Developmental Psychology*, 47(2), 585–591.

61 Steinberg, L. and Monahan, K. C. (2010) 'Adolescents' exposure to sexy media does not hasten the initiation of sexual intercourse', *Developmental Psychology*, 47(2), 562–576.

62 Fishbein, M. and Ajzen, I. (2010) *Predicting and Changing Behaviour*. New York, NY: Taylor & Francis.

63 Gottfried, J. A., Vaava, S. E., Bleakley, A., Hennessy, M. and Jordan, A. (2011) 'Does the effect of exposure to TV sex on adolescent sexual behaviour vary by genre?', *Communication Research*, 20(10), 1–23.

64 O'Hara, R. E., Gibbons, F. X., Gerrard, M., Li, Z. and Sergeant, J. D. (2012) 'Greater exposure to sexual content in popular movies predicts earlier sexual debut and increased sexual risk taking', *Psychological Science*, 18 July, E-publication.

65 Bender, S. S. and Kosunen, E. (2005) 'Populations at risk across the lifespan and teenage contraceptive use in Iceland: A gender perspective', *Public Health Nursing*, 22(1), 17–26; Crosby, R. A., DiClemente, R. J., Wingood, G. M., Sionean, C., Cobb, B. K. and Harrington, K. (2000) 'Correlates of unprotected vaginal sex among African American female adolescents: Importance of relationship dynamics', *Archives of Pediatrics and Adolescent Medicine*, 154(9), 893–899; Tanfer, K., Cubbins, L. A., Billy, J. O. G. (1995) 'Gender, race, class and self-reported sexually transmitted disease incidence', *Family Planning Perspectives*, 27, 196–202.

66 Levinson, R. A., Jaccard, J. and Beamer, L. (1995) 'Older adolescents' engagement in casual sex: Impact of risk perception and psychosocial motivations', *Journal of Youth and Adolescence*, 24(3), 349. Manning, W. D., Longmore, M. A. and Giordano, P. C. (2005) 'Adolescents' involvement in non-romantic sexual activity', *Social Science Research*, 34, 384–407.

67 Lowry, D. T. and Shidler, J. A. (1993) 'Prime time TV portrayals of sex, "safe sex" and AIDS: A longitudinal analysis', *Journalism Quarterly*, 79(3) 628–637; Lowry, D. T. and Towles, D. E. (1989) 'Prime time TV portrayals of sex, contraception and venereal diseases', *Journalism Quarterly*, 66(2), 347–352.

68 Kelley, P., Buckingham, D. and Davies, H. (1999) 'Talking dirty: Children, sexual knowledge and television', *Childhood*, 6(3), 221–242.

69 Silverman-Watkins, L. T. and Sprafkin, J. N. (1983) 'Adolescents' comprehension of televised sexual innuendoes', *Journal of Applied Developmental Psychology*, 4, 359–369.

70 Karniol, R. (2001) 'Adolescent females' idolization of male media stars as a transition into sexuality', *Sex Roles*, 44(1–2), 61–77.

71 Steele, J. R. (1999) 'Teenage sexuality and media practice: Factoring in the influences of family, friends and school', *Journal of Sex Research*, 35(4), 331–341.

72 Brown, J. D., Halpern, C. T. and L'Engle, K.I. (2005) 'Mass media as a sexual super peer for early maturing girls', *Journal of Adolescent Health*, 36(5), 420–427.

73 Solderman, A. K., Greenberg, B. S. and Linsangan, R. (1988) 'Television and move behaviors of pregnant and non-pregnant adolescents', *Journal of Adolescent Research*, 3(2), 153–170.

74 Peterson, R. and Kahn, J. (1995) 'Media preferences of sexually active and inactive youth', *Sociological Imagination*, 32(1), 29–43.

6

MUSIC AND SEXUALIZATION

Music videos were originally introduced as a promotional device for music artists seeking wider public exposure to their music. Videos either focused on performances or integrated songs with story-telling.[1] Early 'performance' videos depicted the artists singing their songs or playing their instruments in studio or concert settings. Eventually, production formats developed in terms of narrative complexity and depicted actors in support of the artists playing out specific roles. These 'concept' music videos did not simply represent a platform for the music but integrated musical compositions with dramatic narratives – music videos told stories. Soon, the visual imagery became as important as the music in this production context. Artists were rated by their markets not just in terms of the quality of their latest musical creations, but also for the originality of their videos. From early on, sex became a prominent thematic component of these videos. It is not specifically the depiction of sexual themes within music videos that is problematic, but perhaps more the way in which sex is used as a vehicle for distinctive portrayals of women in a highly sexualized way. If images that objectify women are also combined with lyrics that reinforce the same messages, the ingredients are put in place to cultivate sexualized perceptions of women.

Although sexual depictions in music videos have not been as graphic as those found in many drama productions made for the cinema or television, they nevertheless have attracted criticism for the stereotyped way in which women tended to be treated.[2] The raw sexuality nature of these video products was often underpinned by sexually explicit lyrics. For observers of music videos, the sex was predominantly masculine in perspective and women were treated as decorative sexual objects whose primary purpose was the (actual or virtual) sexual titillation of men. Occasionally, role reversals would appear in the videos of female artists whose status in the music industry accorded them a masculine-like potency – such as Lady Gaga and Madonna – and who would use attractive young men in similarly decorative roles. In general, however, women's bodies were depicted much more often than men's bodies in a hyper-sexualized fashion.[3]

Concerns have been growing about the exposure of children to sexually explicit music videos on the internet. The British Prime Minister David Cameron summoned music industry representatives and internet service providers to his office in January 2012 to discuss actions that could be taken to prevent children from downloading videos that allegedly glamorized sexual violence and promiscuity.[4] Lobbyists acting on behalf of parents had earlier called for tighter controls over the distribution of such materials and for age-related ratings to be assigned to promotional trailers for these videos.

These concerns have been further reinforced by the actions of some female celebrity icons who have engaged in overtly sexualized displays in promoting their music and not least those who have matured from supposedly innocent and clean-cut child performers to the grown-up market. For four years, American singer and actress Miley Cyrus had starred in the title role of the popular television series *Hannah Montana* as a good-natured schoolgirl who is a pop star outside school hours. Cyrus shocked the world and incurred the ire of many of her teenage fans when, as a 20-year-old aspirant pop icon, she performed a sexually suggestive dance in a revealing costume at the 2013 MTV Video Music Awards ceremony in New York.[5] Worldwide publicity about this 'stunt' as many labelled it misleadingly reinforced the shock value with a photograph showing film actor Will Smith and his son and daughter in the audience with mouths gaping open – only for it to be revealed later that this shot showed their reactions to a performance by Lady Gaga.[6]

A number of writers have warned about the social risks to impressionable children from sexually explicit music lyrics and music video images that promoted themes such as the sexual exploitation of women and the use of drugs and guns. Such content has been aligned with a wider 'cultural toxicity' that has been perceived as prevalent in youth culture and threatens to undermine the innocence of childhood.[7] Feminist writers warned that such mediated debasement of childhood has accelerated across the digital media era that has made contentious sexualized material more widely available for children to access.[8] The sexualized lyrics of rappers might be especially problematic in this context.[9]

Although tools are available to enable parents or guardians to block offensive material, they were not always implemented. Age-restrictive ratings were also used by services such as YouTube, but there was less than complete confidence that such devices successfully prevent children's direct access to such content. The growth in concern about exposure to sexually explicit music content was made more acute by the fact that online sources could be accessed by children via their mobile phones.

Early research: Images and words

Research conducted on music videos throughout the 1980s and 1990s indicated that many, sometimes a clear majority, contained some sexual content.[10] It is not simply the prevalence of sex in these videos that is important in terms of their possible impact, but also the nature and form of that sexual material. The sex tended to consist of touching and kissing, but much of it was implicit rather than graphic. Women, however, were found frequently to be treated as sex objects and this was often manifested in the ways that they were dressed. The women featured were young, attractive and scantily clad and engaged in sexually provocative movements.

Although some music videos were fronted by female artists, in many the women were support acts – often dancers – and were used to decorate the sets as often as to contribute to the music and its presentation. By the mid-1980s, more than half of rock music videos were found to depict women in a sexually provocative way.[11] Women were stereotyped in terms of their social roles, some were downtrodden and nearly one in ten portrayed violence against women. During the 1990s, the amount of sex, sexual explicitness and themes of sexualization became increasingly prominent in music videos.[12]

From 2000, the prevalence of sex and sexualization content in music videos continued to grow, and both song lyrics and the images used in music videos became more explicit.[13] Suggestive sexual activity manifest as erotic styles of dancing, facial expressions of the young women featured in these videos, and their involvement in scenes where they were used as sexually alluring decorations or objects of desire of featured male artists became more regular features.

Explicit sexualization of women in hip hop music

Sexualization themes occurred across a range of music genres. The most explicit sexual content occurred in association with hip-hop, rap and R & B music. Music video artists and their producers began to move beyond extremely suggestive dancing by attractive and scantily attired young women to feature scenes of simulated sexual activity, including oral sex and intercourse. Rap music videos did not stop at the sexual objectification of women, but increasingly came to include themes of women shown in positions of extreme submission to men, including scenes of sexual violence.[14]

Contemporary hip-hop and rap music is characterized by commentaries on social issues and problems that have blighted impoverished communities populated mainly by ethnic minorities. Some of this music conveys religious and political messages that attempt to be constructive in tone, but much of it frequently has themes of extreme violence and is explicitly sexual in nature. Highly sexualized images are described in the lyrics and depicted visually where the music is promoted and performed in video formats. Much of this material derives from black communities and is widely consumed across these communities. A number of sexual scripts have been differentiated in which black girls and women are depicted in stereotyped and often sexualized ways.

Although it originated out of social alienation and the need for young blacks to express their frustrations and hopes for the future, hip-hop/rap music has become big business. The sexualized images have persisted despite the increasingly corporate nature of much of this music. This has led some commentators to observe corporate compliance in the 'commodification' of black women.[15]

Top-selling videos from internationally acclaimed artists such as 50 Cent, Hustlaz, Ict-T, Lil' Jon and Snoop Dogg all contained simulated sexual content that almost invariably treated women as sexual objects. In some music videos, with more restricted circulations but still available to those who know where to find them, non-simulated sexual acts were shown.

Themes based on the degradation of women have characterized gangsta rap (GR) music. In one investigation of nearly 500 GR songs, Edward Armstrong discovered that well over one in five contained lyrics that were unflattering towards women and treated them as little more than objects with the purpose of satisfying base male urges and needs.[16] In an analysis of over 500 music videos that had been broadcast on Black Entertainment Television, Country Music Television, Music Television and Video Hits-1, themes of interpersonal violence occurred in around one in seven videos (15 per cent). The violence was most often perpetrated by male protagonists and women and men were equally likely to be featured as victims. Among white actors in these videos, however, an overwhelming proportion of the victims of violence were women.[17]

Hip-hop comprises a number of sub-genres that focus on different social settings but where among the key differentiating features is the way in which black women are depicted. Booty rap focuses on life around strip clubs and depicts scantily dressed young black women dancing seductively around black male rappers. Gangster rap has a more violent theme and centres on life linked to gangs, alcohol and drugs, and often conveys scripts of sexual violence towards black women.[18]

According to Carolyn West, six sexual scripts can be identified from hip-hop music that represent different types of black woman.[19] These have been called, 'Diva', 'Gold Digger', 'Freak', 'Gangster Bitch', 'Baby Mama' and 'Earth Mother'. The 'diva' typifies an idealized Western notion of female beauty, with women featured who have a slender build, long hair and, although black, a lighter skin tone and tend to be well dressed. They are linked to symbols of wealth. The 'gold digger' is a woman who uses sex for personal economic reasons – to survive, to acquire possessions or simply for a better life. The 'freak' tends to be overtly sexual in appearance and behaviour and is sometimes involved in prostitution or has an adventurous sex life. The 'gangster bitch' tends to be located in poor, violent neighbourhoods and is both sexual and violent in her character. Her boyfriend may be involved in criminal activities and she actively supports him in this. The 'baby mama' is a woman who becomes pregnant or has a child often at a young age and the narratives in which she features tend to show her as pestering the father for money and using child access to manipulate the father. Finally, the 'earth mother' tends to place women centre stage, and they are often depicted by female rap artists whose music characterizations of women can represent extensions of their real life persons as politically active and aware and financially and emotionally independent women.

As the 'earth mother' theme has illustrated, the introduction of sexualization into music videos has not been restricted to male artists. A number of extremely popular female artists, some of whom had clean-cut public personas, have sexed-up their images to extend their fan base. Country music has tended to be the genre least likely to included sex and sexualization themes. Nonetheless, successful female artists such as Faith Hill and Shania Twain have released songs and accompanying videos in which they have used iconic male sexual fantasy representations of women. Sexual references have characterized much of the music of other leading female artists, including Katy Perry, Madonna and Rihanna. These performers have sexually objectified themselves, although one might argue that this has been their choice and the sexualization that is used represents a demonstration of women as powerful sexual beings.

Lady Gaga is probably one of the most prominent artists and she has frequently used explicit sexual content in her music videos. In her video for Alejandro, simulated rough sex and sadomasochism feature prominently. Some songs have sexual themes while others do not. Nevertheless, artists such as Lady Gaga have turned even non-sexually themed songs into sexual ones in her videos. A prime example here is 'Telephone'. The lyrics of the song revolve around a girl partying at a club and being interrupted by phone calls. The music video for this song, however, features themes of nudity, sex and even murder. Lady Gaga has a huge fan base, particularly among teenagers. In 2010 she was voted Best Female Artist by 13- to 19-year-olds at the Teen Choice Awards.

Emerson analysed 56 music videos of male and female performers to uncover the representation of black womanhood.[20] While acknowledging the presence of exploitative images of black women, she also found examples of black women asserting their own power through their sexuality. At the same time, this assertion of their independence and autonomy was placed with a wider context of their musical creativity – a process over which leading black female artists also exhibited considerable personal control. Black women in these videos did not feel a need to hide their sexual appeal but were comfortable showing it off to men and women. Sexy in this context equalled power.

In addition to the sexual images present in music videos, the lyrics of popular songs frequently make references to sexual relationships and sexual behaviour. In one analysis of rap music videos recorded from a number of US cable television channels, Yaunyuan Zhang, Travis Dixon and Kate Conrad of the Department of Communication, University of Illinois, at Urbana-Champaign found that females with extremely thin body shapes were over-represented. Women with small body sizes were especially likely to be present in rap videos with sexual themes. In videos with political themes and where sexual themes were absent or only of peripheral significance, the featured women tended to have larger body sizes.[21]

The same researchers conducted a further investigation of rap music videos and found that they were characterized by dominant themes of materialism and misogyny. The first theme was expressed in terms of overt displays of wealth as evidenced through a lavish high-consuming lifestyle, expensive clothes and jewellery, and top of the range cars. The latter theme tended to take the form of scenes that sexualized women and emphasized the dominance of men over women. This research revealed that rap music videos tended to feature male characters taking the lead in a range of settings and themes, whereas female characters were mostly used as sexual objects. One particularly interesting finding was that even some leading female rap artists adopted a sexualized character and placed themselves in positions of submission.[22]

Concerns have understandably been raised about the implications of this extreme music culture, given its dominant themes, for the sexual socialization, sexual behaviour and self-images of young black women.[23] Many of the themes played out in this music resonate closely with social conditions on the ground for black girls living in deprived, violent neighbourhoods.[24] The images of black women in rap music represent narratives for coping with difficult social circumstances, and despite the submissive or oppressed nature of many of the black female types that appear in this music they could nevertheless provide life scripts that desperate and insecure young black girls internalize for future reference.

Exposure to music videos

Adolescents around the world have been found to display regular exposure to music videos that depict women as sex objects. This exposure cuts across different ethnic and cultural groups. The potential of music to serve as a vehicle for sex and the sexual socialization of young people has been underlined by studies revealing the extent to which sex is a feature of music outputs that are popular among young people.[25]

In the US, teenage African-Americans reported watching over three hours of music video content every day.[26] American Latino students were found to watch a similar amount of music video content on a daily basis.[27] This content is readily available via cable TV channels and the internet. There are numerous music cable channels that provide round the clock access to music video material.

In another large study of American teenagers' media consumption habits and exposure to sexual content across the major mass media, music outputs were found to contain more sex than movies, television, magazines, newspapers or internet sites that had been nominated as popular with a large teenage sample. While 11 per cent of media content analysed was classed as sexual in nature, music outputs were nearly four times as likely (40 per cent) to contain any sexual material. Around one seventh (15 per cent) of the sexual content in music outputs focused on sexual intercourse. A similar proportion of music outputs (17 per cent) featured narratives describing the breakdown of sexual relationships.[28]

Impact of music videos

Music videos contain sex and have displayed a tendency to depict women in highly sexualized and stereotyped ways. Young people are known to engage in widespread and frequent consumption of music videos. In consequence, there is a high probability that most young consumers of these cultural products are exposed to large numbers of sexualized images. Does all this material simply pass over their heads or do they absorb social scripts from it that shape their beliefs about women, sex and intimate relationships?

Female pop stars can provide powerful role models for children and teenagers. These influences can be especially pronounced in the case of artists who themselves initially came to public prominence as children. Two of the biggest female music icons to emerge in the modern era, Britney Spears and Christina Aguilera, began their show business careers as child stars on *The Mickey Mouse Club*. From innocent youngsters in this wholesome entertainment format, both reinvented themselves in their early adult years as recording artists targeting an older market. Sexiness was a major weapon added to their armoury to depict their transition to adulthood and underpin a maturity to their music that would appeal to adult markets.

Both Aguilera and Spears cultivated dramatically changed personal images underlined by the way they dressed, the way they behaved and the types of songs they sang. Initially, they – and especially Spears – gently introduced relatively innocent flirtations with sexual themes, such as in Spears's major hit 'Baby One More Time'. Later on, they both adopted a much more overt sexuality not only with more explicit sexual themes running through their song lyrics, but also by being featured in revealing poses in magazines. Despite these more mature themes, Aguilera and Spears remained popular with younger audiences but now engaged with their fan bases, regardless of their ages, in a much more open, sexual fashion. The use of nude poses represented a voluntary sexual objectification of their physical selves, legitimizing the use of sexiness to define successful maturity from childhood to adulthood for girls.

If music videos can influence young people, what form does this influence take? As we will see, these videos have been linked to the way in which young people regard themselves, as well as their beliefs and opinions about others. They have also been identified as agents in the development of sexual behaviour patterns amongst young people.

In terms of self-perceptions, attention here has focused on the sexual objectification of women in music videos. There is concern that these themes could lead to women and girls in the audience making unfavourable comparisons between themselves and sexually attractive and provocative women featured in these videos. Some researchers have classed music videos alongside other media content, particularly on television and in magazines, that present an objectified body-shape ideal for women. Usually, this ideal emphasizes a thin body shape.

Evidence has emerged that teenage girls are inclined to experience lowered self-esteem after exposure to music videos featuring attractive women with slender bodies. In one controlled experiment, 16- to 19-year-old girls were assigned to three conditions. In one condition they watched three music videos, in a second condition they listened to three songs and in a third condition they learned a list of words. All the girls had been pre-tested about their body self-esteem. After the three interventions they completed a further psychological test designed to measure how they felt about their bodies. The girls who watched the music videos, but not the girls in the other two conditions, displayed increased dissatisfaction with their bodies.[29]

Andsager and Roe developed a typology of music videos from a review of past evidence.[30] They differentiated three thematic domains that defined the nature of music videos and, in turn, might indicate the kinds of influences they could have on consumers. The three themes were sex as metamorphosis, sex as fantasy fulfilment and, finally, sex as power. The sex as metamorphosis theme was used by artists to create a different image of themselves.

This approach might be used by female or male artists who use sex as an attribute to reinvent their image as more grown-up or dangerous than the image for which they were known. This technique might be used by artists who found fame as children or teenagers who wish to demonstrate their maturity as they grow older by encouraging their audiences to see them as being sexual for the first time.

One of the best examples of this phenomenon is Britney Spears who has used sexual imagery to make the transition from innocent teenage pop performer to a more sexually mature artist. The problem here is that in order to get audiences to adopt a more adult image of 'Britney', she adopted highly revealing appearances and suggestive behaviour to shock audiences into seeing her differently. While this may be rationalized as necessary to achieve a complex rebranding, it also presented sexualized images to her young fan base that objectified the female form (her own).

The sex as fantasy theme in music videos has often taken the form of male fantasy scenarios involving women dressed provocatively, taking on suggestive roles as a dominatrix, nurse, or schoolgirl, and other socially stereotyped male sexual fantasy figures. In their videos, male artists will feature female role models of this kind as objects of voyeurism and desire. Female artists often adopt these female roles themselves to invoke similar male responses.

Under the sex as power theme, artists – usually male ones – utilize sex to demonstrate power over women. Women are featured scantily clad with camerawork focusing on their physical attributes. Female artists may put themselves on display through revealing a lot of flesh and acting out clearly sexual scenarios. One significant difference here is that they will tend to use their sexuality as a source of their power over others, particularly men. They present their physical bodies as objects of male desire, but determine how much of them men are allowed access to.

Researchers have reported cases of young black girls making references to some of these themes and female types in their conversations with each other and in their self-descriptions on their social media sites.[31] Girls will describe themselves as 'bitches' – a term frequently used in relation to young black women in hip-hop music. They will also make sexual self-references that adopt explicit sexual labels of women as integral aspects of their online identities. In addition, they will expand upon these self-images to infer their sexual experience and availability.[32] Counter-balancing this, some black teenage girls have adopted a polarized position as sexually pure or chaste and take pride in their virginity, which is worn as a badge of self-control and independence.[33]

In an experiment conducted with African-American adolescents, participants were randomly assigned to view either non-violent rap videos in which women were shown in sexually subordinate roles or no videos at all. All participants also read a verbal description of a scene in which a teenage male perpetrator committed date rape on a teenage female victim. Participants were asked to give their opinions about the date rape episode and the acceptability of the behaviour that was described. The attitudes of male participants did not differ between conditions in which rap videos were viewed or no videos were viewed. In contrast, teenage females who watched rap videos displayed greater acceptance of the date rape behaviour than did those who saw no videos at all.[34]

Sexual beliefs and attitudes

Exposure to music videos with sexual themes has been found to influence people's beliefs about sexual behaviour in society and their attitudes towards sex in general. Watching these videos can give people exaggerated impressions about the normality of sexual promiscuity and might, in turn, encourage them to adopt more liberal attitudes towards sex.[35] One of the main concerns about music videos that depict women in a highly sexualized way is that they can, through repeat exposure, cultivate distorted attitudes and beliefs about women. Greater acceptability of sexual promiscuity, which was linked to heavier consumption of music videos, was found to be prevalent among female college students rather than just men. Male college students who watched music videos a lot, meanwhile, displayed stronger sex-role stereotyping.[36] Young men in America who reported regular consumption of music videos also displayed more tolerant attitudes towards sexual harassment.[37]

Exposure to a sexually charged music video (by Madonna) triggered more liberal post-viewing sexual attitudes among university undergraduates than did a more romantically themed music video (by Amy Grant).[38] In a subsequent experimental study, a sexually themed music video starring a male artist (Michael Jackson) also elicited more assertive sexual attitudes among university undergraduates than did a music video with no sexual content.[39] In a further experiment conducted with 12- to 15-year-olds, those who watched music videos with sexual content later displayed greater acceptance of premarital sex than did controls who watched non-sexual video material.[40]

A further study reported that opinions about women can be influenced by watching and listening to music videos with sexually explicit themes.[41] The researchers divided a small sample of US university students into those who watched and listened to a set of music videos featuring black female artists rapping about sexual enticement, or singing about romantic love. Afterwards, all participants were shown pictures of black and white women and were asked to evaluate them. Male participants rated the black women more harshly than did female participants. Opinions were more negative about the rappers singing about sexual enticement than about the artists singing romantic love songs. The rappers were rated as more sexually active and promiscuous than the romantic love singers.

Yuanyuan Zhang, Laura Miller and Kristen Harrison found that exposure to music videos with sexual themes was correlated with acceptance of premarital sex and sex as recreation. Regular reported watching of these videos was also associated with beliefs that women are sexual objects and should be sexually subordinate to men and that it is acceptable for men to have multiple sexual partners.[42]

Jeremiah Strouse and his colleagues surveyed a sample of 214 American teenagers still at school about their consumption of music videos and their current sexual activity.[43] The researchers obtained further information about the types of families and households with whom these teenagers lived. Girls who reported watching music videos were more likely to agree that premarital sex was acceptable than were their same-sex peers who did not watch this form of entertainment. This relationship was especially strong for girls who came from less happy and stable family backgrounds. There was no link between claimed viewing of music videos and opinions about premarital sex among boys. The broad conclusion here was that girls from poorer and less structured families were more at risk from engaging in early sexual activity and might also be drawn to music videos. What is less clear is whether exposure to music videos *per se* also contributed to teenage girls' opinions about sex before marriage or, indeed, whether this effect, if it did exist, was confined to specific types of videos that had sexual themes.

Patricia Greenfield, professor of psychology at UCLA, and her colleagues carried out a series of experiments with pre-teenage children, teenagers and young adults up to 29 years.[44] They tested listeners' abilities to understand and explain the lyrics of the Bruce Springsteen song 'Born in the USA' and Madonna's 'Like a Virgin'. Springsteen's music was more to the tastes of young adults, while pre-teens and teens preferred Madonna. Understanding of specific terms used in 'Like a Virgin' improved significantly with age. Those in their late teens and 20s showed almost universal ability to explain what specific turns of phrase in this song meant, while amongst the pre-teens an overwhelming majority (around four in ten) were unable to do this. Even fewer pre-teens were able to explain Madonna's feelings in this song. Once youngsters had reached their teens they were more able to relate to this song.

All the above research about music videos and attitudes and beliefs concerning sex derived from surveys in which samples of respondents provided information about their viewing habits and attitudes, and beliefs about sexual matters via questionnaires. Statistical tests were then computed on these self-report data to identify degrees of association between exposure to music videos and sex-related attitudes or beliefs. What this evidence does not confirm for us is whether watching music videos, even if they contain portrayals that treat women as sex objects, can cause specific sexualized attitudes and beliefs to emerge.

To measure and understand this type of relationship, a different methodology is needed in which the researchers can control people's exposure to specific video materials to find out whether watching sexualized content can trigger sexualized beliefs and attitudes. Experimental research of this type has been used to study this question. One American investigation carried out with youngsters aged 12 to 14 years invited some of them to watch MTV tapes for no more than one hour. Compared with others who did not watch these tapes, the MTV viewers were more likely to approve of premarital sex.[45] In a later study, American college students were recruited to watch a music video that had sexual content and were subsequently found to give stronger endorsements to sexually promiscuous attitudes than were a matched group of students who did not watch this tape.[46]

Sexual behaviour

As we have seen, there is evidence that the use of sexualized content in music videos can shape viewers' and listeners' opinions about the artists and more generic beliefs about their gender and race. Are the influences of music videos ultimately translated into behavioural outcomes? Behavioural effects can take different forms. Specific portrayals can serve as role models that trigger imitative behaviour in observers. For most psychologists who specialize in the study of human behaviour, however, the mass media influence behaviour in a less direct way by providing rich sources of behavioural 'scripts' from which observes can learn. These scripts represent cognitive memories of sequences of behaviour that are acted out in visualized scenarios. Exposure to these scripts can result in them being 'internalized' or memorized so that they can be called upon in the future whenever we are confronted by a situation in our own lives that requires us to act in a certain way.[47]

Hence, if music videos frequently depict women presented as sexual objects in sexually submissive roles in scenarios where men are powerful and dominant and express their power through sexual exploitation of compliant women, they provide a source of misogynistic scripts or, worse, social scripts that represent and legitimize sexual aggressiveness and exploitation. Hip-hop music, in particular, has attached glamour to sexual promiscuity and using sex as a commodity that buys social status and funds materialism.[48] Does the constant consumption of this material cultivate a set of social perceptions in young ethnic minority girls that encourages them to adopt lifestyles that put them at further risk in terms of their health or social security? Some reassurance has emerged from studies that have indicated that some black girls have rejected these social scripts and the ideas of subservient femininity and dominant masculinity they present.[49]

In fact, black adolescent girls reject hip-hop's depictions of sexually available women and other associated gender stereotypes.[50] One observation has been that some black girls have created oppositional scripts of their own, such as the 'Sister Saviour' concept that embraces the code that sex should take place only within marriage.[51] Yet, despite these alternative socially constructive scripts, other black adolescent girls continued to see value in the need for play on their female sexuality and to use it as a social weapon when circumstances warranted. Rather than adopting one extreme position – complete sexual openness and promiscuity versus chastity outside wedlock – there was recognition that there were occasions when a more conservative image was appropriate and others when the need to be sexy was advantageous.[52]

Carol Pardun, Kelly L'Engle and Jane Brown of the University of North Carolina surveyed adolescents in the US and assessed them for their level of sexual activity, romantic relationships and music tastes. The more these American teenagers reported listening to music with lyrics that contained sexual references, the more likely they were to be sexually active.

This initial study provided some insights into possible relationships between listening to music lyrics and young people's sexual behaviours, but it did not establish causality. While it is possible that exposure to popular music with lyrics that contain sexual references could trigger adolescents to become sexual, it is equally feasible to interpret these findings in the opposite direction. That is, young people who have become sexually active, for other reasons, also display a stronger taste for listening to music that makes references to sex.

In a subsequent report, the same research group reported a survey with white and black American teenagers in which their exposure to sexualized media was related to their reported sexual behaviour. Although the teenagers' exposure to sexual content in music videos was measured in this study, it was aggregated with their exposure to sexual content in magazines and in movies and television pro-grammes. The authors of this research reported that a greater amount of exposure to sexual content in the media at age 12 to 14 years predicted a greater likelihood of having had sexual intercourse two years later when other social factors were statistically cancelled out, but this occurred only for white teenagers. Teenagers' exposure to sexual content in music outputs may have contributed to this sexual behaviour outcome, but this study did not show the extent to which music had an independent influence on the onset of teenagers' sexual activity.[53]

A follow-on analysis by the same research group differentiated between consumption of sexual content in different media and the reported sexual behaviours of teenagers. Consumption of sexual content through music emerged as the most powerful predictor across all media of sexual activity, including onset of sexual intercourse.[54]

Steven Martino and his colleagues at the RAND Corporation conducted a study over several years in which a sample of 12- to 17-year-olds were surveyed three times about their sexual experiences and tastes in music.[55] Out of 1461 adolescents who were contacted initially, 1242 completed all three waves of interviews. Follow-up interviews after initial contact were conducted after one year and again after three years. As well as answering questions about whether they were sexually active and in what ways, these young interviewees indicated how often they listened to the music of a number of musical artists.

The participants were asked if they had ever had sexual intercourse, which in this case was defined as penetrative vaginal intercourse. In addition, further ques-tioning explored, for those who had not yet had full sexual intercourse, how far along the coital continuum they had got. The questioning here asked participants whether they had kissed, 'made out' (or kissed for a long time), touched a breast/ had a breast touched, touched genitals/had genitals touched, and finally given or received oral sex. They were scored on this five-point scale for their degree of sexual experience if they had not yet had full sexual intercourse.

Key music measures comprised interviewees' indications as to whether they had ever listened to the music of 16 male and female music artists from across a range of music genres who were among the top-selling music performers of the time. Each artist's most recently released music album was independently analysed for its sexual content and the data generated were added to interviewees' music-listening data. Sexual content was classified in two ways. The first was for the degree of explicitness – that is, whether references were made to explicit sexual acts or whether sexual references were more subtle. The second was for whether the sexual references were degrading or non-degrading to women.

Songs with degrading lyrics towards women tended to be more sexually explicit and nearly all dealt with themes of casual sex. These songs were mostly performed by rap artists.

When the researchers examined relationships between reported listening to music types and sexual behaviour, they found that those listening to music with lyrics that were sexually degrading to women were more likely subsequently to have begun to have sexual intercourse or to have progressed along the sexual continuum in their degree of sexual activity. This relationship persisted when they controlled statistically for a range of social and demographic factors known also to predict early onset of sexual behaviour. Level of reported exposure to music that contained sexual lyrics that were non-degrading (or respectful) towards women was not statistically related to changes in sexual habits.

The idea that young people might be influenced in their sexual behaviours by listening to music with lyrics that make sexual references derives from a theory known as social cognition theory. This theory, in turn, derives from earlier social learning theory that claimed that we learn by observing the behaviours of others. Early theorizing focused on whether observers would copy specific behaviours of others, especially when they had witnessed those behaviours being rewarded. The initial demonstrations of this effect tended to measure immediate or short-term influences of observed behaviour. However, it does not always follow that observed behaviour can affect how we ourselves behave only when an opportunity to re-enact it occurs immediately. There are occasions when we might adopt a pattern of behaviour in a social setting that we originally witnessed elsewhere a long time ago. Recognition that this longer-term effect of imitative learning can occur led psychologists to modify the original theory such that the learning that takes places may occur at a cognitive level in the form of memories of previously experienced sequences of behaviours, otherwise known as 'scripts'.[56] Such scripts might then be triggered at a future date by relevant social cues and the behaviour physically reproduced by us.

Scripts concerned with behaviour can be learned even without direct observation of the behaviour concerned. Hence, we can learn verbal descriptions of behaviour sequences and convert these into imagined scenarios that we can visualize in our imaginations. According to some researchers, such scripts might be learned from media content.[57] Song lyrics might qualify as behavioural triggers in this context.[58]

Despite earlier observations that female music artists believe that by being sexual in their videos they are not forfeiting social or sexual power to men, Monique Ward, Ann Merriwether and Alison Caruthers found that young male viewers in their teens and 20s focused on the sexual attributes of these female forms.[59] It is unclear, therefore, whether their preoccupation with the sexual attributes of female artists or female support to male artists led to these portrayals being interpreted as iconic representations of feminine power. Female artists may believe that their videos allow them to demonstrate their power as women and as sexual beings, but for young men there is often a tendency, nonetheless, to focus on these women as sexual objects rather than autonomous performers deserving of their respect.

Impact upon male listeners and viewers

There has been a lot of focus in the sexualization literature on the impact of mediated sexualization upon girls or women. The position of boys or men has tended to be investigated less often. In the context of music mediation of sexual themes, young black men have confirmed that the depictions of hip-hop lyrics and videos has some resonance with reality in the way they represent the nature of gender relations.[60] One feature of this is that black gender relations are often shown as adversarial in hip-hop videos and this can confirm expectations among young black men that this is the way such relationships will play out in real life.[61]

Of greater concern are the depictions of gender conflicts that take the form of sexual violence. Rape has been a visible theme in gangster rap, with lyrics explicitly advocating male violence against women as justified in the context of sexual interactions. Other more worrying sub-themes involve gang rape and rape of under-age girls.[62] There is no compelling empirical evidence that exposure to this kind of material triggers sexual violence in young men. There is evidence of a worrying level of self-reported participation in gang rape, however, among black adolescent boys.[63] Girls can also absorb lessons from the sexually violent music scripts, and the extent of exposure to them has been correlated with levels of acceptance of date violence amongst young black women.[64]

Further evidence has emerged that regular viewing of rap music videos that contain highly sexualized themes was associated over time with a greater propensity among adolescent black girls to have more sexual partners and to have acquired sexually transmitted diseases.[65] Regular consumption of this type of music was also linked to other risky behaviours such as drug-taking and alcohol consumption.[66]

As we saw earlier, Yuanyuan Zhang and her colleagues at the University of Illinois at Urbana Champaign ran a survey with undergraduate students to find out whether watching music videos with sexual themes was linked with their attitudes towards sexual relations and most especially with holding double standards about male and female sexuality.[67] Respondents were asked to indicate how much they agreed or disagreed with attitudes such as 'It is important that the men be sexually experienced so as to teach the women' and 'A woman who is sexually active is less likely to be considered a desirable partner.'

The researchers measured the extent to which they had watched each of 75 music videos that had been pre-rated by a separate sample of students in terms of their sexual explicitness. The videos endorsed were combined with their sexual content scores such that each student's reported viewing experience could be weighted in terms of the degree of sexual material to which they had been exposed.

Stronger endorsement of both premarital sexual permissiveness and of sexual double standards was found to be closely associated with being male, already sexually active, and with watching music videos with greater amounts of explicit sexual content. Hence, those students who reported watching greater amounts of sexually laced music videos held more recreational opinions about sex and more stereotyped views about female and male sexuality. Within the double standards assessment, women who were sexually outgoing and liberal were also regarded as less desirable in some ways because they made themselves so readily available. The risk here is that if music videos frequently depict women as having these qualities, the lessons learned by impressionable young observers could be that all women can be characterized in this way.

Another study by Zhang and her colleagues Travis Dixon and Kate Conrad found evidence that greater consumption of rap music videos among African-American college students was less likely to result in the belief that rap music is degrading to women.[68] These researchers noted that earlier analyses of rap music had revealed common sexual themes, sometimes tinged with violence, and highly visible sexualized portrayals of women. From a sample of more than 100 rap music videos, they found that two broad types of production could be distinguished. One type was characterized by dominant themes of materialism and misogyny. Here there were conspicuous depictions of affluence and wealth combined with portrayals of male dominance over women. In the second type, the principal themes comprised political awareness, expression of culture (in this case, black culture), disaffection with mainstream society and the importance of the local community. The latter genre emphasized the importance of black cultural identity and community in a world in which the mainstream often marginalized that community. The relevance of this study to the current discussion was in its findings that when appearances by women were systematically related back to the different themes, it was the misogyny theme that emerged as the best predictor of female appearances. This confirmed that in these music videos, women were depicted in highly sexualized roles in which their main purpose was to service the needs of men.[69]

Brian Primack and his colleagues surveyed 14- to 15-year-olds about their music listening habits and favourite artists.[70] Previous analyses had provided data on the extent to which the music of various artists contained sexual material that was either degrading or non-degrading to women.[71] A calculation of each respondent's exposure to sexual content in music lyrics was made based on information about their hours of weekly listening and proportion of songs by their favourite artist that contained sexual references of different kinds. Adolescents' sexual behaviour was measured in terms of whether they had ever had sexual intercourse or, if not, whether they had engaged in other sexual practices other than intercourse, from kissing through to oral sex. The researchers found – as others had done – that teenagers' reported exposure to music with degrading sex was related to their propensities to be sexually active and to had have sexual intercourse. Exposure to music with non-degrading sexual themes did not exhibit any significant relationship with sexual activity. These findings were found both for teenage boys and girls.

Research has shown us that sex linked to music might be a factor involved in shaping young people's attitudes to sex and, in turn, to their own sexual practices. This only becomes a serious social problem if there is accompanying evidence that the opportunities for such effects to occur are widespread. Thus, it may be true that youngsters with specific music preferences are drawn to music that is infiltrated with antisocial sexual content. If it is apparent, however, that the music diets of many youngsters could potentially contain this sort of material, then the problem of sexual content that degrades women is scaled up.

Analyses of popular songs have shown that there could be a problem here. One study of 279 songs identified through *Billboard* magazine as the most popular of the day (in 2005) found than over one third (37 per cent) contained references to sex. More significantly, two-thirds of those songs contained degrading references to women. This sort of content was most likely to be found in rap music, but was also prevalent in country music and in rhythm and blues and hip-hop music. Songs with degrading sexual material were also more likely to contain references to substance abuse and violence.

The words of songs can invoke unpleasant behavioural dispositions towards women just as much as video enactments of sexual exploitation. Men who listened to music with sexually violent themes were more likely than those who did not to report experiencing behavioural problems with their female partners.[72]

Summary and conclusions

Music and sex have been closely inter-related from the early days of popular song-writing as intimate human relationships have often provided the inspiration to musicians and writers. Music is also a popular form of entertainment among young people. Developing a taste for specific genres of music can play an important part in defining social identity among children and teenagers and is often linked to the type of social background from which they have emerged and the reference groups to which they wish to belong.

Some genres of music are characterized by explicit sexual references. As a result of the emergence of music videos to showcase music artists and their work, the sexual aspects of music can become even more explicit in that lyrics are accompanied by visual narratives that display overt sexual content. This content often takes the form of appearances by scantily clad young women and varied simulations of sexual activity. Male artists, in particular, have produced videos that regularly depict sexually objectified representations of women. In addition, some well-known female artists have adopted sexually objectified images for themselves as a form of personal sexual empowerment – that is, they display themselves in a sexual way that is under their control.

Concerns have been raised about the possible effects of music content and especially when songs are accompanied by the release of videos. Research evidence has so far indicated the exposure to such material has been found among some samples of young people to display significant degrees of statistical association with holding more sexually open and even promiscuous beliefs and to earlier onset of sexual activity. Some evidence has also emerged that specific male attitudes towards female sexuality that readily embrace more objectified impressions of women have also been linked to reported levels of exposure to sexually explicit songs and music videos. What is not clear from the evidence to emerge so far is whether exposure to sex in music causes sexualized attitudes and beliefs about women or encourages young people to become sexually more adventurous and to do so at an earlier age. Nevertheless, even if the statistical relationships observed so far can be explained, in part, by selective exposure by those young people who exhibit sexualized beliefs or promiscuity for other reasons, regular exposure to highly sexualized music content could provide social scripts that, when internalized, serve only to reinforce pre-existing sexualized psychological profiles.

Notes

1 Brown, J. D. and Campbell, K. (1986) 'Race and gender in music videos: The same beat but a different drummer', *Journal of Communication*, 36, 94–106.
2 Andsager, J. and Roe, K. (2003) '"What's your definition of dirty baby?" Sex in music videos', *Sexuality & Culture: An Interdisciplinary Quarterly*, 7(3), 79–97.
3 Ward, L. M., Merriwether, A. and Caruthers, A. (2006) 'Breasts are for men: Media, masculinity ideologies and men's beliefs about women's bodies', *Sex Roles*, 55, 703–714.
4 Woolf, M. (2012) 'Cameron calls in music bosses over explicit videos', *The Sunday Times*, 1 January, p9.
5 Harlow, J. (2013) 'Fallen angel', *The Sunday Times*, 1 October, p16.
6 Peacock, L. and Kerr, I. (2013) 'MTV Music Video Awards 2013: Why everybody's talking about Miley Cyrus and that performance', *The Telegraph*, 27 August, www.telegraph.co.uk/women/womens-life/10267842/, accessed 7 October 2013.
7 Palmer, S. (2006) *Toxic Childhood: How the Modern World is Damaging Our Children and What We Can Do about It*. London, UK: Orion.
8 Walkerdine, V. (1997) *Daddy's Girl*. Cambridge, MA: Harvard University Press; Ringrose, J. and Walkerdine, V. (2008) 'Regulating the abject', *Feminist Media Studies*, 8(3), 227–246.
9 Lamb, S. and Brown, L. M. (2006) *Packaging Girlhood: Rescuing Our Daughters from Marketers' Schemes*. New York, NY: St Martin's Press.
10 Baxter, R., De Reimer, C., Landini, A., Singletary, M. W. and Leslie, L. (1985) 'A content analysis of music videos', *Journal of Broadcasting & Electronic Media*, 29(3), 333–340; Sherman, B. L. and Dominick, J. R. (1986) 'Violence and sex in music videos: TV and rock 'n' roll', *Journal of Communication*, 36, 79–93.
11 Vincent, R. C., Davis, D. K. and Bronskowski, L. A. (1987) 'Sexism on MTV: A content analysis of rock videos', *Journalism Quarterly*, 64, 750–755; Vincent, R. C. (1988) 'Clio's consciousness raised? Portrayal of women in rock videos re-examined', *Journalism Quarterly*, 65, 155–160.
12 Seidman, S. A. (1992) 'An investigation of sex-role stereotyping in music videos', *Journal of Broadcasting & Electronic Media*, 36, 209–216; Sommers-Flanagan, R., Sommers-Flanagan, J. and Davis, B. (1993) 'What's happening on music television? A gender role content analysis', *Sex Roles*, 28, 745–753; Strasburger, V. C. and Hendren, R. O. (1995) 'Rock music and rock music videos', *Pediatric Annals*, 24, 97–103; Gow, J. (1996) 'Reconsidering gender roles on MTV: Depictions in the most popular music videos of the early 1990s', *Communication Reports*, 9, 151–161; Seidman, S. A. (1999) 'Revisiting sex-role stereotyping in MTV videos', *International Journal of Instructional Media*, 26, 11–22.

13 Arnett, J. J. (2002) 'The sounds of sex: Sex in teens' music and music videos', in J. Brown, R. Walsh-Childers and J. Steele (Eds.) *Sexual Teens, Sexual Media*, pp253–264, Hillsdale, NJ: Erlbaum.

14 Sommers-Flanagan, R., Sommers-Flanagn, J. and Davis, B. (1993) 'What's happening on music television', *Sex Roles*, 28(11/12), 745–753; Conrad, K., Dixon, T. L. and Zhang, Y. (2009) 'Controversial rap themes, gender portrayals and skin tone distortion: A content analysis of rap music videos', *Journal of Broadcasting and Electronic Media*, 53(1), 134–156.

15 Sharpley-Whiting, T. D. (2007) *Pimps Up, Ho's Own: Hip Hop's Hold on Young Black Women*. New York, NY: New York University Press.

16 Armstrong, E. G. (2001) 'Gangsta misogyny: A content analysis of the portrayals of violence against women in rap music, 1987–93', *Journal of Criminal Justice and Popular Culture*, 8(2), 96–126.

17 Rich, M., Woods, E. R., Godman, E., Emans, S. J. and DuRant, R. H. (1998) 'Aggressors and victims: Gender and race in music video violence', *Pediatrics*, 101(4), 669–673.

18 Cole, J. B. and Guy-Sheftall, B. (2003) *Gender Talk: The Struggle for Women's Equality in African American Communities*. New York, NY: Ballantine Publishing Group.

19 West, C. M. (2009) 'Still on the auction block: The (s)exploitation of black adolescent girls in rap(e) music and hip-hop culture', in S. Olfman (Ed.) (2009) *The Sexualization of Childhood*, pp89–102. Westport, CT: Praeger.

20 Emerson, A. R. (2002) 'Where my girls at? Negotiating black womanhood in music videos', *Gender & Society*, 16, 115–135.

21 Zhang, Y., Dixon, T. and Conrad, K (2010) 'Female body image as a function of themes in rap music videos: A content analysis', *Sex Roles*, 62, 787–797.

22 Conrad, K., Dixon, T. and Zhang, Y. (2009) 'Controversial rap themes, gender portrayals and skin tone distortion: A content analysis of rap music videos', *Journal of Broadcasting & Electronic Media*, 53(1), 134–156.

23 Stephens, D. P. and Phillips, L. D. (2003) 'Freaks, Gold Diggers, Divas and Dykes: The sociohistorical development of adolescent African American women's sexual scripts', *Sexuality & Culture*, 7, 3–47.

24 Martyn, K. K. and Hutchinson, S. A. (2001) 'Low-income African-American adolescents who avoid pregnancy: Tough girls who rewrite negative scripts', *Qualitative Health Research*, 11, 238–256.

25 Sun, S. W. and Lull, J. (1986) 'The adolescent audience for music videos and why they watch', *Journal of Communication*, 36, 115–125; Wingood, G. M., Di Clemente, R. J., Bernhardt, J. M. et al. (2003) 'A prospective study of exposure to rap music videos and African-American female adolescents' health', *American Journal of Public Health*, 93, 437–439.

26 Ward, L. M., Hansborough, E. and Walker, E. (2005) 'Contributions of music video exposure to black adolescents' gender and sexual schemes', *Journal of Adolescent Research*, 20, 143–166.

27 Rivadeneya, R., Ward, M. L. and Gordon, M. (2007) 'Distorted reflections: Media exposure and Latino adolescents' conception of self', *Media Psychology*, 9, 261–290.

28 Pardun, C. J., L'Eagle, K. L. and Brown, J. D. (2005) 'Linking exposure to outcomes: Early adolescents' consumption of sexual content in six media', *Mass Communication & Society*, 8(2), 75–91.

29 Bell, B. T., Lawton, R. and Dittmar, H. (2007) 'The impact of thin models in music videos on adolescent girls' body dissatisfaction', *Body Image*, 4(2), 137–145.

30 Andsager, J. and Roe, K. (2003) *op. cit.*

31 Stephens, D. P. and Phillips, L. D. (2003) *op. cit*; Stokes, C. E. (2007) 'Representin' in cyberspace: Sexual scripts, self-definition and hip hop culture in Black American adolescent girls' home pages', *Culture, Health and Sexuality*, 9, 169–184.

32 Stokes, C. E. (2007) *ibid.*

33 Stokes, C. E. (2007) *ibid.*

34 Johnson, J. D., Adams, M. S., Ashburn, L. and Reed, W. (1995) 'Differential gender effects of exposure to rap music on African American adolescents' acceptance of teen dating violence', *Sex Roles*, 33, 597–605.

35 Strouse, J. S. and Buerkel-Rothfuss, N. L. (1987) 'Media exposure and the sexual attitudes and behaviours of college students', *Journal of Sex Education and Therapy*, 13, 43–51.

36 Ward, L. M. (2002) 'Does television exposure affect emerging adults' attitudes and assumptions about sexual relationships? Correlational and experimental conformation', *Journal of Youth and Adolescence*, 31, 1–15.

37 Strouse, J. S., Goodwin, M. P. and Roscoe, B. (1994) 'Correlates of attitudes towards sexual harassment among early adolescents', *Sex Roles*, 31, 559–577.

38 Calfin, M. S., Carroll, J. L. and Schmidt, J. (1993) 'Viewing music-videotapes before taking a test of premarital sexual attitudes', *Psychological Reports*, 72, 475–481.

39 Kalof, L. (1999) 'The effects of gender and music video imagery on sexual attitudes', *Journal of Social Psychology*, 139, 378–385.

40 Greeson, L. E. and Williams, R. A. (1986) 'Social implications of music videos for youth: An analysis of the content and effects of MTV', *Youth and Society*, 18, 177–189.

41 Gan, S., Zillmann, D. and Millbrook, M. (1997) 'Stereotyping effect of black women's sexual rap on white audiences', *Basic and Applied Social Psychology*, 19(3), 381–399.

42 Zhang, Y., Miller, L. E. and Harrison, K. (2008) 'The relationship between exposure to sexual music videos and young adults' sexual attitudes', *Journal of Broadcasting and Electronic Media*, 52(3), 368–386.

43 Strouse, J. S., Buerkel-Rothfuss, N. I. and Long, E. (1995) 'Gender and family as moderators of the relationship between music video exposure and sexual permissiveness', *Adolescence*, 30, 505–521.

44 Greenfield, P. M., Bruzzone, I., Koyamatsu, K., Satuloft, W., Nixon, K., Brodie, M. and Kindsdale, D. (1987) 'What is rock music doing to the minds of our youth? A first experimental look at the effects of rock music lyrics and music videos', *Journal of Early Adolescence*, 7, 315–329.

45 Greenson, J. L. and Williams, R. A. (1986) 'Social implications of music videos for youth', *Youth & Society*, 18, 177–189.

46 Calfin, M. S., Carroll, J. L. and Schmidt, J. (1993) 'Viewing music video tapes before taking a test of premarital sexual attitudes', *Psychological Reports*, 72, 475–481.

47 Bandura, A. (1994) 'Social cognitive theory of mass communication', in J. Bryant and D. Zillmann (Eds.) *Media Effects: Advances in Theory and Research*, pp61–90. Hillsdale, NJ: Erlbaum; McCormick, N. B. (1987) 'Sexual scripts: social and therapeutic implications', *Sex and Marital Therapy*, 2, 3–27.

48 Edwards, J. M., Iritani, B. J. and Hallfors, D. D. (2006) 'Prevalence and correlates of exchanging sex for drugs or money among adolescents in the United States', *Sexually Transmitted Infections*, 82, 354–358.

49 Ward, L. M., Hansborough, E. and Walker, E. (2005) 'Contributions of music video exposure to Black adolescents' gender and sexual schemas', *Journal of Adolescent Research*, 20, 143–166.

50 Stephens, D. P. and Few, A. L. (2007) 'Hip hop honey or video ho: African American preadolescents' understanding of female sexual scripts in Hip Hop culture', *Sexuality and Culture*, 11, 48–69; Squires, C. R., Kohn-Wood, L. P., Chavous, T. and Carter, P. L. (2006) 'Evaluating agency and responsibility in gendered violence: African American youth talk about violence and hip hop', *Sex Roles*, 55, 725–737.

51 Stephens, D. P. and Phillips, L. D. (2003) *op. cit.*

52 Squires, C. R., Kohn-Wood, L. P., Chavous, T. and Carter, P. L. (2006) *op. cit.*

53 Brown, J. D., L'Engle, K. L., Pardun, C. I., Guo, G., Kenneavy, K. and Jackson, C. (2005) 'Sexy media matter: exposure to sexual content in music, movies, television, and magazines predicts black and white adolescents' sexual behaviour', *Pediatrics*, 117, 1018–1027.

54 Pardun, C. J., L'Eagle, K. L. and Brown, J. D. (2005) 'Linking exposure to outcomes: Early adolescents' consumption of sexual content in six media', *Mass Communication & Society*, 8(2), 75–91.

55 Martino, S. M., Collins, R., Elliott, M. N., Strachman, A., Kanouse, D. E. and Berry, S. H. (2006) 'Exposure to degrading and non-degrading music lyrics and sexual behaviour among youth', *Pediatrics*, 118, 430–441.

56 Bandura, A. (1994) 'Self-efficacy', in V. S. Ramachaudran (Ed.) *Encyclopedia of Human Behaviour*, vol 4, pp71–81. New York, NY: Academic Press.

57 McCormick, N. B. (1987) *op. cit*; Ward, L. M. (1995) 'Talking about sex: Common themes about sexuality in prime-time television programmes children and adolescents view most', *Journal of Youth & Adolescence*, 24, 595–615.

58 Christenson, P. G. and Roberts, D. E. (1998) *It's Not Only Rock & Roll: Popular Music in the Lives of Adolescents*. Cresskill, NJ: Hampton Press.

59 Ward, L. M., Merriwether, A. and Caruthers, A. (2006) *op. cit.*

60 Wade, B. and Thomas-Gunnar, C. (1993) 'Explicit rap music lyrics and attitudes toward rape: The perceived effects on African American college students' attitudes', *Challenges: A Journal of Research on African American Men*, 58, 51–60.

61 Ward, L. M., Hansborough, E. and Walker, E. (2005) *op. cit.*

62 Armstrong, E. G. (2001) 'Gangsta misogyny: A content analysis of the portrayals of violence against women in rap music: 1987–93', *Journal of Criminal Justice and Popular Culture*, 8, 96–126; Adams, T. M. and Fuller, D. B. (2006) 'The words have changed but the ideology remains the same: Misogynistic lyrics in rap music', *Journal of Black Studies*, 36, 938–957.

63 Like, T. Z. and Miller, J. (2006) 'Race, inequality, and gender violence: A contextual examination', in R. D. Peterson, L. J. Krivo and J. Hagan (Eds.) *The Many Colors of Crime; Inequalities of Race, Ethnicity, and Crime in America*, pp137–176. New York, NY: New York University Press; West, C. M. (2009) 'A thin line between love and hate? Black men as victims and perpetrators of dating violence', *Journal of Aggression, Maltreatment & Traumas*, 16(3), 238–257.

64 Johnson, J. D., Adams, M. S., Ashburn, L. and Reed, W. (1995) 'Differential gender effects of exposure of rap music on African American adolescents' acceptance of teen dating violence', *Sex Roles*, 33, 597–605.

65 Wingood, G. M., DiClemente, R. J., Renhardt, J. M., Harrington, K., Davies, S. L., Robillard, A. and Hook, E. W. (2003) 'A prospective study of exposure to rap music videos and African American female adolescents' health', *American Journal of Public Health*, 93, 437–439.

66 Peterson, S. H., Wingood, G. M., DiClemente, R. J., Harrington, K. and Davies, S. (2007) 'Images of sexual stereotypes in rap videos and the health of African American female adolescents', *Journal of Women's Health*, 16, 1157–1164.

67 Zhang, Y., Miller, L. E. and Harrison, K. (2008) *op. cit.*

68 Dixon, T., Zhang, Y. and Conrad, K. (2009) 'Self-esteem, misogyny and Afrocentricity: An examination of the relationship between rap music consumption and African American perceptions', *Group Processes and Intergroup Relations*, 12, 345–360.

69 Conrad, K., Dixon, T. and Zhang, Y. (2009) 'Controversial rap themes, gender portrayals and skin tone distortion: A content analysis of rap music videos', *Journal of Broadcasting & Electronic Media*, 53(1), 134–156.

70 Primack, B. A., Douglas, E. L., Fine, M. J. and Dalton, M. A. (2011) 'Exposure to sexual lyrics and sexual experience among urban adolescents', *American Journal of Preventive Medicine*, 36(4), 317–323.

71 Primack, B. A., Gold, M. A., Schwartz, E. B. and Dalton, M. A. (2008) 'Degrading and non-degrading sex in popular music: a content analysis', *Public Health Reports*, 123(5), 593–600.

72 Fischer, P. and Greitemeyer, T. (2006) 'Music and aggression: The impact of sexual-aggressive song lyrics on aggression-related thoughts, emotions and behaviour toward the same and the opposite sex', *Personality and Social Psychology Bulletin*, 32, 1165–1175.

7

ADVERTISING AND SEXUALIZATION

Sex has been used to sell in advertising for a long time.[1] Advertising appeals directed at boys focus more on behavioural action, while those directed at girls focus more on how they look and their interpersonal relationships with others.[2] Sex is used to sell many different types of products. For some types of products, sex, often manifest also with nudity, may be relevant. Hence, an advertisement that depicts a naked female in a shower using a soap product might contain imagery deemed to be sexual, but at the same time is providing a legitimate demonstration of the use of the product. The suggestion that a male deodorant product makes men sexually irresistible to women may be stretching credulity, but uses sex in a way that is relevant to the humorous sales pitch employed. The use of sex *per se* in advertising is less of a problem than when it treats women as objects. Advertising across all mainstream media has time and again been found to treat women differently from men. Not only have they been used to advertise products that emphasize different social or life roles for each gender, there has also been a tendency to objectify women more than men. Women are not just presented as objects, but more specifically as sex objects.

It is not difficult to work out why advertisers use sexually attractive actors and models. Physical attractiveness can enhance the effectiveness of persuasive messages. If the person trying to persuade us to buy a product is someone we find attractive, we are more likely for that reason alone to believe what they say and to follow up on their recommendations.[3] On a more basic perceptual level, sex attracts our attention. Thus, for advertisers trying to make their brands stand out in a crowded commercial marketplace, using attractive models wearing no clothes is virtually guaranteed to make people look.[4]

Portraying women as sex objects may attract the attention of consumers, but it converts them symbolically, at least, into objects or things as distinct from human beings.[5] One of the techniques used to underline the objectification of women is to show only part of a woman's body rather than the whole of it. Thus, many advertisements may depict a woman's naked torso from the rear or the side or might show a pair of shapely legs rather than showing the whole person.[6] The absence of a head or face, in particular, dehumanizes the model by removing a significant part of her being that we generally refer to in making a personality assessment. Thus, we see only body parts. There may be enough exposure of the female form to draw our attention, but we are unable to evaluate the person depicted as a whole and see her instead as a collection of parts.[7]

Representations of gender

We need to begin by being clear about what we mean by 'sexualization' in advertising. Over many years, a great deal of research evidence has been compiled that shows differences in how men and women have been treated in advertisements. This observation holds true for all kinds of advertising across all kinds of media. Most of the research derives from studies of advertising on television and in magazines. This has been largely because for many years these were the primary advertising vehicles, especially for advertising targeted at girls and women. The differences in treatment or use of men and women in commercial selling settings were manifest both in the way in which each gender was presented and in the behaviours they displayed. Such differences were not invariably defined by sex in the sense of sexual attractiveness or sexual behaviour. Nevertheless, sexualization was a prominent and recurring feature of the treatment of women because for a long time they were much more likely to be sexually objectified in advertisements than were men.

Television advertisements have been exposed as prime purveyors of images and messages that focus on the sexualization of women. During the early days of television in the 1950, 1960s and 1970s, when women appeared in advertisements, they occupied a few narrowly defined stereotypes of being physically attractive and sexually appealing, yet domesticated and dependent on men.[8]

It was not just that women were more likely to be seen in house-wifey roles than as successful career professionals, they were also less likely than were men to be product demonstrators or product authorities, except for a narrow range of domestic products.[9]

Even during those times of the day when women outnumbered men in televised advertisements because the television audience comprised mainly women, women were still not given wider opportunities in the world of advertising and were mainly depicted in a narrow range of domestic roles in which they depended on the advice provided by male authority figures.[10] Such patterns of gender representation in advertising traversed national boundaries.[11]

Even when girls and boys were shown in advertisements, gender stereotypes were preserved intact. Girls and boys were used as endorsers or demonstrators for different product types deemed to be gender appropriate. They showed different behavioural characteristics, with boys being more likely to engage in outdoor and competitive play than girls.[12] Children themselves have been found to display gender stereotyping when asked to judge different advertisements for previously unknown gender-neutral products in terms of whether the production techniques used meant that the messages were targeted at boys or girls. Fast-paced production techniques with loud, exciting music were seen as masculine-type advertisements, and productions that used slower-paced delivery and soft music were classed as more feminine.[13] Towards the end of the 1980s, trend analyses of advertisements began to report that traditional sexism in advertising in the way that women were treated was starting to weaken. This was evidenced, in particular, in an increase in the proportion of advertisements that showed women as working. Just as the old adage that 'a woman's place is in the home' was no longer true for society, this fact was reflected rather more in the way that advertisers depicted women when they were used as product demonstrators or endorsers.[14]

Sexual objectification in advertisements

The sexual objectification of women in advertising was observed from early on within this broader gender stereotyping context. From the 1950s, researchers noted that women in magazine and television advertisements were objects defined by their beauty and sexual attractiveness.[15] Women are more likely to be depicted or shown in a state of undress than are men in advertisements.[16] Even if they do not show women with no clothes on, advertisers focus on the sexiness of women when promoting products.[17]

Some product categories are worse than others in this context. Among the sexist advertisements are those for beer. While around half of television advertisements, in general, have been shown to display women in limited and largely decorative roles, this pattern applies to three-quarters of beer adverts.[18]

This type of imagery has been labelled as exploitative because it feeds stereotypical male fantasies about women and their sexual availability. There is also a follow-on concern that some women may take such depictions of their own sex as role models to which they should aspire in terms of their own appearance and behaviour.[19] Rather than leading to relationship success for women, however, such imitation may ultimately lead only to disappointment if they fail to live up to these media ideals.[20]

The sexualization of women was not restricted to advertising on television. It has been just as prevalent in magazine advertising.[21] The use of sex in magazine advertising increased from the mid-1960s to the mid-1980s, and the sexual content of advertisements became more explicit. There was more nudity or suggestive dress that exposed a lot of flesh. There were also more explicit references to sex in advertising appeals, together with implied sex acts. It was, of course, mainly female models who were nude or photographed in sexually inviting poses.[22]

On television, advertising was generally more restrained. The use of sex in advertising increased over time but remained at a low level compared with print media. American media researcher Carolyn Lin reported that only a minority of around 12 per cent of televised advertisements in mainstream network television used sexual themes or showed any nudity.[23]

Popular magazines aimed at mainstream consumer groups and particular ones aimed at teenage girls and young women carry large quantities of advertising. Whether considering magazines designed for general readerships or one targeted at female or male readerships, the sexualization of women occurs frequently in advertisements throughout all these types of publications.

In magazines such as *Time* and *Vogue*, for instance, around four in ten advertisements contained sexualizing depictions of women between 1995 and 2002.[24] In general, women are used as objects to be looked at or as a decorative background to the advertised brands.

Sexualized images of women have tended to be far more commonplace in men's magazines than in women's magazines.[25] Regardless of the ethnicity of the target readership (black or white men or women), sexualization of women was measured as being three times as likely in advertisements in men's magazines as it was in women's magazines. However, women were also far more likely than men to be depicted nude, partially nude or in purely decorative poses in women's magazine advertisements.[26] In popular men's magazines such as *Maxim* and *Stuff*, about eight out of ten women depicted in advertising-related photographs were shown as sex objects.[27]

Rudman and Verdi found that female models were much more likely than male models to be shown in submissive sexually exploitative positions.[28] Other research found that women were three times as likely as men to be dressed provocatively in magazine advertisements.[29] Further studies confirmed that women were largely used as decorations. Between the early 1980s and early 2000s, women were shown provocatively dressed or undressed with progressively far greater frequency (28 per cent of depicted women in 1983 and 49 per cent in 2003).[30]

Some researchers have examined the way in which women have been represented in advertisements over time using an analytical framework developed by Erving Goffman.[31] Analyses of advertising in magazines found evidence that stereotyping in the ways women had been displayed in advertising had persisted over several decades.[32] Goffman's coding framework focused on different parts of the body and postural elements. He examined the position of the hands and feet, facial expressions and position of the head, as well as the size of those depicted. Thus, it was not simply the visible prevalence of women relative to men that was an important signifier of how they were treated and the impressions they might therefore convey to consumers, but the nature of their appearance as indicated by their physical characteristics and behaviours. Goffman's analysis was restricted to magazine advertisements so 'behaviour' was frozen in a photographic image. Nevertheless, it was often possible to measure specific gestures and expressions and to infer from this whether women were being shown in an authoritative or submissive fashion and the extent to which this occurred when they were on their own or depicted with men.

One interesting comparison of the way in which women were visually presented in advertisements in popular magazines in 1979 and 1991 reported that in terms of many body image features, there was little change. Of most relevance to the theme of this book, the two most significant findings were that there was a notable increase in the prevalence of women in magazine advertisements wearing body-revealing clothes or no clothes at all (nudity), and accompanying this were more sexually suggestive gestures and expressions.[33]

One of the ways that advertisers objectify women is by focusing on their bodies rather than their faces and by showing only parts of their body. This technique is used much less often when men are featured in advertisements.[34] In fact, with men, advertisers are more likely to feature their faces rather than their bodies.[35] The use of sexy part-body shots has been especially popular in advertisements for underwear, perfume and clothing. However, it was also found to be used with advertisements for cars and power tools.[36]

More recent research that examined men's and women's fashion magazines showed that the continuing depiction of women in advertisements in sexually objectified ways has been relentless.[37] A sample of nearly 2000 magazine advertisements was compiled from a pool of more than 4000 advertisements in 60 publications covering six genres: women's magazines, men's magazines, news and business magazines, entertainment magazines, special interest magazines and adolescent girls' magazines. The advertisements selected for analysis were those that depicted women. The researcher in this case focused on whether the featured woman was treated as a sex object. This meant that her sexuality was being used to promote the product. They also catalogued how the woman was dressed and whether she could have been considered a 'victim'. This was determined by whether any inferred or explicit act of violence was directed against her, whether she was being tricked or lied to, whether she was depicted in any form of activity and whether she appeared distressed.

Just over half of the advertisements that featured women also depicted those women as sex objects. This treatment was true of three-quarters of advertisements featuring women in men's magazines. Hence, not only was the sexual objectification of women fairly normative in all major magazine types, including those targeted at women and teenage girls, but it was the dominant style of presentation of women in advertisements in magazines targeted specifically at men. The sexual objectification of women was present in nearly two-thirds of advertisements featuring women in women's glamour magazines such as *Bazaar*, *Cosmopolitan*, *Elle*, *Essence*, *Glamour*, *Marie Claire* and *Vogue*.

Slightly less than one in ten of advertisements featuring women across these magazines portrayed them as victims. Hence, women were far less likely to be presented in magazine advertisements as victims than as sex objects. Fashion magazines were the most likely to contain advertisements that presented women as victims (17 per cent of all advertisements with women). There was some evidence that sexual objectification and victimization of women did occur together. In fact, in a clear majority of advertisements in which women appeared as victims (73 per cent), they were also treated as sex objects. This was only a small proportion of the total number of advertisements found in these magazines, but it nonetheless indicates a tendency on the part of advertisers to depict mainly sexually alluring women as victims of male dominance. Before we feel too concerned for women, however, another measure determined whether women were shown as aggressors. There were fewer (3 per cent) advertisements of this sort among those that contained women. Once again, though, in around three-quarters of those advertisements in which women were shown as aggressor, they were also depicted in a more sexualized way.

One interpretation put forward for the links between female victimization and sexualization is that the victimizing of women might be conceived as a backlash against the growing power of women in society.[38] Women were also sometimes portrayed as aggressor, but less often than they were shown as victims. In both cases, however, the advertisements that feature these two types of female portrayal were only a tiny proportion of all advertising messages in magazines. Regardless of whether women are shown in dominant, submissive or neutral positions in advertisements, advertisers frequently treat them in highly sexualized ways. The social capital that is therefore attached to women's sexiness is repeatedly reinforced in this way and this message is distributed both to men and women, and begins to permeate youth female culture through teen magazines.

Many similar patterns of male and female representation have been found in television advertisements. The difference here is that in television advertisements, the question is which parts of the female and male forms do the camera movements dwell on? While video footage can show continually changing shots and angles, one analysis found that the camera still tended to settle on men's faces more than those of women in televised advertisements. In contrast, the camera spent more time focused on different parts of women's bodies, such as their chests, buttocks and legs.[39] In a sample of beer commercials, the camera focused on women's chests in nearly half the ads, while it focused on men's chests in only about one quarter of these cases.

Historically, evidence has emerged that in mainstream advertising the use of sexualized images of children has been fairly rare. In one investigation of advertisements in men's magazines over a 40-year period, less than 2 per cent of advertisements depicted children in a sexual way. Where such images did occur, however, an overwhelming majority (85 per cent) depicted girls.[40]

Public opinion about sex in advertising

A 1999 US poll for *Adweek* reported that most people (70 per cent) felt there was too much sexual imagery in advertising.[41] Despite the popularity of using sex in advertising, this approach may not always be effective. Although sexual content can draw in a consumer's attention, it can also cause significant distraction of attention away from the principal promotional message. Consumers may devote so much cognitive effort to looking at images of nudity or sexual behaviour that the remainder of the advertising message is missed.[42]

Public opinion about the use of sexual content in advertising is important. Adverse public reactions to nudity or explicit sexually themed material can become attached to advertised brands with disastrous commercial consequences. Moreover, in some countries, advertisers could find themselves falling foul of media regulations if they cause widespread offence to people.

We know that sex can help to sell by attracting consumers' attention. Sex, and more especially sexualization, may not make the advertising message more acceptable or more memorable. There are some parts of the population that are particularly sensitive to sexually themed sales pitches. Unnecessary sexual objectification of women in advertising can invoke especially strong negative reactions from older female consumers.[43] Consumers, in general, react strongly to advertisements that go too far in their use of sexual themes even though some degree of sex might be perceived as potentially relevant for specific types of product.[44]

We should be careful therefore not to draw blanket conclusions about the public acceptability of the use of sex in advertising. Research was conducted in the UK in the 1990s to determine the limits of public tolerance for sex in advertising.[45] Public opinion was mediated by the nature of the product as well as the nature of the sexual content. One key aspect of this study was to determine the acceptability of nudity in advertising. Where the nudity was logically used, such as when advertising a bath product for which the user would normally be unclothed, it was deemed more acceptable. When the nudity was not in any way relevant to the way in which the product would normally be used – such as in advertisements for motor vehicles – nudity was regarded as more problematic. What also made an impact upon viewers' opinions was when sex and nudity were combined. Thus, images showing a completely nude female from behind or even some side-angle shots were judged to be acceptable. Exposure of female breasts, however, caused concern even when the nudity was relevant to the product.

Effects of sexualization in advertising

The use of sexualization themes in advertisements can have both commercial and social impact. By commercial impact we mean whether a particular advertising technique enhances the impact of the messages upon consumers by rendering it easier to remember or by promoting positive attitudes towards the advertisement or the brand being advertised. The evidence has been that the commercial effects are mixed. In some instances, sexual themes can make the advertisement work better and in others in can reduce its impact. The social impact of advertising concerns whether subtle social messages contained in the text or narratives or in the picture content of advertisements can be conveyed to consumers, thus changing their social attitudes, beliefs or even the way in which they behave.

Putting sex into advertisements can draw in consumers' attention but does not necessarily make the advertisement or information about the brand more memorable. Inserting a scantily clad female model into an advertisement may make men in the audience sit up and take more notice, and may also attract the eye of women, though not necessarily for the same reasons. The use of such imagery can create an impression that use of the advertised brand could be associated with a more successful and sex-filled lifestyle. It is possible, then, that if a product is linked often enough with sexual attractiveness this might rub off on the brand, and for consumers for whom sexual attractiveness has high social capital, this style of advertising might create a highly positive impression about the brand.

The use of sexually attractive models in magazine advertisements for cars was found to enhance consumers' feelings and evaluations of the advertised brands.[46] Interestingly, this effect worked equally well among both female and male consumers. Similar effects have also been observed in advertisements for coffee and perfume.[47] Attractiveness does not, however, equal nudity. Attractiveness can help to create a positive halo effect around the brand, while nudity alone may be less effective in this respect.[48]

The problem is that while a positive impression might be created at the point of exposure to the advertisement, is it retained for very long afterwards? Marketing researchers have found that, regrettably for advertisers, often it is not. With advertising in print media, for example, the presence of a nude female – whether relevant to the product or not – can draw in consumers' attention, but can also subsequently lead to poorer brand recall.[49] One explanation for this outcome is that the presence of an attractive and partially clothed or nude model distracts the consumer's attention from information about the brand.[50] Brad Bushman reported that sex in TV advertisements disrupted recall of brand information.[51]

Increasing the sexualization quotient of an advertisement has also produced mixed results. An attractive and naked female was found to be just as distracting when shown in a head and shoulders shot as when shown fully nude.[52] Evidence has also emerged that increasing levels of nudity can sometimes create a more unfavourable opinion about the advertisement and brand.[53] When celebrity endorsers are used, however, it is better for the advertising if they are perceived by consumers as attractive.[54]

In the end, what is important is whether the use of attractive and nude female models is perceived as congruent with the purpose of the advertising and of the particular brand being promoted. Having a beautiful female model demonstrate the use of a body oil was seen as effective, while using a similar model to advertise a ratchet wrench set was not.[55] Thus, there must be a clear and logical relationship between a glamorous and sexy model and the product. If this connection is not seen, the advertisement loses credibility and authority for consumers.

The influence of sexual appeals on consumers' responses to advertisements was investigated by Annie Lang and her colleagues at Indiana University. In a series of laboratory-based studies, they examined the effects of sexual appeals in billboard advertisements on observers' length of attention, recall of the advertisements and advertised brands, emotional arousal, attitudes towards the advertising, and intentions to purchase.[56]

College undergraduates viewed images of billboard advertisements on a television screen. They could determine the duration of exposure and could bring up each image by pressing a key on a computer console. The billboard commercials were classified as containing sex or not sex. Sexual appeals were determined by how men and women in the images were visually displayed. A further distinction was made in terms of whether they promoted alcohol or not. Measurements included the length of time spent looking at the billboard, facial expressions while looking, and physiological measures of facial movements, heart rate and galvanic skin response.

Billboards with sexual appeals attracted male participants' attention longer than did those without sexual appeals, but made no difference in this respect to women observers. There was no effect of sexual appeals on heart rates for either gender. Sexual appeals did not cause observers to smile more, but billboards without sexual appeals caused the observers to smile less than at baseline. Emotional arousal as measured by galvanic skin response increased for men when used with general products but decreased when used with alcohol products. These results were reversed for women who were more aroused by sexual appeals when used in alcohol advertisements but not in advertisements for other products.

In a second experiment, largely the same design was used with further enhancements. The billboard images were projected onto a wall rather than viewed on a TV screen and viewing took place in groups, rather than as individual viewing alone. Physiological measures were not feasible in a group setting so participants rated their emotional arousal verbally. Duration of attention was replaced in this experiment by a test of ability correctly to recognize which billboard advertisements had been seen once all viewing had finished. Verbal intention to purchase an advertised product was also measured.

Overall recognition performance was not affected by sexual appeals. However, sexual appeals did enhance recognition specifically of alcohol advertisements. Billboard advertisements with sexual appeals did not make observers feel significantly more emotionally aroused, but they were rated more favourably. This latter effect was significant for alcohol advertising, but not for other product advertising. The presence of sexual appeals also rendered observers more likely to express an intention to purchase the advertised products.

In a third experiment, college students saw billboard advertisements project onto a screen positioned to the right of another screen on which they played a computer driving game. The appearances of billboard images were controlled by the researchers and occurred every 34 seconds for 7 seconds. At the end of the driving video, participants were taken to an adjacent room where they were tested for brand recognition and recall, and intention to buy and use the advertised products.

Billboard advertisements with sexual appeals were better recognized, although they took longer to recognize billboards with sexual appeals. Recall of both advertisements and brands was better from those billboards with sexual appeals. Intentions to use products were not generally influenced by sexual appeals.

Sometimes, to be effective in advertising, the use of sex must be subtle. Although consumers may react favourably to advertisements that contain overt sexual appeals, those messages may ultimately be less well recalled by consumers later on. A sexually attractive model or actress can become a focal point and distract consumers' attention to the extent that other information about the advertised brand is missed.[57]

Sexualized themes in advertisements can have unanticipated or unplanned effects on people. Leaving aside their commercial impact, advertisements frequently convey important cultural messages that can shape the way in which people perceive the world around them. Sexually themed scenarios or images in advertisements can present social scripts to anyone who watches them that can shape attitudes and beliefs about female and male attractiveness, sexual relationships and moral values. The sexual objectification of women in advertisements through the use primarily of models with specific body shapes or facial features can set norms of attractiveness or impressions about women that are absorbed into the wider social consciousness. Some of the effects that arise out of these subtle cultural messages can influence the way some men regard women and most of them can have profound effects on how some women perceive themselves.

The representation of the female physical form is perhaps the most visible and 'in your face' source of cultural influence here. A lot of research evidence has emerged to show that when exposed to advertisements that contain images of models with slim body shapes, women can experience reduced self-esteem about their own shape and may even believe they are bigger than they really are. These effects are especially likely to occur among teenage girls and young adult women who are sensitive about the way they look.[58]

Advertisements that feature highly attractive female product endorsers with very slender body shapes can represent a source of idealized body images that female consumers believe they must emulate. Such images can affect the self-esteem of women who already feel uncertain about their own bodies and who have a propensity to make comparisons between themselves and other people.[59] One interesting study showed that when advertising that contains thin female models is embedded in television programmes that feature slim female actors, the effects of the body perceptions of women in the audience can be even more pronounced.[60]

Restrictions in the range of roles occupied by women in advertisements compared with those in which men are featured can reinforce certain gender stereotypes that, in turn, can place women at a social disadvantage. If women are always shown as homemakers in advertisements, then that is how they may eventually be perceived in society. If women are shown as sex objects, this could mean they are seen as only good for one thing in the eyes of some men. Turning this effect on its head, these depictions can mean that men (and possibly also women themselves) have greater difficulty accepting the idea of women occupying more serious positions in society, such as, for example, in terms of careers or in politics.[61]

Sexual objectification in advertisements and attitudes towards women

As we saw earlier in this chapter, sexism has characterized the depictions of women in advertisements across various mass media. This has taken the form of disproportionately showing women in domestic home-making roles as housewives and mothers, while less often compared with men showing them in other settings, particularly ones associated with success and authority in the workplace.[62]

Concern was voiced about these portrayals of women because it was felt that such stereotypes could form part of the gender socialization of children.[63] The hypothetical concerns that arose from studies of representations of women and girls in advertisements were reinforced by evidence that women who were frequently exposed to these commercial messages exhibited greater self-consciousness and anxiety in social settings and poorer expectations for personal achievement.[64] Further evidence has emerged from earlier observations that advertising stereotyped women in terms of their social and occupational roles; this pattern has shifted with women being shown in a wider range of roles.[65] Although advertisements started to represent more accurately the changing social and economic fortunes of women, a further development was observed in the way in which women were treated. An increase was recorded in the prevalence of sexually exploitative depictions of women.[66] More focus was placed on female sexual attractiveness and advertising images and narratives presented more overt sexualized representations of women.[67]

When asked, women were found to find offence in these portrayals.[68] Despite female consumers' rejection of overtly sexualized portrayals of their gender by advertisers, questions have been asked about whether these messages about female sexuality nevertheless hit home and influence the way in which women perceive themselves and the way that women are perceived by men.

One particular concern has centred on how men's attitudes towards female sexuality might be influenced by sexualized depictions of women in advertising. Exposure to sexually explicit media portrayals of women that present a narrow view of female sexuality has been found to influence the way in which men think about women as sexual beings. These portrayals can create a climate of opinion and belief that regards women as sexually submissive and receptive to dominant and even coercive male sexual overtures.[69] Can sexualized representations of women in advertisements shape distorted impressions of female sexuality? Can these depictions of women influence both male and female consumers?

In one investigation of these questions, researchers randomly assigned a sample of male and female American university undergraduates aged between 17 and 39 years to three different conditions in which they saw and evaluated magazine advertisements that depicted women in a highly sexualized way, in a non-traditional counter-stereotypical way, or which showed the products only with no women present.[70] The advertisements had been selected from wide circulation of men's, women's and general interest magazines such as *Cosmopolitan*, *Gentlemen's Quarterly*, *Newsweek*, *Sports Illustrated*, *Time* and *Vogue*. After completion of this exercise, all participants completed four scales from Burt's Sexual Attitude Survey. These scales were designed to measure people's endorsement of gender-role stereotypes; beliefs about the degree to which women are manipulative and scheming; acceptance of violence in interpersonal relationships; and beliefs about women and rape.

Comparisons were made between students assigned to the three advertisement exposure conditions and between males and females in the sample. The findings showed that overall, men displayed more stereotyped beliefs about women than did women themselves, believed that women could be adversarial and scheming in relationships more than did women, were more accepting of violence in relationships than were women, and were more inclined than were women to believe that women enjoy being raped. All these beliefs were significantly stronger among men who had viewed advertisements that treated women as sex objects than among men in the other advertisement exposure conditions. The researchers placed particular focus here on the adversarial relationship and rape myth acceptance findings because they indicated that when men are fed a diet of advertisements in which women are treated as sex objects, they appear to change their impressions of women, becoming much more cynical about them. More seriously, exposure to this type of advertising also seemed to be able, at least in the short term, to encourage men to be more accepting of sexual violence against women.

Future considerations

Sex and sexualization have been prominent and prevalent features of advertising across all the major media. For advertisers, sex sells. There is some evidence to back up this belief. Sexual content in advertisements can draw in consumers' attention. This effect on its own is seen as important in increasingly crowded media advertising environments in which huge numbers of brands are competing for consumers. Initial attention to a commercial message, however, is only the first step along a chain of events that result in the end-goal – namely, the purchase and consumption of the advertised brand.

The difficulty advertisers can experience with sexual themes is that sex can dominate an advertisement to a point where the consumer pays too little attention to the remainder of the message. This can result in poorer impact in terms of consumers' reception of product-related information that may play a significant part in persuading consumers to choose the advertised brand over other brands. Worse still, the sexual content might be so attention grabbing that it steals all the consumer's attention away from the advertised brand to a point where the brand itself is not remembered.[71]

Another risk run by advertisers who include sexual content in their commercial messages is that consumers may fail to see the relevance of it. Quite apart from whether the sex distracts the consumer's attention away from the brand, there is another important step of creating a positive attitude towards the brand and also towards the advertisement. If consumers believe that sex is being used in a very crude fashion to grab their attention, they may reject the advertisement for use of gratuitous sex, which for some consumers may be seen as offensive and for others it might be regarded as patronising. Either way, a negative impression of the advertisement will follow and this might, in turn, transfer onto the advertised brand.[72] This might also reduce consumers' purchase intentions towards brands.[73]

As we have seen, there are spin-off effects of the use of sex in advertising. These effects are perhaps the most relevant of all to the primary theme of this book, which is to examine the sexualization of childhood. The way in which women have been treated by advertisers has been a source of debate and social concern for many years. Sexuality in advertisements can often be a disguised form of sexism, which raises issues linked to political correctness.[74]

Stereotyped treatment of the genders – particularly in the ways in which they are visibly represented – can create a climate of personal dissatisfaction among consumers if and when they make comparisons between themselves and the actors and models they see in advertisements. Young women can be especially susceptible to these social comparison effects. Some women are preoccupied with the way they look and will evaluate others in terms of appearance.[75] Women who show the greatest levels of concern about their body shape and weight, for instance, will be drawn to make constant comparisons with other women, including those shown in advertisements. Very often, these comparisons will be unfavourable, leading female consumers to critique their own appearance in less than flattering ways.[76]

Young women often devote disproportionate attention to their own appearance and come to believe that this is the primary dimension on which they should be judged as a person. In their use of sexual themes, frequently manifest in the form of exceptionally attractive female models, advertisers play to these insecurities by providing unattainable physical appearance ideals. If these appearance themes are registered not just by young women as they enter adulthood but also by pre-teenagers who have yet to reach physical maturity, the stage could be set for these insecurities to be internalized by school-age girls at a time of life when it would be psychologically healthier for them to be free of such worries.

Notes

1 Trachtenberg, J. A. (1986) 'It's become part of our culture', *Forbes*, May, 134–135.
2 Moniek, B. and Valkenburg, P. M. (2008) 'Appeals in television advertising: A content analysis of commercials aimed at children and teenagers', *Communications*, 27(3), 349–364.
3 Patzer, G. L. (1985) *The Physical Attractiveness Phenomenon*. New York, NY: Plenum Press.
4 Chaiken, S. (1979) 'Communicator physical attractiveness and persuasion', *Journal of Personality and Social Psychology*, 37, 1387–1394.
5 Bem, S. L. (1993) *The Lenses of Gender: Transforming the Debate on Sexual Inequality*. New Haven, CT: Yale University Press.
6 Archer, D., Iritani, B., Kimes, D. and Barrios, M. (1983) 'Face-ism: Five studies of sex differences in facial prominence', *Journal of Personality and Social Psychology*, 45, 725–735.
7 Kilbourne, J. (Lecturer) and Winderluch, R. (Producer and Director) (1979) *Killing Us Softly*. [Film]
8 Caballero, M. J., Lumpkin, J. and Madden, J. (1989) 'Using physical attractiveness as an advertising tool: An empirical test of the attraction phenomenon', *Journal of Advertising Research*, 20, 800–821; Ferrante, C. L., Haynes, A. M. and Kingsley, S. M. (1988) 'Image of women in television advertising', *Journal of Broadcasting & Electronic Media*, 32, 231–237; Knill, B., Pesch, M., Pursey, G., Gilpin, P. and Perloff, R. (1981) 'Sex role portrayals in television advertising', *International Journal of Women's Studies*, 4, 497–506.
9 Manstead, A. R. S. and McCulloch, C. (1981) 'Sex role stereotyping in British television advertisements', *British Journal of Social Psychology*, 20, 171–180; McArthur, L. Z.

and Resko, B. G. (1975) 'The portrayal of men and women in American television commercials', *Journal of Social Psychology*, 97, 209–220.

10 Knill, B., Persch, M., Pursey, G., Gilpin, P. and Perloff, R. (1981) *op. cit.*

11 Furnham, A. and Voli, V. (1989) 'Gender stereotypes in Italian television advertisements', *Journal of Broadcasting & Electronic Media*, 33(2), 175–185; Gilly, M. C. (1988) 'Sex roles in advertising: A comparison of television advertisements in Australia, Mexico and the United States', *Journal of Marketing*, 52(2), 75–85.

12 Smith, P. K. and Bennett, S. (1990) 'Here come the steel monsters!', *Changes*, 8(2), 97–105.

13 Huston, A. C. Greer, D., Wright, J. C., Welch, R. and Ross, R. (1984) 'Children's comprehension of televised formal features with masculine and feminine connotations', *Developmental Psychology*, 20, 707–716.

14 Sullivan, G. L. K. and O'Connor, P. J. (1988) 'Women's role portrayals in magazine advertising: 1958–83', *Sex Roles*, 18, 181–188.

15 Verkateson, M. and Losco, J. (1975) 'Women in magazine ads', *Journal of Advertising Research*, 15(5), 49–54.

16 Lin, C. A. (1997) 'Beefcake versus cheesecake in the 1990s: Sexist portrayals of both genders in television commercials', *Harvard Journal of Communication*, 8, 237–249.

17 Signorielli, N., McLeod, D. and Healy, E. (1994) 'Gender stereotypes in MTV commercials: The beta goes on', *Journal of Broadcasting & Electronic Media*, 38, 91–101.

18 Rouner, D., Slater, M. D. and Domenech-Rodruguez, M. (2003) 'Adolescent evaluation of gender role and sexual imagery in television advertisements', *Journal of Broadcasting & Electronic Media*, 47, 435–454.

19 Downs, A. C. and Harrison, S. K. (1985) 'Embarrassing age spots or just plain ugly/ Physical attractiveness stereotyping as an instrument of sexism on American television commercials', *Sex Roles*, 13(1/2), 9–19.

20 Lafky, S., Duffy, M. and Berkowitz, D. (1996) 'Looking through gendered lenses: Female stereotyping in advertisements and gender role expectations', *Journalism Quarterly*, 73, 379–388.

21 Schorin, G. A. and Vanden Burgh, B. G. (1985) 'Advertising's role in the diffusion of country-western trend in the US', *Journalism Quarterly*, 62, 515–522; Soley, L. C. and Kurzband, G. (1986) 'Sex in advertising: A comparison of 1964 and 1984 magazine advertisements', *Journal of Advertising*, 13, 46–64; Sullivan, G. and O'Connor, O. (1988) *op cit.*

22 Plous, S. and Neptune, D. (1997) 'Racial and gender biases in magazine advertising: A content analysis study', *Psychology of Women Quarterly*, 21, 627–644.

23 Lin, C. (1998) 'Use of sex appeals in prime-time television commercials', *Sex Roles*, 38, 461–475.

24 Lindner, K. (2004) 'Images of women in general interest and fashion advertisements from 1955 to 2002', *Sex Roles*, 51, 409–421.

25 Baker, C. N. (2005) 'Images of women's sexuality in advertisements: A content analysis of black- and white-oriented women's and men's magazines', *Sex Roles*, 52, 13–27.

26 Reichert, T. and Carpenter, C. (2004) 'An update on sex in magazine advertising: 1983–2003', *Journalism & Mass Communication Quarterly*, 81, 823–837.

27 Krasas, N. R., Blauwkamp, J. M. and Wesselink, P. (2008) '"Master your Johnson": Sexual rhetoric in *Maxim* and *Stuff* magazines', *Sexuality & Culture*, 7, 98–119.

28 Rudman, W. J. and Verdi, P. (1993) 'Exploitation: Comparing sexual and violent imagery of females and males in advertising', *Women & Health*, 20, 1–14.

29 Reichert, T., Lambiase, J. Morgan, S., Carstarphan, M. and Zavoina, S. (1999) 'Cheesecake and beefcake: No matter how you slice it, sexual explicitness in advertising continues to increase', *Journalism and Mass Communication Quarterly*, 76(1), 7–20.

30 Reichert, T. and Carpenter, C. (2004) *op. cit.*

31 Goffman, E. (1978) *Gender Advertisements*. Cambridge, MA: Harvard University Press.

32 Busby, L. J. and Leichty, G. (1993) 'Feminism and advertising in traditional and non-traditional women's magazines, 1950s – 1980s', *Journalism Quarterly*, 70, 247–264; Bell,

P. and Milic, M. (2002) 'Goffman's gender advertisements revisited: Combining content analysis and semiotic analysis', *Visual Communication*, 1(2), 203–222.

33 Kang, M.-L. (1997) 'The portrayal of women's images in magazine advertisements: Goffman's gender analysis revisited', *Sex Roles*, 37, 979–996.

34 Archer, D., Iritani, B., Kimes, D. and Barrios, M. (1983) *op. cit*; Dodd, D., Harcar, V., Foerch, B. and Anderson, H. (19809) 'Face-ism and facial expressions of women in magazine photos', *The Psychological Record*, 39, 325–331.

35 Sullivan, G. and O'Connor, O. (1988) *op. cit.*

36 Boddewyn, J. and Kunz, H. (1991) 'Sex and decency issues in advertising: General and internal dimensions', *Business Horizons*, 34, 13–20.

37 Stankiewicz, J. and Rosselli, F. (2011) 'Women as sex objects and victims in print advertisements', *Sex Roles*, 58(7/8), 579–589.

38 Frost, L. (2001) *Young Women and the Body: A Feminist Sociology*. London, UK: Palgrave.

39 Hall, C. C. and Crum, M. J. (1994) 'Women and "body-isms" in television beer commercials', *Sex Roles*, 31(5/6), 329–337.

40 O'Donohue, W., Gold, S. R. and McKay, J. S. (1997) 'Children as sexual objects: Historical and gender trends in magazines', *Sexual Abuse: Journal of Research & Treatment*, 9, 291–301.

41 Dolliver, M. (1999) 'Is there too much sexual imagery in advertising?', *Adweek*, 15 March, 21–22.

42 Lang, A., Wise, K., Lee, S. and Cai, X. (2003) 'The effects of sexual appeals on physiological, cognitive, emotional and attitudinal responses for product and alcohol billboard advertising', in J. Lambiase and T. Reichert (Eds.) *Sex in Advertising: Perspectives on Erotic Appeal*, pp107–132. Mahwah, NJ: Erlbaum.

43 Johnson, D. K. and Satow, K. (1978) 'Consumers' reactions to sex in TV commercials', in H. K. Hunt (Ed.) *Advances in Consumer Research*, vol 5, pp411–414. Chicago, IL: Association for Consumer Research.

44 Warwick, Walsh & Miller, Inc. (1981) *Study of Consumer Attitudes toward TV Programming and Advertising*. New York, NY: Warwick, Walsh & Miller, Inc.

45 Independent Television Commission (1995) *Nudity in Television Advertising*. London, UK: Independent Television Commission.

46 Smith, G. and Engel, R. (1968) 'Influence of a female model on perceived characteristics of an automobile', in *Proceedings of the 76th Annual Convention of the American Psychological Association*, pp681–682. Washington, DC: American Psychological Association.

47 Baker, M. J. and Churchill, G. A. Jr. (1977) 'The impact of physically attractive models on advertising evaluations', *Journal of Marketing Research*, 14, 538–555.

48 Alexander, W. M. and Judd, B. Jr. (1978) 'Do nudes in ads enhance brand recall?', *Journal of Advertising Research*, 18(1), 47–51.

49 Baker, S. (1961) *The Effects of Pictures on the Subconscious: Visual Persuasions*. New York, NY: McGraw-Hill; Courtney, A. E. and Whipple, T. W. (1983) *Sex Stereotyping in Advertising*. Lexington, MA: D.C. Heath and Company.

50 Steadman, M. (1969) 'How sexy illustrations affect brand recall', *Journal of Advertising Research*, 9(1), 15–19.

51 Bushman, B. (2005) 'Violence and sex in television programs do not sell products in advertisements', *Psychological Science*, 70, 247–264.

52 Alexander, W. M. and Judd, B. Jr. (1978) *op. cit.*

53 LaTour, M. S., Pitts, R. E. and Snook-Luther, D. C. (1991) 'Female nudity, arousal and ad response: An experimental investigation', *Journal of Advertising*, 19, 51–62.

54 Kamins, M. A. (1990) 'An investigation into the "Match-Up" hypothesis in celebrity advertising: When beauty may be only skin deep', *Journal of Advertising*, 19, 4–13.

55 Peterson, R. A. and Kerin, R. A. (1977) 'The female role in advertisements: Some experimental evidence', *Journal of Marketing*, 41, 59–63.

56 Lang, A., Wise, K., Lee, S. and Cai, X. (2003) *op. cit.*

57 Severn, J., Belch, G. E. and Belch, M. A. (1990) 'The effects of sexual and non-sexual advertising appeals and information level of cognitive processing and communication effectiveness', *Journal of Advertising*, 19(1), 14–22.

58 Heinberg. L. J. and Thompson, J. K. (1992) 'Social comparison: gender, target importance ratings and relation to body image disturbance', *Journal of Social Behaviour and Personality*, 7, 335–344; Ogden, J. and Mundray, K. (1996) 'The effect of the media on body satisfaction: The role of gender and size', *European Eating Disorders Review*, 4, 171–181; Stice, E. and Shaw, H. E. (1994) 'Adverse effects of the media portrayed thin-ideal on women and linkages to bulimic symptomatology', *Journal of Social and Clinical Psychology*, 13, 288–308.

59 Irving, L. (1990) 'Mirror images: Effects of the standard of beauty on the self and body esteem of women exhibiting varying levels of bulimic symptoms', *Journal of Social and Clinical Psychology*, 9, 230–242; Thornton, B. and Maurice, J. (1997) 'Physique contrast effects: Adverse impact of idealised body images for women', *Sex Roles*, 37, 433–439.

60 Myers, P. N. and Biocca, F. A. (1992) 'The elastic body image: The effect of television advertising and programming on body image distortion in young women', *Journal of Communication*, 42(3), 108–133.

61 Schwartz, N., Wagner, D., Bannert, M. and Mathes, L. (1987) 'Cognitive accessibility of sex roles concepts and attitudes toward political portrayals: The impact of sexist ads', *Sex Roles*, 17(9–10), 593–601.

62 Bretl, D. J. and Cantor, J. (1988) 'The portrayal of men and women in U.S. television commercials: A recent content analysis and trends over 15 years', *Sex Roles*, 18, 595–609; Geis, F. L., Brown, V., Jennings, J. and Porter, N. (1984) 'TV commercials as achievement scripts for women', *Sex Roles*, 10, 513–525; Sullivan, G. L. and O'Connor, P. J. (1988) *op. cit.*

63 Macklin, M. C. and Kolbe, R. H. (1984) 'Sex-role stereotyping in children's advertising: Current and past tends', *Journal of Advertising*, 13, 34–42; Schwartz, N. and Markham, W. T. (1985) 'Sex-role stereotyping in children's toy advertisements', *Sex Roles*, 17, 593–601.

64 Geis, F. L., Brown, V., Jennings, J. and Porter, N. (1984) *op. cit*; Gould, S. J. (1987) 'Gender differences in advertising response and self-consciousness variables', *Sex Roles*, 16, 215–225.

65 Ferrante, C. L., Haynes, A. M. and Kingsley, S. M. (1988) 'Images of women in television advertising', *Journal of Broadcasting & Electronic Media*, 32, 231–237.

66 Sullivan, G. L. and O'Connor, P. J. (1988) *op. cit.*

67 Soley, L. C. and Kurzbard, G. (1986) 'Sex in advertising: A comparison of 1964 and 1984 magazine advertisements', *Journal of Advertising*, 15, 46–64.

68 DeYoung, S. and Crane, F. G. (1992) 'Females' attitudes toward the portrayal of women in advertising: A Canadian study', *International Journal of Advertising*, 11, 249–255.

69 Check, J. V. P. and Malamuth, N. M. (1983) 'Sex-role stereotyping and reactions to depictions of stranger versus acquaintance rape', *Journal of Personality and Social Psychology*, 45, 344–356; Malamuth, N. M. and Donnerstein, E. (Eds.) (1984) *Pornography and Sexual Aggression*. Toronto, Canada: Academic Press.

70 Lanus, K. and Covell, K. (1995) 'Images of women in advertisements: Effects on attitudes related to sexual aggression', *Sex Roles*, 32 (9/10), 639–649.

71 Belch, G. A., Belch, M. A and Villareal, A. (1987) 'Effects of advertising communications: Review of research', in J. Sheth (Ed.) *Research in Marketing*, vol 9, pp59–117. New York, NY: JAI Press; Percy, L. and Rossiter, J. R. (1992) 'Advertising stimulus effects: A review', *Journal of Current Issues and Research in Advertising*, 14, 75–90.

72 Simpson, P. M., Horton, S. and Brown, G. (1996) 'Male nudity in advertisements: A modified replication and extension of gender and product effects', *Journal of the Academy of Marketing Science*, 24, 257–262.

73 La Tour, M. S. and Henthorne, T. L. (1994) 'Ethical judgements of sexual appeals in print advertising', *Journal of Advertising*, 23, 81–90.

74 Miller, C. (1992) 'Publisher says sexy ads are OK, but sexist ads will skin sales', *Marketing News*, November, 26, 8–9.
75 Beebe, D. W., Hornbeck, G. N., Schober, A., Lane, M. and Rusa, K. (1996) 'Is body focus restricted to self-evaluation? Body focus in the evaluation of self and others', *International Journal of Eating Disorders*, 20, 415–422.
76 Streigel-Moore, R. H., McASvoy, G. and Rodin, J. (1986) 'Psychological and behavioural correlates of feeling fat in women', *International Journal of Eating Disorders*, 5, 935–947.

8

PORNOGRAPHY AND SEXUALIZATION

Concerns about childhood sexualization, early onset of sexual activity, and consequent effects on self-image, social stereotyping, personal health and social risks, particularly among girls, have almost inevitably led to debates about the availability of sexually explicit material. One of the major areas of concern in this field is the availability of sexual content to which children can gain access in which sexual behaviours are graphically described or depicted. This content, generally known as 'pornography', is widespread. In the pre-digital era, pornographic materials had restricted access. The most graphic depictions could only be obtained via licensed premises. Other softer forms of pornography might be distributed via generally available media channels or retail outlets, but were still largely hidden from view behind encrypted access routes or on the top shelves of shops. With the emergence and dramatic growth of the internet, however, sexual content has become both more widely available and more easily accessed by all.

Pornographic sites represent a small proportion of all the websites accessible on the internet, but attract a disproportionate flow of online traffic. Sites such as Pornhub, YouPorn and RedTube are among the most visited websites.[1] Visitors gain free access to hard core pornographic material. There are no controls over access, which means than anyone, including children, can view these sites. Every day, there are millions of hits directed towards pornography online. This means that the internet has come to be classified as a highly sexualized medium.[2]

There has been growing concern about the impact of pornography upon children. This concern has been driven by its availability on the internet and the fact that has been consistently confirmed by research, that young people around the world report that they regularly go online.[3] There are plenty of opportunities for children and teenagers to see pornography online both intentionally and accidentally.[4] Pornography has been regarded as putting children at increased risk both of being victims of unwanted sexual attention and sexual abuse and of becoming perpetrators of extreme, abusive and criminal sexual practices.[5] Children have a right to expect adults to behave responsibly towards them and to play a part in reducing the sexual risks to which they might be exposed as a result of their access to pornography. Children also need protection from adults who may seek to groom them for sexual purposes.[6]

This concern has been amplified by high-profile media campaigns led by prominent newspapers. In the UK, the *Daily Mail* has been a vocal opponent to pornography and has focused its effort, in particular, on lobbying government to impose tighter restrictions over the internet, which is a source of readily accessible hard-core pornographic material. According to the *Daily Mail*, content classification schemes, parental warnings and voluntary blocking devices are not sufficient. Instead, there ought to be an automatic block on websites that display explicit sexual material. Among the reasons for this move is evidence that exposure to online pornography is cultivating warped attitudes towards sex that, in turn, encourage inappropriate early sexual behaviour. Research evidence was cited allegedly showing that significant minorities of teenage girls reported unwanted sexual advances and sexual touching at school.[7]

Further evidence collated from police forces across the UK indicated marked increases in arrests of children under 13 for suspected rape. Out of 39 police forces (from a total of 52) that responded to the *Daily Mail's* enquiries, 31 forces stated they had arrested children aged between 10 and 13 years on suspicion of rape in the previous year. As the newspaper's report outlined: 'According to the figures, 357 children aged 18 and under were found guilty of a range of sex crimes, including rape, sexual assaults on other children, grooming, incest and taking or possessing indecent photographs of minors'.[8] The same report recounted a story of a 12-year-old boy who raped a 9-year-old girl after allegedly watching hard core pornography on the internet. The boy showed to the police the online porn sites he had visited and claimed he had copied them to 'feel more grown up'.

Research with young people in the UK aged 9 to 19 years found that of those who went online at least once a week, nearly four in ten (38 per cent) had seen a pop-up advertisement for a porn site, more than one in three (36 per cent) had ended up on a porn site by accident, and one in four (25 per cent) had received porn junk mail. Perhaps even more seriously, one in ten had visited porn sites on purpose (10 per cent) or had been sent pornographic images by someone they knew (9 per cent).[9] In a UK Sex Education Survey run by online polling agency YouGov in 2008, more than one quarter of teenage boys aged 14 to 17 years were found to be accessing pornography every week. One in 20 were found to be accessing it every day. More than half had viewed porn online, via their mobile phones, and in other media. Many children and teenagers also had exposure to porn adverts that popped up while they were online looking at other material.[10]

Research from around the world has confirmed that children's exposure to pornography online is a global phenomenon.[11] The growth in prevalence of porn online has undoubtedly contributed to findings that have shown that rates of unwanted or accidental exposure to internet pornography have been on the increase.[12] More worrying, perhaps, are data that have indicated more young people are deliberately seeking out pornographic content when they go online.[13] This material tends to be used for immediate sexual gratification, but the longer lasting effects of repeated exposure to such material cannot be ignored or underestimated.[14]

There has been much debate about pornography and its effects upon those who watch it – whether children or adults. Pornography has its defenders who have argued that it is simply another form of entertainment, albeit a form that shows sexually explicit material.[15] Some commentators have even attached educational or therapeutic benefits to films and videos that depict real sex and argue that they can broaden people's minds about sex and the joy it can bring to people's lives.[16] A much more prevalent view is that pornography can cause real social harms by emphasizing and even glorifying the degradation of women. Pornographic films depict women as sexually voracious, willing to do anything to please men and are blatantly treated as dehumanized sexual objects whose sole purpose is the sexual gratification of men.[17]

In pornography, sex is generally shown devoid of any wider social context and most especially as part of a loving, romantic relationship. The sex is often shown in close-up and from different angles and positions, and even when apparently physically pleasurable for those taking part is devoid of genuine affection or emotional connection.[18] While sexual intercourse as an expression of a loving relationship may form only part of the sexual interaction, with partners gently building up to eventually physical coupling, in pornography, foreplay is minimal and most of the camerawork focuses on penetrative sex with the partners moving in an orchestrated way through a series of positions.[19] As we will see later, however, much pornographic sex portrays women as passive vessels whose main purpose is to deliver sexual gratification to dominant male partners. The women featured in pornography are sexually objectified and in some of the more extreme forms of the genre they are almost totally dehumanized. The treatment of sex as an activity designed to deliver sexual pleasure devoid of any meaningful emotional relationship and of women as objects that can deliver this carnal pleasure has raised important questions about the lessons that might be learned by children and teenagers who are exposed to this material during critical periods in their psychological development.

Research among adolescents in The Netherlands has shown that internet pornography can potentially send out a range of different messages about sexual relations and instil sexual attitudes and beliefs in young people that differ from one they may have learned from their families. Such mixed messages about sex and sexual relations can lead to a degree of 'sexual uncertainty' among adolescents.[20]

There is also a compelling body of research evidence that has indicated the sexual violence towards women shown in pornographic films (and even in some non-pornographic films) can produce changes in the way young men perceive women and, more seriously, can lead to them displaying less sympathy towards victims of rape. At the same time, they called for greater leniency towards men accused of committing rape.[21] We will examine this evidence in more detail later in this chapter.

One of the core issues that need to be unravelled when discussing the potential effects of 'degrading' portrayals on women in pornography is what we mean by degrading. For some psychologists who have specialized in the study of media effects on audiences, degrading pornography is defined very much in terms of the overt and visible ways that women are treated in explicit films and videos. This material often depicts women as highly promiscuous, willing to have sex with any man who comes along, and willing to do so in an animalistic way without any apparent emotional connection. According to one leading researcher in this field, Dolf Zillmann, degradation springs from the treatment of 'women as sexually insatiable and socially nondiscriminating in the sense that they seem eager to accommodate the sexual desires of any man in the vicinity and as hyper-euphoric about any kind of sexual stimulation'.[22]

The sexual domination of women by men has been a prominent theme of pornographic films and videos for many years. Even during the 1970s and 1980s, sexually explicit films that were commercially available with restricted ratings were found frequently to contain scenes in which sex and violence were combined. While some evidence indicated that sexual violence was most prevalent in films with the most restrictive ratings,[23] elsewhere the rating level was found to make little difference.[24] Violence against females in a sexual context occurred in scenes that depicted women having sex with one other man or with multiple male partners or even with other women. Women, however, were far more often shown as the recipients of sexual violence than as perpetrators.

One investigation of X-rated videos in the US during the 1980s reported that more than half contained rape scenes. In nine out of ten cases, a woman victim was raped by a man, and in one in ten instances a woman was raped by another woman.[25]

A particularly unsavoury genre of explicit movies that became popular from the 1980s is the 'slasher movie'. These movies had storylines dominated by violence and the infliction of pain. They also usually contained scenes that depicted the violent sexual victimization of women. Although women were found to present themselves as willing sexual partners for any man in standard pornographic films, they were nevertheless depicted as willing participants. In the slasher movie, in contrast, the female victim is subordinated to a male attacker generally against her will. In these productions, male attackers are shown as enjoying inflicting pain on their victims and camera shots focus extensively on the pain and suffering of the female victims.

Research into slasher films found, however, that the victims of these films were as likely to be male as female.[26] It also emerged that although sex and violence were sometimes mixed together in these videos, usually this was not the case. Although there was some evidence that close-up shots of females being tortured were longer in duration than for terrorized male victims, the violence meted out to both was not generally sexual in nature.[27]

Children accessing sexual content on the internet

The emergence of the internet has magnified concerns about pornography because of the volume of explicit sexual content that can be found on the internet, the ease with which it can be located by anyone, especially children, and because in an unregulated environment material that is illegal can be accessed on a mass scale that would not be so readily available through other distribution channels.

Pornographic content is not generally targeted at children and teenagers, but it is sought out by them. With the onset of digital technology that allows people to capture and resend content obtained online, new forms of extreme sexual content have emerged produced by the senders themselves. As young people become more sexually curious during adolescence, it should come as no surprise that they seek out pornographic material wherever they can. In past generations this urge was sated with pornographic magazines. Today, far more diverse content can be accessed with the click of a mouse. Furthermore, in the unregulated online environment, content of the most extreme kinds can be accessed, including material that depicts illegal behaviours.

Evidence of the seriousness of pornography for children has come from different sources. In the UK, the *Daily Mail*, the most widely read mid-market newspaper in the country, reported a dramatic rise in the numbers of children telephoning a helpline called ChildLine after exposure to hard-core pornography on the internet.[28] It was reported that counsellors had to deal with more than 50 telephone calls a month on this subject, a 34 per cent year-on-year increase. During 2011 to 2012, ChildLine reported that a total of 641 counselling sessions had been carried out with children who had been exposed to emotionally upsetting pornographic images online, which compared with 478 the year before.

In the same report, the founder of ChildLine and former TV presenter Esther Rantzen said that hard-core porn videos that could be readily accessed online were warping children's understanding of normal sexual relations. One worrying trend believed to be a knock-on effect of exposure to internet porn was the growing pressure placed on teenage girls by their boyfriends to post sexual images of themselves online, usually via their mobile phones. While believing their boy-friends only used these images for private consumption, instead the pictures fre-quently ended up being forward on to other boys or even being publicly displayed on open-access social media sites. Many of the helpline calls came from girls who had engaged in this phenomenon of 'sexting'. One earlier UK study by parent advice charity Family Lives had found evidence that girls as young as 11 had taken part in intimate webcam sessions.

Of course, the statistics provided by help services such as ChildLine about the prevalence of exposure of children to pornography are based on self-selected samples of youngsters who have sought support. We need to know whether such exposure really is widespread and, if so, how prevalent it is across the child and teenage population. Then we need to know why youngsters engage in porn-related activ-ities, whether these consist of searching for porn videos over the internet or actively posting sexual images of themselves or others online. Case study evidence has identified individuals who have had first-hand experience of phenomena such as the posting of sexual images of themselves, but what do we know about the scale of this behaviour and the reasons why teenage boys and girls engage in it? More generally, how harmful is graphic sexual imagery to children and teenagers?

Does this material play a critical role in the development of sexual attitudes and beliefs and can it shape the sexual conduct of young people?

Sonia Livingstone is Professor of social psychology at the London School of Economics and director of the Kids Online Network. In a 25-country survey conducted across the European Union, she probed large samples of children and teenagers about their online experience and, in particular, asked them questions about exposure to explicit sexual imagery on the internet.[29] In total, more than 25,000 young people were surveyed. She found considerable variations in online behaviour and experiences between the participating countries. Nonetheless, it was also clear that growing numbers of youngsters were reporting exposure to pornographic imagery.

Around one in seven (14 per cent) of 9- to 16-year-olds said they had seen sexual images on websites. This experience was reported only by 1 in 20 (5 per cent) nine- and ten-year-olds, but this figure grew to one in four (25 per cent) for 15- and 16-year-olds. More poignantly, 8 per cent of those aged 11 to 16 years claimed specifically to have seen images of people having sex and where genitals were exposed. A tiny percentage (2 per cent) claimed to have witnessed images of violent sexual activity online. On this evidence, online pornographic experiences were reported only by minorities of children. Perhaps more significant, however, was the finding that among those who had seen explicit sex on the internet, one in three (32 per cent) had found these images upsetting.

Among 9- to 16-year-olds, around one in seven (15 per cent) claimed to have 'seen or received sexual messages on the internet'. This experience was reported by no nine- and ten-year-olds, but was mentioned by more than one in five (22 per cent) of 15- and 16-year-olds. Exposure to sexting, whether as a sender or receiver, was much less widespread (just 3 per cent across all age groups – but reported by 5 per cent of 15- to 16-year-olds).[30]

Research by the Australian Research Centre in Sex, Health and Society surveyed young people's use of pornography in 12 countries and reached a conclusion that regular exposure to this material could alter the way in which boys viewed girls. Watching porn a lot was associated with beliefs that casual sex is perfectly acceptable behaviour and that there is nothing wrong with sexually harassing girls.[31]

Emotional reactions to explicit sexual content

Before we look at social scientific evidence concerning the different ways in which exposure to pornography can produce lasting effects on young people, we will examine what is known about the immediate responses of children to explicit sexual content. Many youngsters around the world have been found to react unfavourably to pornography.[32] As we saw earlier in this chapter, research among children and teenagers across Europe reported that around one in seven (14 per cent) of youngsters aged between 9 and 16 years had reportedly seen sexual images via the internet. A small proportion (2 per cent) admitted to watching graphic sexual content online. Many (46 per cent) stated they had been upset by this content.[33]

Reactions to pornography tend to differ between girls and boys. Girls are more often upset by explicit sexual images than are boys. In contrast, boys are more likely than girls to report feeling a sense of excitement when seeing this type of content. Girls are more likely to say they felt embarrassed when they saw explicit sexual material.[34]

Impact of explicit sexual content

As well as concerns about the role pornography might play in triggering premature interest in sex among children, there are even more serious concerns about specific harmful effects this material might have. Many of the most serious concerns stem from the risk that graphic sexual content depicts women as willingly participating in casual sex and in sex of a violent nature. Much evidence has emerged that exposure to extreme pornographic depictions, combined with violence in which women are on the receiving end, can distort the beliefs, attitudes and sexual intentions of young men towards women as sexual objects. Indeed, it is the objectification and dehumanization of women in these settings that is as critical as the overt behaviour itself in presenting the wrong messages to men about women's sexual preferences.

Pornography is both sexually explicit and tends more often than not to depict women as sexually receptive and preoccupied with the sexual satisfaction of dominant male sexual partners. Although much mainstream pornographic content depicts mutually consenting sex, more extreme forms of sexual activity are readily accessible, including sex that is sadomasochistic and violent in nature. Women are usually the victims.[35] Over time, pornographic content that is available online has become more extreme in nature and is frequently sought out by young males.[36]

Among the outcomes of showing women as willing recipients of aggressive sex are that it objectifies women and can create the impression among those who watch this material that such behaviour is normal. As they reach sexual maturity, young men may come to regard women as sexual objects whose primary purpose is to cater to their own sexual desires and gratifications.[37]

Establishing the impact of pornography upon young people's sexual beliefs, attitudes and behaviours has been tackled from different perspectives over the years. It would be unwise to take all of the mounting body of evidence at face value. One reason for this is that studies in this field vary in their methodological rigour. Not all methodologies are appropriate for testing hypotheses concerning the degree to which sexual beliefs, attitudes and behaviours displayed by children or adults are causally shaped by exposure to pornographic images.

Studies that have used experimental methodologies in which exposure to pornography and subsequent cognitive, emotional or behavioural reactions among participants are controlled by researchers can technically test cause–effect hypotheses. To do this, however, they must impose stringent controls over the pornographic experiences of participants and this can usually only be achieved under highly contrived exposure conditions. The characteristics of experiments call into question their 'ecological validity', which means that the conditions under which tests of porn effects are carried out do not model real world scenarios under which people normally consume and respond to pornography.

Experiments conducted under tightly regimented laboratory conditions also generally measure only immediate or short-lasting reactions to pornography and therefore do not shed much light on the kinds of longer-term effects repeated exposure to such material might have.[38] Longer-term effects have usually been explored via survey methodologies. With these studies, however, participants provide verbal self-reports about their past exposure to pornography and about their sex-related beliefs, attitudes, practices and preferences. This type of research can reveal degrees of statistical association between these different variables but cannot confirm whether they are causally connected. Thus, a strong correlation between a survey respondent saying that they regularly consume pornography and the number of sexual partners they have had or the age at which they first had sexual intercourse could indicate that porn exposure triggered sexual activity or that sexual activity, having been triggered by something else, led respondents to seek out porn perhaps for ideas about sexual technique or to enhance the mood before engaging in intercourse.[39]

Ultimately, it seems likely that simply searching for some kind of direct link between pornography exposure and specific cognitive, emotional or behavioural reactions may distract attention from understanding a more complex bi-directional relationship; this relationship involves the interplay between naturally emergent sexual urges underpinned by the biological and psychological development of young people, and the development of an internalized body of sexual experience that derives from mediated sources of sexual content and sexual conversations and behavioural interactions with others.[40]

Impact upon sexual attitudes and beliefs

Evidence has emerged that exposure to pornography can condition attitudes and beliefs about women and their enjoyment of specific forms of sex on the part of young men. What people think and feel about sex, sexual relations and the normative expectations held about each gender in the context of sexual relationships can be shaped by exposure to pornography. There is substantial research evidence that has been collected from different cultural settings around the world to back up this statement. Furthermore, a great deal of this empirical evidence has derived from samples of teenagers and young adults – age groups that are becoming sexually active, still defining their personal identity, and learning how to behave in different social settings. Both genders have been found to display susceptibilities to the influences of pornography when exposed to it.

One of the initial concerns about liberal exposure to explicit sexual content among children and teenagers has been that the casual way in which sex is depicted in pornography might cultivate more permissive attitudes towards sex. This concern has been borne out by research evidence accumulated over several decades.

Controlled exposure studies have reported that when college students were shown sequences from pornographic films, their opinions about sexual infidelity and promiscuity often did change towards the more liberal end of the spectrum compared with matched peer groups who were shown film clips that did not depict sexual behaviour.[41]

Even though it is not clear whether attitude changes that have been measured under carefully constructed and controlled research experiments can be regarded as normative reactions to pornography that will occur in the outside world, there is evidence from different cultures in different parts of the world that exposure to the kinds of casual sexual couplings that are typical of pornographic portrayals are statistically associated with more permissive attitudes about sex and sexual relations. Adolescents in Taiwan who reported exposure to online pornography held more positive attitudes about sex outside marriage – in a society where this kind of behaviour is normatively discouraged.[42] Swedish adolescents who had a history of exposure to internet porn were found to be more accepting of casual sex than those of their peers who did not watch this material.[43]

Thoughts about women and sex

A great deal of researchers' attention has been devoted to the way in which young male consumers of pornography are affected by it. There is no doubt, however, that women themselves are concerned that pornography is potentially harmful to their own sex. The nature of this opinion can vary with the religious and political standpoint of the women making these judgements. One study of American women who were either feminists or held fundamentalist religious beliefs (Baptists, Jehovah's Witnesses, Mormons and Pentecostals) found that the fundamentalists denigrated pornography as degrading and dehumanizing to women. The feminists also held some of these concerns but were also sympathetic to freedom of speech defences against censorship.[44]

In a subsequent study from the same lead researcher, male and female college students viewed and evaluated a series of sexually explicit clips from different films and videos. In general, if a woman was depicted as subordinating herself to a man, this was classified as 'degrading' both for male and female viewers. The sexual objectification of women and themes of so-called 'penis worship' in these films was also classed as degrading for women. There was less concern, however, about portrayals in which a high-status woman has sex with a lower-status male in the sense that she was not regarded as being reduced to a purely sexual object in this context.[45]

The potential of pornographic films and videos to influence people can be measured at a number of different psychological levels. There is obviously a concern that ultimately watching women being degraded in explicit sexual scenes might turn men into potential rapists. Measuring behavioural effects of this material is very difficult for experts, no matter how good they are at doing research, because of the restrictions of ethical rules. Causality research requires that interventionist experiments are carried out, but ethical rules will not permit researchers to expose participants in their studies to conditions under which they might be harmed and turned into a potential risk to others. Nevertheless, media researchers have been very creative in developing methodological designs that can measure changes in the psychological state of people that may be contingent on watching pornography. This research often begins by finding out whether watching pornography triggers specific thoughts about women or about sex. It can then proceed to an examination of whether people's attitudes towards women and sex can be changed as a result of exposure to certain types of pornographic portrayal.

For example, how do people's thoughts compare when asked what they think about pornographic portrayals in which a women is raped and in one version displays terror and abhorrence and in another version becomes sexually aroused. For young men watching these scenes, the version in which the woman becomes aroused is less likely to be regarded as rape. This reaction provides important insights into what men define as rape. While in a purely legal sense, if a woman is coerced to have sex against her will, such action would be classed as rape. However, if she subsequently displays some pleasure, the behaviour of her male assailant is excused because even though he has forced his victim to have sex, if he has also apparently given her pleasure, this means that his behaviour is justified and acceptable.

It has also emerged that once this revised opinion of one instance of rape has occurred, it can carry over to subsequent similar experiences. Neil Malamuth of the University of California, Los Angeles, is one of the foremost experts in this area. He conducted many creative interventionist studies during the 1980s and 1990s on the potential effects of exposure to pornography on the sexual attitudes of young men. In one set of studies, he invited male college students to watch different versions of a film portrayal of rape in which the female victim displays either great distress or arousal after initial distress. He and his colleagues found that young men who viewed the version in which the victim eventually became sexually aroused did not see this as 'rape'. Even more significantly, when all these young men watched a second rape portrayal, those who had initially seen the rape arousal version of the first rape scene also held fewer and weaker negative opinions about the second rape scene compared with young men who had watched an earlier rape scene in which the woman victim was distressed.[46]

The thoughts that can be triggered in men towards rape scenes can be stored away and influence other attitudes and beliefs they hold about women and sex. Regular watching of pornography in which women are treated as sex objects and more especially in which women are raped can result in the cultivation of generally negative attitudes towards women as sexual beings.[47] Of further concern is that if men already hold callous attitudes towards women and regard them as little more than sex objects – perhaps because of other experiences during their childhood and adolescence, or exposure to pornography that treats women as sex objects and willing recipients of coercive sex – they may have these attitudes confirmed and strengthened.[48] In particular, exposure to pornography in which women are sexually degraded can even result in men believing that women really enjoy being raped.[49]

Not all the evidence that has emerged over the years has supported these outcomes. This fact can be an inconvenient nuisance for those who wish to use the empirical evidence to support arguments for tighter regulation of pornography or of movies, more generally, that contain explicit sexual content, but needs to be addressed if a balanced view about the possible effects of pornography is to be achieved.

In a study of around 200 men who were invited to watch sexually explicit videos that they could choose for themselves, the nature of their attitudes towards coercive sex (or rape) that occurs between a man and his wife was assessed. The men were asked whether they would define this type of behaviour as wrong and to what extent it should be punished. They were given a range of options here from doing nothing because it was a private matter between husband and wife to more severe penalties, including varying terms of imprisonment. No evidence emerged from this analysis that the pornography viewing habits of the men made any difference to their opinions on this issue.[50]

With this study, the male participants were asked to choose their own videos to watch. This raises a question about how carefully matched they were in terms of the nature of the material they viewed. Other researchers have investigated whether there is a link between dosage of exposure to sexual violence and the attitudes that men subsequently form about women, especially in sexual contexts. Surveys have found that statistically significant links can occur between the amount of pornography men see, whether in magazines or films, and their propensity to believe that women enjoy being raped.[51]

One of the most creative series of studies that investigated whether watching pornographic films and videos can influence male attitudes towards women, sex and rape was conducted by Professor Ed Donnerstein, Professor Dan Linz and their colleagues at the University of California, Santa Barbara. Their research was carried out with male college students who had undertaken extensive psychological pre-tests designed to establish the stability of their personalities. Only the most stable personalities were chosen for the main part of the study.

There were two parts to Donnerstein and Linz's studies, which as far as the participants were concerned were not connected. Within the university setting for this research two different departments contacted the students for what appeared to be two different studies. In the first part, the participants were invited to view and evaluate a movie each day for five days. Some participants only saw films that contained sexual violence and others saw films that contained no material of this kind. A battery of evaluative scales was provided that included ratings of how violent, offensive and degrading to women each film was perceived to be.

In the second part of the study that occurred about a week later, the participants were invited to view a video recording of a fictional rape trial. Afterwards they were asked to give their opinions about the trial, the victim of the alleged rape, the perpetrator and the verdict. Donnerstein and Linz found that those young men who had viewed the week-long diet of sexually violent films tended to display far more sympathy for the accused in the rape trial and less sympathy for the victim than did their peers who had watched only non-sexually violent films. There had been evidence in the first part of the study that those men exposed to the sexually violent films found these films less violent and offensive and less degrading to women with progressive exposures. They then theorized that this apparent desensitization to sexual violence transferred across to their judgements about a rape trial on which they were invited to offer their opinions.[52]

In follow-on research by the same researchers, tests were run for the effects on young men of watching either violent sexual scenes or non-violent sexual scenes. They also differentiated between the men in terms of their pre-existing attitudes towards women to make comparisons between men who held rape-myth beliefs and men who did not hold such beliefs. In both cases, they were subsequently invited to watch and evaluate the same film clips in which women were verbally and physically abused by men. On this occasion, the reactions of the men in the audience to the scenes of women being attacked differed not only as a function of the diet of viewing they had been fed, but also in terms of their pre-existing attitudes towards women.

Only the men who already held callous and cynical attitudes towards women and rape were apparently affected by watching films in which women were violently abused, whereas men who did not believe beforehand that women enjoyed being raped were not influenced. In this case, the men who were influenced by sexually violent scenes were less sympathetic towards women being verbally or physically attacked by men. Perhaps even more significant was the finding that men who initially rejected rape myth beliefs displayed more cynical views towards a woman being attacked by a man if they had been fed a diet beforehand of non-violent sexual scenes depicting sexually promiscuous women.

These findings show, then, that men who already hold sympathetic views about violence towards women can have these beliefs strengthened by watching films depicting sexual violence. Even men who did not initially sign up to the idea that women enjoy being treated violently by men exhibited greater sympathy to this viewpoint after watching pornography, and the pornography worked best if the sex was non-violent but in which the women participants were treated in a sexually objectified way.

Despite appearing on the surface to offer compelling empirical evidence that men's attitudes towards women and sex can be shaped by violent and non-violent pornography, the work of Donnerstein and Linz has not gone unchallenged by other experts. One weakness in the design was that it did not include a control group of young men who saw no films at all, and another observation was that some participants might have made a link between the two phases of the study and also guessed what the researchers were hoping to find. If this was true, they may have responded in the second stage in a way consistent with the researchers' hypotheses. Another factor was that in the video of the fictional rape trial, details about the events leading up the alleged assault, including whether the accused and victim had been sober beforehand and whether the female victim was sexually promiscuous or not, were unclear.[53]

In a further test of this particular methodology, Professor James Weaver invited both female and male students to watch diets of sexually violent films or films with no such content before giving their opinions about written descriptions of three legal cases involving physical or sexual assault against women in an apparently separate exercise. Weaver made sure that relevant details about each fictional legal case were provided to ensure that the participants could reach unambiguous judgements about the culpability of the perpetrator and victim in each instance. In two of these cases, the male perpetrator's behaviour was described as clearly unjustified, while in the third case, mitigating circumstances for his actions were given. The reactions of young female and male college students varied with the nature of their viewing diet and with the circumstances described in the legal cases.

Weaver also found that by getting participants to go beyond simple ratings of the films in the first stage, participants thought more carefully about whether women were depicted in disparaging or degrading ways. Female college students who had their attention drawn to the degrading nature of sexually violent films were sympathetic towards the female victim in two of the assault cases where the circumstances were clearly explained, but had less sympathy towards the female victim in the case where the reasons for the alleged assault were more ambiguous. Male college students who had seen sexually violent films beforehand had less sympathy towards women victims of assault in all cases.[54]

Repeated exposure to images and scripts in pornography that depict women as sexually available and promiscuous receptacles of men's sexual desires, and willing to engage in a variety of sexual acts with partners whom they do not know can lead to their internalization by young men at a crucial stage in their psychological development. Such images might also put teenage girls and young women under pressure to adopt some of these characteristics in their own sex lives and to succumb to male pressure to engage in sexual acts with which they are not comfortable. Raw sex divorced from a surrounding narrative that places it in the context of a growing or established relationship between partners with emotional commitments to each other presents a social learning framework in which participants and, most especially, women become dehumanized. It creates a normative setting in which the act of sex becomes a behaviour designed to provide immediate gratification to a purely physical urge rather than an expression of love and devotion.

Later investigations of young people's responses to sexually explicit material found on the internet, conducted in a number of different countries, have noted that regular exposure to pornography can change viewers' attitudes towards sex and women. It can lead to a cheapening of female sexuality and create a mind-set among men and women that could encourage more promiscuous behaviour. Among young men, a diet of pornography might shift their opinions about women so that they come to believe that all women enjoy casual sexual couplings and want to be dominated by men.[55] Regular exposure to explicit sexual material was found to lead male Dutch adolescents to be more likely to regard women as sex objects.[56] At the same time, it might put young women under pressure to comply with new norms, even though it cuts against their true feelings about being sexual.[57] One investigation with teenagers in America reported that exposure to pornography could change the attitudes of both female and male viewers about male dominance and female submission in sexual relations in line with the way in which each gender played out their sexual roles in sexually explicit materials.[58] There is even greater concern about the potential effects of pornography when portrayals that depict women in a degrading fashion also turn violent. Research has emerged that when young men watch women being treated violently in scenes of sexual intercourse, it can cultivate a sense that coerciveness in sex is acceptable.[59]

Boys' and girls' and sexual attitudes

The empirical evidence from experimental studies has been borne out by surveys of boys' and girls' attitudes to sex. Girls are being encouraged in sex education programmes to resist pressures to engage in sex when they do not want to. Such lessons also teach that sex should be part of an established and loving relationship. This attitude towards sex was regarded by many young men as a specifically female orientation towards sex.[60]

The ways in which young people react to pornography are varied and have been measured via different research methods and techniques. Some evidence derives from the reports on youngsters themselves about their experiences with graphic sexual content found on the internet. Other evidence has explored degrees of association between reported online user behaviour and sexual attitudes, beliefs and behaviour. Yet other studies have attempted to measure direct cause–effect relations between exposure to pornographic material and individuals' sexual attitudes and responses. Because of ethical constraints that are placed on researchers when investigating potentially risky attitudes and behaviours, however, interventionist research has generally been restricted to adult participants.

The European Union Kids Online survey examined the prevalence of European children's experiences with explicit sexual content on the internet.[61] As well as ascertaining the extent of reported exposure to sexual content, the researchers also probed further for the children's reactions to it. These further questions were asked of children aged 11 to 16 years. Among this age group, just over one in ten (11 per cent) said they saw images or videos of someone naked on the internet. Of those who reported this experience, approaching one third (30 per cent) said they were bothered by what they saw. One in two (50 per cent) said they had talked to someone else about these images. Fewer than one in ten of this age group (8 per cent) said they had seen images or videos of someone's private parts and the same percentage reported seeing images or videos of someone having sex. In these two instances, around one in four said they had been bothered by what they saw and around half of them said they had talked to another person about these experiences.

Even in societies where sexual activity among young people outside marriage occurs at a low level, evidence has emerged that exposure to pornography is linked to being sexually active. Yumiko Nishimura of Kyoto University in Japan reported a survey of young men and women in Mauritius aged between 15 and 24 years. Three in ten young men (31 per cent) and one in ten (10 per cent) of young women volunteered that they had ever had penetrative sexual intercourse. For most of these young people, their first sexual experiences tended to occur at around the age of 17 or 18. Neither men nor women indicated the use of condoms. There were social life factors that statistically indicated increased likelihood of being sexually experienced. The most significant of these were visiting night clubs and drug use. Young men, though not young women, who were sexually active were more likely than those who were not to have watched pornographic films.

The researchers here recommended that Mauritian authorities should consider tighter controls over the availability of pornography which could be accessed not just through the internet (more difficult to control), but also through video rental stores on the island (easier to control). These findings do not show that pornography was a trigger mechanism for the onset of teenage sexual behaviour, but if sexually active males demonstrate an appetite for pornography there may be concerns that if these videos provide sexual scripts (particularly involving unsafe sexual practices) for young men, they could still encourage risky behaviour.

Surveys with children can be used to identify the potential of exposure to inappropriate pornographic content. It has been amply demonstrated that the opportunity for such exposure is widespread on the internet. While this fact alone is worrying for many and although such material is also regarded by critics as offensive, we must also ask what types of effects of exposure to pornography online might be expected to occur with children?

The use of the internet as a conduit through which to access standard pornographic material that is displayed either in photographic images or in video footage on websites might be expected to result in effects similar to those already measured in relation to porn obtained offline. Viewers see the content on a screen, just as they would with a pornographic video played back over a television set via a video-recording and playback device. The only difference between the offline and online experience is the mode of access to the material. There are two other major elements, however, to the online world.

First, there are more opportunities in increasingly digitized entertainment environments to find more and more extreme pornographic material that is banned in the offline world and available only through black markets to consumers 'in the know' in terms of sources of supply. On the internet, the barriers to access illegal pornographic content are often removed and children can view material that is fit for no one's consumption.

Second, the digital world is interactive and this means that consumers can gain more control over the things they see on screen and may even be able to control them – for instance, in interactive game environments. Research with young adult males – again American college students – found that erotic materials engaged with interactively did not have any more powerful effects than watching standard film or video footage in which women were shown in sexually explicit scenes.[62]

This research was carried out during the mid-1990s in the early days of the internet and when interactive games were not as sophisticated in terms of their narratives and production techniques as they are today. It was argued by the authors at the time that despite theories predicting that watching women behave in sexually promiscuous fashion in porn films might encourage men to believe that women in real life are similarly inclined, there is an alternative perspective on this. In this case, we can say that the behaviour of actors in porn films is at odds with most men's real life experiences with women, that these portrayals are seen as having little relevance in terms of providing lessons about real women.

All this, of course, could be true; but in terms of the interactive world, as the veracity of computer game environments grows, with computer-generated characters increasingly having the appearance of real human actors, and the growing sophistication of storylines and character development in these environments, their ability to draw in players psychologically is likely to increase. The potency of these environments to allow players to embed themselves in different sexual scripts where they have a high level of direct control over on-screen action could create a setting in which extreme behavioural actions that are experienced are produced by others, but are self-generated. Under these circumstances, the sexual scripts themselves could become much more deeply and permanently embedded in the player's psyche.

Sexual attitudes and beliefs can be turned inwards in terms of the way in which young people perceive themselves. We have seen in earlier chapters how the sexualization of childhood can be manifest in distorted self-images and that these effects are most pronounced among girls. Pornography not only depicts sexual behaviour in highly stylized ways, it also presents a distinctly stereotyped view of women. This stereotyping does not just take the form of submissive sexual behaviour on the part of women, but is also exhibited in their physical appearance. Porn actresses are generally either very slender or have voluptuous upper bodies typified by large breasts that have frequently been augmented by plastic surgery.

Children and teenagers have been found to pick up lessons about appearance and behaviour from pornography. Both boys and girls can acquire internalized views about how a woman should look and behave in a sexual context. At the same time, these stereotypes are not invariably accepted without question or criticism. Research among Swedish teenagers has found that adolescent porn consumers recognize double standards in terms of the way in which sexually adventurous women are perceived as compared with men. Sexual promiscuity among women is often criticized, while among men it is regarded more positively.

Commenting on the appearance of the typical porn actress, some Swedish teenagers remarked that silicon-enhanced breasts lost their appeal after a while and teenage boys indicated that they preferred a more natural feminine appearance. When invited to reflect on the depictions of the genders and sexual activity, Swedish teenagers felt that pornography raised unrealistic sets of expectations. While some were dismissive of these representations of sex, for others, pornographic portrayals raised anxieties about their own appearance and sexual performance.[63]

Pornography and sexual behaviour

Ultimately, concerns about pornography have centred on how exposure to explicit sexual content might shape the actual sexual practices of young people. Does pornography trigger earlier onset of sexual activity? Do regular users of porn begin to have full sexual intercourse at an earlier age? Does regular consumption of porn encourage young people to become more sexually adventurous and promiscuous?

Teenagers in a number of countries have told researchers that they feel they can learn about sexual practices from pornography.[64] We have seen already that adolescents known to have a history of watching pornography demonstrated more positive attitudes towards promiscuous sexual behaviour, but many of these same samples indicated a greater willingness to behave in a sexually promiscuous way themselves.[65] The important question here, however, is whether it is not only attitudes towards sexual practices that are affected by pornography, but also actual sexual behaviour.

Research in a number of countries has indicated that young people who watch pornographic content tend to be more sexually active and are sexually active earlier than their peers who do not consume it.[66] Regular viewing of sexually explicit movies was found to be significantly correlated with having multiple sexual partners among African-American teenage girls aged 14 to 18 years.[67]

Self-report evidence of possible behavioural effects of exposure to pornography on the sex lives of teenagers has emerged in Sweden. This research also indicated problems that can arise in interpreting self-reports of behaviour because they are not always consistent. Virtually all the boys (98 per cent) and most of the girls (76 per cent) in this research said they had seen pornography. Three-quarters of these teenagers had had sexual intercourse and almost the same percentage had used contraception. Most of these young people (71 per cent) said they believed that pornographic depictions did influence the sexual behaviours of their peers, but only a minority (29 per cent) believed that they had been influenced themselves. What also emerged was that those who were the most frequent consumers of pornography tended also to report having started sexual relations at an earlier age.[68]

Later research confirmed the link between exposure to sexually explicit material on the internet and age of first sexual experience. Young people who have experienced online pornography the most tend also to be the ones who started having sexual relations earlier.[69] The early onset of sexual behaviour, including oral sex and penetrative intercourse, has been observed to occur among both male and female adolescents who report regular exposure to internet pornography. One investigation of American teenagers found that a majority of the males and a large minority of females said they had initially seen explicit sexual material online by the age of 14 and began sexual relations during the following year.[70] Not only do teens who have been exposed to internet pornography become sexually active earlier, they are also more likely to engage in riskier sexual practices. This includes casual and unprotected sex with different partners.[71]

There have also been contradictory findings that have failed to support any link between consumption of online pornography and teenagers' sexual behaviours. One Swiss study found that adolescents in that country had seen sexually explicit content online and some teens had consumed this material from an early age. Their history of porn consumption seemed to make little or no difference to the age at which they became sexually active, how many sexual partners they had had or whether they engaged in risky sexual practices.[72]

Behavioural inclinations towards women

As we have seen, exposure to pornography that objectifies women or degrades them sexually may be able to shape men's thoughts about women and sex. One of the most worrying themes in pornography is the depiction of violent sexual behaviour in which women are usually depicted as the victims of coercive sex. We have already reviewed evidence that has indicated that exposure to this type of material can affect male attitudes towards women and towards the use of force in sex.

Ethical constraints mean that researchers cannot try to manipulate the behaviour of the people they study where to do so might put others at risk. Instead, it has been necessary to rely on people's reports about their own behaviour as a proxy for real observed behaviour. From opinions about whether rape is acceptable or whether women enjoy being forced to have sex, some researchers have gone further and asked people in their studies whether they might be more likely to commit rape themselves if they think they could get away with it. This propensity is then linked back to other self-reports about their history of viewing violent and nonviolent pornography.

The data here are generally collected through self-completion questionnaires that are conducted anonymously so as to enhance the likelihood that participants will answer honestly without fear of being uncovered in terms of any socially inappropriate inclinations they might have. Using this approach, evidence has emerged that young men who reported a relatively regular diet of pornographic material with sexually violent themes and who also already held callous attitudes towards women displayed the greatest propensity to use force against women.[73] Of course, this research only measured degrees of correlation between violent urges towards women and reported exposure to sexually violent pornography and such data cannot prove that a cause–effect relationship exists here.

In addition, some researchers have used more 'qualitative' approaches in which small samples of young people have been interviewed at length, either one to one or in small groups, about their exposure to explicit sexual materials and whether they have sensed any influences of such materials on their own behaviour. These personal attributions about behaviour are not always reliable indicators of actual behaviour because researchers can never be sure whether teenagers whom they interview will be totally honest about how they behave in their own sex lives. Nonetheless, these interview studies can provide insights into the behavioural inclinations of young people and how these might be influenced by pornography.

Even limited duration diets of exposure to sexually violent videos were observed to produce shifts in the attitudes held by young men about rape.[74] The early evidence indicated that this effect of violent pornography could occur even among young men with no prior history of aggressive behaviour. Subsequent research, however, has found that antisocial reactions to sexual violence are most acute among men who already display predispositions to behave in this way.

There are adolescent and young adult males who display a 'risk profile' that comprises a set of reported behavioural predispositions towards aggression, in general, and more especially towards the use of aggression in their sexual relations with women. These individuals often seek out pornography and develop a preference for depictions of coercive sex. They tend to show the most positive emotional reactions to sexually violent content and are more accepting of the use of violence against women.[75] One Canadian study with 14-year-old boys found that there was a significant level of correlation between exposure to pornography and agreement that it was acceptable to hold a girl down and force her to have sex.[76] Adolescent boys with aggressive predispositions and who watch sexually violent material have been found to exhibit an increased likelihood of engaging in coercive sex and made more sexually aggressive remarks when interviewed.[77]

Further evidence from American adolescents revealed that, over time, those youngsters who had regularly consumed pornography and material of a sexually violent nature were more likely to engage in sexually harassing behaviour.[78] Similar findings emerged from a study of teenagers in Italy.[79] Only slightly more comforting findings emerged from a larger-scale survey of US teenagers, which found that for most male respondents there was no evidence that exposure to violent sexual materials made them more likely to behave in a sexually aggressive manner. For those male teens who exhibited psychological predispositions towards sexual aggression and who also consumed more pornography, there was a significantly enhanced likelihood that they would show sexually violent behaviour in their own lives.[80]

A follow-up survey by the same researchers several years later that observed the same teenagers over three years confirmed earlier findings that male teens who displayed sexually violent dispositions at the outset were many times more likely to become sexually violent if they had consumed a regular diet of sexually violent pornography.[81] One of the key factors in terms of the influence of sexually violent content on adolescents is that they may have few alternative models of how to behave from their own sexual experiences. If they already experience pathological tendencies, they may also be particularly sensitized to depictions of coercive sex.[82]

There have been specific concerns raised about the impact of pornography upon at-risk teenagers who already display emotional disturbance or sociopathic tendencies. These young people may already experience difficulties in their social relationships with others. They may have caregivers who are not their parents or live in households in which there is a lack of emotional and financial stability. Their background may therefore have already predisposed them to hold distorted views about sexual relations. Youngsters with problematic personality profiles can be drawn to sexually explicit materials for escape and entertainment as much as out of curiosity. If their psychological profiles have predisposed them to commit sexual offences, some forms of pornographic portrayal – especially ones that promote promiscuity or coercive sex – may only serve to fuel their pathological urges further.[83] Although we may be talking here about a tiny minority of young people, the possibility that this group, which perhaps is responsible for a disproportionate number of sexual offences, could pose higher social risks through their exposure to pornography raises serious questions about the control of pornography production, distribution and consumption.

Porn: Concerns and need for regulation

As we have seen from the evidence reviewed in this chapter, pornography can be and often is readily accessed by teenagers and pre-teenage children. There are widespread concerns about the psychological effects of pornographic material on young people. These concerns have centred on the immediate distress that exposure to explicit sexual content can cause to children, the beliefs and attitudes they develop about sex, and the nature of their own emergent sexual behaviour.

Parents have openly expressed serious concerns about the risks that the internet can pose for their children. The European Union Kids Online study surveyed children and also questioned their parents about their children's involvement with the internet. Across all parents surveyed with children aged 9 to 16, this research found that one in three said they 'worried a lot' both about their child being contacted by strangers online and about their child seeing inappropriate material there.[84] Given that nearly one in three children in this survey reported that they had ever made contact with someone they had never met face to face on the internet, and about half this number admitted seeing sexual images online, these concerns have some substance. Given the further finding from this survey that nearly six in ten (59 per cent) children who used the internet also had their own social network site profile posted online, European youngsters were clearly enthusiastically seeking to use the internet to generate social contacts. Three-quarters of young social media users restricted who could have access to their profiles; one in four allowed anyone to see their sites.

Despite parents' concerns, many know little about how their children use the internet or what kinds of images they encounter there. Even when children see sexual material online and talk to other people about this, it is clear from the extent to which the parents of those children are aware of these experiences that parents are not children's first port of call when they want to talk about graphic imagery they have seen online. Sonia Livingstone and her colleagues reported that only around one third of parents of 11- to 16-year-olds who had said they had seen images of someone naked, someone's private parts or someone having sex on the internet were aware that their child had had such experiences.[85]

This lack of parental awareness is brought into sharper focus in the presence of evidence that while most exposure to pornography online is accidental, growing numbers of children deliberately seek out explicit sexual materials on the internet as they grow older. One American survey of adolescents aged 12 to 18 years found that just 8 per cent said they had intentionally sought out pornography online over the previous year.[86] Nearly nine in ten of these youngsters were male and aged over 14. Other social factors linked to the search for explicit online sex by young people were having a weak emotional bond with their carer, frequent coercive discipline and a history of delinquent behaviour in the offline world. Before we conclude that the risk of seeking out pornography online is restricted to young people from socially, psychologically and environmentally disadvantaged backgrounds, however, another important finding emerged. Young people who had reported accidental exposure to online porn were more than 2.5 times as likely to seek it out in the future as were peers who reported no accidental exposure to it.

Despite the serious worries that have been voiced about the harms that can be caused to children by pornography, some researchers and commentators have suggested that pornography can have positive and beneficial psychological and social effects. It can provide valuable information about sexual practices for young people as they become sexually active themselves.[87] Pornography can also pose a challenge to restrictively conservative social attitudes towards sexual behaviour and what might be defined as 'normal' sexual behaviour and relationships.[88] The last point has been seen as being especially poignant in relation to public debates about the rights of people with different sexual orientations.[89]

Notes

1 Ropelato, J. (2006) 'Internet pornography statistics', Top Ten Reviews.com, internet-filter-review.toptenreviews.com/internet-pornographystatistics.html.
2 Cooper, A., Boies, S., Haheu, M. and Greenfield, D. (1999) 'Sexuality and the internet: The next revolution', in F. Muscarella and L. Szuchman (Eds.) *The Psychological Science of Sexuality: A Research Based Approach*, pp519–545. New York, NY: Wiley; Peter, J. and Valkenburg, P. M. (2006a) 'Adolescents' exposure to sexually explicit online material and recreational attitudes toward sex', *Communication Research*, 56, 639–660.
3 Lawsky, D. (2008) 'American youth trail in internet use: Survey', *Reuters*, 24 November, http://www.reuters.com/article/2008/11/24/us-internet-youth-idUS-TRE4AN0MR20081124; Lenhart, A., Purcell, K., Smith, A. and Zickur, K. (2010) 'Social media & mobile internet use among teens and young adults', Pew Internet and American Life Project, http://www.pewinternet.org/Reports/2010/Social-Media-and-Young-Adults.
4 Mitchell, K. J., Wolak, J. and Finkelhor, D. (2007) 'Trends in youth reports of sexual solicitations, harassment and unwanted exposure to pornography on the internet', *Journal of Adolescent Health*, 32, 601–618.
5 Flood, M. (2009) 'The harms of pornography among children and young people', *Child Abuse Review*, 18, 384–400.
6 Russell, D. and Purcell, N. (2005) 'Exposure to pornography as a cause of children sexual victimization', in N. Dowd, D. Singer and R. Wilson (Eds.) *Handbook of Children, Culture and Violence*. Thousand Oaks, CA: Sage, pp59–84.
7 Martin, D. (2012) 'School groping surge blamed on net porn', 14 November, *Daily Mail*, 17.
8 Bentley, P. (2012) 'Internet porn and the rape suspects aged 10', *Daily Mail*, 19 November, 1–2.
9 Livingstone, S., Bober, M. and Helsper, E. (2005) *Internet Literacy Among Children and Young People: Findings from the UK Children Go Online Project*. London, UK: LSE Research Online, http://www.eprints.lse.ac.uk/archive/00000397, accessed 24 December 2012.
10 YouGov (2008) *Teen Sex Survey*, September, http://www.parenting.signposts.org.uk/assetss/downloads/Teen%20Sex%20Survey, accessed 24 December 2012.

11 Bonino, S., Ciairano, S., Rabaglietti, E. and Cattelino, E. (2006) 'Use of pornography and self-reported engagement of sexual violence among adolescents', *European Journal of Developmental* Psychology, 3, 265–288; Flood, M. (2007) 'Exposure to pornography among youth in Australia', *Journal of Sociology*, 43, 45–60; Johansson, T. and Hammaren, N. (2007) 'Hegemonic masculinity and pornography: Young people's attitudes toward and relations to pornography', *Journal of Men's Studies*, 15, 57–70; Lo, V. and Wei, R. (2005) 'Exposure to internet pornography and Taiwanese adolescents' sexual attitudes and behaviour', *Journal of Broadcasting and Electronic Media*, 49, 221–237.

12 Mitchell, K., Wolak, J. and Finkelhor, D. (2007) 'Trends in youth reports of sexual solicitations, harassment and unwanted exposure to pornography on the internet', *Journal of Adolescent Health*, 32, 601–618.

13 Cameron, K., Salazar, L., Bernhardt, J., Burgess-Whitman, N., Wingood, G. and Di Clemente, R. (2005) 'Adolescents' experiences with sex on the web: Results from online focus groups', *Journal of Adolescence*, 28, 535–540.

14 Nosko, A., Wood, E. and Desmarais, S. (2007) 'Unsolicited online sexual material: What affects our attitudes and likelihood to search for more?', *The Canadian Journal of Human Sexuality*, 16, 1–10; Sabina, C., Wolak, J. and Finkelhor, D. (2008) 'The nature and dynamics of internet pornography exposure for youth', *Cyberpsychology & Behavior*, 11, 691–693.

15 Kaplan, H. S. (1984) 'Have more fun making love', *Redbook*, July, 88–89, 166; Stoller, R. (1976) 'Sexual excitement', *Archives of General Psychiatry*, 33, 899–909; Wilson, W. C. (1978) 'Can pornography contribute to the prevention of sexual problems?', in C. B. Quals, J. P. Wincze and D. H. Barlow (Eds.) *The Prevention of Sexual Disorders: Issues and Approaches*, pp159–79. New York, NY: Plenum Press.

16 Goldstein, A. (1984) 'The place of pornography: Packaging eros for a violent age, [Comments to a forum held at the new School for Social Research in New York City, moderated by L. H. Lapham]', *Harper's*, November, pp31–39, 42–45.

17 Brownmiller, S. (1975) *Against Our Will: Men, Women and Rape*. New York, NY: Simon and Schuster; Diamond, S. (1985) 'Pornography: Image and reality', in V. Burstyn (Ed.) *Women against Censorship*, pp40–57. Vancouver, BC: Douglas & McIntyre.

18 Brown, D. and Bryant, J. (1989) 'The manifest content of pornography', in D. Zillmann and J. Bryant (Eds.) *Pornography; Research Advances and Policy Considerations*, pp3–24. Hillsdale, NJ: Lawrence Erlbaum Associates; Prince, S. (1990) 'Power and pain: Content analysis and the ideology of pornography', *Journal of Film & Video*, 42(2), 31–41; Slade, J. (1984) 'Violence in the hard-core pornographic film: An historical survey', *Journal of Communication*, 26, 16–33.

19 Cowan, G., Lee, C., Levy, D. and Snyder, D. (1988) 'Dominance and inequality in X-rated videocassettes', *Psychology of Women Quarterly*, 12, 299–312; Peter, J. and Valkenburg, P. M. (2009) 'Adolescents' exposure to sexually explicit internet material and notions of women as sex objects: Assessing causality and underlying processes', *Journal of Communication*, 35, 579–601.

20 Peter, J. and Valkenburg, P. M. (2008b) 'Adolescents' exposure to sexually explicit internet material, sexual uncertainty, and attitudes toward uncommitted sexual exploration: Is there a link?', *Communication Research*, 56, 579–601.

21 Weaver, J. B. (1987) *Effects of Exposure to Horror Film Violence on Perceptions of Women*, PhD thesis, Indiana University, *Dissertation Abstracts International*, 48(10), 2482-A; Zillmann, D. and Weaver, D (1989) 'Pornography and men's sexual callousness toward women', in D. Zillmann and J. Bryant (Eds.) *Pornography; Research Advances and Policy Considerations*, pp95–125. Hillsdale, NJ: Lawrence Erlbaum Associates.

22 Zillmann, D. and Weaver, D. (1989) *ibid*, p135.

23 Palys, T. S. (1986) 'Testing the common wisdom: The social content of video pornography', *Canadian Psychology*, 27, 22–35.

24 Yang, N. and Linz, D. (1990) 'Movie ratings and the content of adult videos: The sex-violence ratio', *Journal of Communication*, 40(2), 28–42.

25 Cowan, G., Lee, C., Levy, D. and Snyder, D. (1988) *op. cit.*

26 Linz, D., Donnerstein, E. and Penrod, S. (1988) 'Effects of long-term exposure to violent and sexually degrading depictions of women', *Journal of Personality and Social Psychology*, 55, 758–768; Weaver, J. (1991) 'Responding to erotica: perceptual processes and dispositional implications', in D. Zillmann & J. Bryant (Eds.) *Pornography; Research Advances and Policy Considerations*, pp329–354. Hillsdale, NJ: Lawrence Erlbaum Associates.

27 Molitor, F. and Sapolsky, B. S. (1993) 'Sex, violence and victimisation in slasher films', *Journal of Broadcasting & Electronic Media*, 37(2), 233–242.

28 Martin, D. (2012) 'Scarred by online porn', *Daily Mail*, 24 August, 1, 4.

29 Livingstone, S., Olafsson, K., O'Neill, B. and Donoso, V. (2012) 'Towards a better internet for children', EU Kids Online, June, www.eukidsonline,net.

30 DeAngelis, T. (2007) 'Children and the internet: Web pornography's effect on children', *Monitor on Psychology*, 38(10), 50.

31 Flood, M. (2009) *op. cit.*

32 Aisbett, K. (2001) *The Internet at Home: A Report on Internet Use in the Home.* Sydney, Australia: Australian Broadcasting Authority; Thornburgh, D. and Lin, H. (2002) *op. cit.*

33 Livingstone, S. and Helsper, E. (2010) 'Balancing opportunities and risks in teenagers' use of the internet: The role of online skills and internet self-efficacy', *New Media & Society*, 12, 309–329.

34 Kaiser Family Foundation (2001) *Generation Rx.com: How Young People Use the Internet for Health Information.* Menlo Park, CA: Henry J. Kaiser Foundation; Sabina, C., Wolak, J. and Finkelhor, D. (2008) *op. cit.*

35 Flood, M. (2009) *op. cit.*

36 Garlick, S. (2010) 'Taking control of sex? Hegemonic masculinity, technology and internet pornography', *Men and Masculinities*, 12(5), 597–614.

37 Peter, J. and Valkenburg, P. (2006) 'Adolescents' exposure to sexually explicit material on the internet', *Communication Research*, 56, 639–660; Peter, J. and Valkenberg, P. (2007) 'Adolescents' exposure to sexualized media environment and their notions of women as sex objects', *Sex Roles*, 56, 381–395.

38 Thornburgh, D. and Lin, H. (Eds.) (2002) *Youth, Pornography and the Internet.* Washington, DC: National Academy Press.

39 Hald, G. (2006) 'Gender differences in pornographic consumption among young heterosexual Danish adults', *Archives of Sexual Behaviour*, 35, 577–585; Janghorbani, M. and Lam, T. (2003) 'Sexual media use by young adults in Hong Kong: prevalence and associated factors', *Archives of Sexual Behaviour*, 32, 545–553.

40 Johansson, T. and Hammaren, N. (2007) 'Hegemonic masculinity and pornography: Young people's attitudes toward and relations to pornography', *Journal of Men's Studies*, 15, 57–70.

41 Zillmann, D. (1994) 'Erotica and family values', in D. Zillmann, J. Bryant and A. C. Huston (Eds.) *Media, Children and the Family: Social Scientific, Psychodynamic and Clinical Perspectives*, pp199–214. Hillsdale, NJ: Lawrence Erlbaum Associates.

42 Lo, V.-H. and Wei, R. (2005) 'Exposure to internet pornography and Taiwanese adolescents' sexual attitudes and behaviour', *Journal of Broadcasting & Electronic Media*, 49, 221–237.

43 Haggstrom-Nordin, E., Hanson, U. and Tyden, T. (2005) 'Association between pornography consumption and sexual practices among adolescents in Sweden', *International Journal of STD & AIDS*, 16, 102–117.

44 Cowan, G., Chase, C. J. and Stahly, G. B. (1989) 'Feminist and fundamentalist women's attitudes toward pornography control', *Psychology of Women Quarterly*, 13, 97–112.

45 Cowan, G. and Dunn, K. E. (1994) 'What themes in pornography lead to perceptions of the degradation of women?', *Journal of Sex Research*, 31(1), 11–21.

46 Malamuth, N. M. (1984) 'Aggression against women: Cultural and individual causes', in N. M. Malamuth and E. Donnerstein (Eds.) *Pornography and Sexual Aggression*, pp19–52. New York, NY: Academic Press; Malamuth, N. M. and Check, J. V. P. (1983)

'Sexual arousal to rape depictions: Individual differences', *Journal of Abnormal Psychology*, 92, 35–67.

47 Check, J. V. P. and Guloien, T. H. (1989) 'Reported proclivity for coercive sex following repeated exposure to sexually violent pornography, non-violent dehumanising pornography and erotica', in D. Zillmann and J. Bryant (Eds.) *Pornography: Research Advances and Policy Consideration*, pp159–184. Hillsdale, NJ: Lawrence Erlbaum Associates.

48 Malamuth, N. M. and Check, J. V. P. (1983) *op. cit.*

49 Malamuth, N. M. (1984) *op. cit.*

50 Davies, K. A. (1997) 'Voluntary exposure to pornography and men's attitudes towards feminism and rape', *Journal of Sex Research*, 34(2), 131–137.

51 Check, J. V. P. (1984) 'The effects of violent and nonviolence pornography', (Contract No. 955V, 19200-3-0899). Ottawa, Ontario: Canadian Department of Justice; Koss, M. P. and Dinero, T. E. (1988) 'Predictors of sexual aggression among a national sample of male college students', in R. A. Pentky and V. L. Quinsey (Eds.) *Sexual Aggression: Current Perspectives. Annals of the New York Academy of Sciences*, pp133–147. New York, NY: New York Academy of Sciences; Malamuth, N. M. and Check, J. V. P. (1985) 'The effects of aggressive pornography on beliefs in rape myths: Individual differences', *Journal of Research in Personality*, 19, 299–320.

52 Linz, D. (1985) *Sexual Violence in the Media: Effects on Male Viewers and Implications for Society*. PhD thesis, University of Wisconsin, Madison; Linz, D., Donnerstein, E. and Penrod, S. (1984) 'The effects of multiple exposures to filmed violence against women', *Journal of Communication*, 3493, 130–147.

53 Weaver, J. (1991) 'Responding to erotica: Perceptual processes and dispositional implications', in J. Bryany and D. Zillmann (Eds.) *Responding to the Screen: Reception and Reaction Processes*, pp329–354. Hillsdale, NJ: Lawrence Erlbaum Associates.

54 Weaver, J. B. (1991) 'Responding to erotica: Perceptual processes and dispositional implications', in J. Bryant and D. Zillmann (Eds.) *Responding to the Screen: Reception and Reaction Processes*, pp329–354. Hillsdale, NJ: Lawrence Erlbaum Associates.

55 Koss, M. P. and Dinero, T. E. (1988) *op. cit.*

56 Peter, J. and Valkenburg, P. M. (2009) *op. cit.*

57 Zillmann, D. (1989) 'Effects of prolonged consumption of pornography', in D. Zillmann and J. Bryant (Eds.) *Pornography: Research Advances and Policy Considerations*, pp117–157. Hillsdale, NJ: Lawrence Erlbaum Associates; Zillmann, D. and Bryant, J. (1982) 'Pornography, sexual callousness and the trivialisation of rape', *Journal of Communication*, 32(4), 10–21.

58 Brown, J. D. and L'Engle, K. L. (2009) 'X-rated sexual attitudes and behaviours associated with US early adolescents' exposure to sexually explicit media', *Communication Research*, 36(1), 129–151.

59 Check, J. V. P. and Guloien, T. H. (1989) *op. cit.*

60 Ringrose, J. and Renold, E. (2012) 'Slut-shaming, girl power and "sexualisation": Thinking through the politics of the international SlutWalks with teen girls', *Gender and Education*, 24(3), 333–343.

61 Livingstone, S., Olafsson, K., O'Neill, B. and Donoso, V. (2012) *op. cit.*

62 Barak, A. and Fisher, W. A. (1997) 'Effects of interactive computer erotica on men's attitudes and behaviour towards women: An experimental study', *Computer in Human Behavior* (1393), 353–369.

63 Haggstrom-Nordin, E., Sandberg, J., Hanson, U. and Tyden, T. (2006) 'It's everywhere! Young Swedish people's thoughts and reflections about pornography', *Scandinavian Journal of Caring Science*, 20, 386–393; Lofgeren-Martenson, L. and Mansson, S. (2010) 'Lust, love, and life: A qualitative study of Swedish adolescents' perceptions and experiences with pornography', *Journal of Sex Research*, 47, 568–579.

64 Alexy, E. M., Burgess, A. W. and Prentky, R. A. (2009) 'Pornography use as a risk marker for an aggressive pattern of behaviour among sexually reactive children and adolescents', *Journal of the American Psychiatric Nurses Association*, 42, 442–453; Hunter, J. A.,

Figueredo, A. J. and Malamuth, N. M. (2010) 'Developmental pathways into social and sexual deviance', *Journal of Family Violence*, 25, 141–148.

65 Peter, J. and Valkenburg, P. M. (2006) *op. cit.*; Peter, J. and Valkenburg, P. M. (2007) *op. cit*; Peter, J. and Valkenburg, P. M. (2008) *op. cit.*

66 Huston, A., Waretella, E. and Donnerstein, E. (1998) *Measuring the Effects of Sexual Content in the Media: A Report to the Kaiser Family Foundation.* Menlo Park, CA: Henry J. Kaiser Family Foundation; Strasburger, V. and Wilson, B. (Eds.) (2002) *Children, Adolescents and the Media.* Thousand Oaks, CA: Sage; Ward, L. (2003) 'Understanding the role of entertainment media in the sexual socialization of American youth: A review of empirical research', *Developmental Review*, 23, 347–388.

67 Wingwood, G., DiClemente, R., Harrington, K., Davies. S., Hook and Oh, M. (2001) 'Exposure to X-rated movies and adolescents' sexual and contraceptive-related attitudes and behaviours', *Pediatrics*, 107, 1116–1120.

68 Haggstrom-Nordin, E., Hanson, U. and Tyden, T. (2005) *op. cit.*

69 Kraus, S. W. and Russell, B. (2008) 'Early sexual experiences: The role of internet access and sexually explicit material', *CyberPsychology & Behaviour*, 11, 162–168.

70 Brown, J. D. and L'Engle, K. L. (2009) *op. cit.*

71 Braun-Courville, D. K. and Rojas, M. (2009) 'Exposure to sexually explicit web sites and adolescent sexual attitudes and behaviours', *Journal of Adolescent Health*, 45, 156–162; Brown, J. D., Keller, S. and Stern, S. (2009) 'Sex, sexuality, sexting and sexed; Adolescents and the media', *The Prevention Researcher*, 16(4), 12–16.

72 Luder, M. T., Pittet, I., Berchtold, A., Akre, C., Michaud, P. A. and Suris, J. C. (2010) 'Associations between online pornography and sexual behaviour among adolescents: Myth or reality?', *Archives of Sexual Behaviour*.

73 Demare, D., Briere, J. and Lips, H. M. (1988) 'Violent pornography and self-reported likelihood of sexual aggression', *Journal of Research in Personality*, 22, 140–155.

74 Linz, D. (1989) 'Exposure to sexually explicit materials and attitude to rape: A comparison of study results', *Journal of Sex Research*, 26, 50–84.

75 Malamuth, N. M. and Huppin, M. (2005) 'Pornography and teenagers: The importance of individual differences', *Adolescent Medicine*, 16, 315–326.

76 Check, J. (1995) 'Teenage training: The effects of pornography on adolescent males', in L. R. Lederer and R. Delgado (Eds.) *The Price We Pay: The Case against Racist Speech, Hate Propaganda and Pornography.* New York, NY: Hill and Wang, pp89–91.

77 Alexy, E. M., Burgess, A. W. and Prentky, R. A. (2009) *op. cit.*

78 Brown, J. D and L'Engle, K. L. (2009) *op. cit.*

79 Bonino, S., Ciarano, S., Rabaglietti, E. and Cattelino, E. (2006) *op. cit.*

80 Ybarra, M. L. and Mitchell, K. J. (2005) 'Exposure to internet pornography among children and adolescents: A national survey', *CyberPsychology & Behaviour*, 8, 473–486.

81 Ybarra, M. L., Mitchell, K. J., Hamburger, M., Diener-West, M. and Leaf, P. J. (2011) 'X-rated material and perpetration of sexually aggressive behaviour among children and adolescents: Is there a link?', *Aggressive Behaviour*, 37, 1–18.

82 Hunter, J. A., Fugeuredo, A. J. and Malamuth, N. M. (2010) *op. cit.*

83 Hunter, J. A., Fugeuredo, A. J. and Malamuth, N. M. (2010) *op. cit*; Ybarra, M. L. and Mitchell, K. J. (2005) *op. cit.*

84 Livingstone, S., Olafsson, K., O'Neill, B. and Donoso, V. (2012) *op. cit.*

85 Livingstone, S., Olafsson, K., O'Neill, B. and Donoso, V. (2012) *op. cit.*

86 Ybarra, M. L. and Mitchell, K. J. (2005) *op. cit.*

87 Helsper, E. (2005) *R18 Material: Its Potential Impact on People Under 18 – An Overview of the Available Literature.* London, UK: London school of Economics and Office of Communications, www.ofcom.org.uk/research/radio/reports/bcr/r18, accessed 30 November 2012.

88 McNair, B. (1996) *Mediated Sex: Pornography and Postmodern Culture.* London, UK: Arnold.

89 Hillier, L., Kurdas, C. and Horsley, P. (2001) *'It's Just Easier': The Internet as a Safety-Net for Same Sex Attracted Young People.* Melbourne, Australia: Australian Research centre in Sex, Health and Society, LaTrobe University.

9

DIGITAL SOCIAL MEDIA AND SEXUALIZATION

During the 21st century, the world of communications changed dramatically as the internet and associated World Wide Web penetrated almost every society and enabled ordinary people to access huge quantities of information at the touch of a button or click of a mouse, to engage in a wide range of transactions that previously had been conducted face to face, by telephone or letter, and to become self-publicists. It is the self-publicity aspects of online technologies that have opened up a range of new settings in which sexualization of children can occur. The openness of the internet means that it enjoys freedom from regulations that restrict the activities of other media. Its accessibility also means that it can empower ordinary people in terms of being able to reach a multitude of others and to upload their content without being restricted by the editorial gatekeepers who control the regular mass media. More than this, the emergence of wireless technology that can match wired technology in terms of transmission capacity means that people can be connected to others all the time even while on the move.

As with many new technologies, the young were dominant among the early adopters of the internet and have also taken readily to mobile communications. From an early age most kids have mobile phones.[1] Now they can use their phones not only to make voice calls, but also to download and upload content in the form of words and pictures. These technologies can have many social benefits in terms of ensuring that children can maintain contact with their parents when out with their friends, enabling users to make arrangements with others without the need to find a fixed location, landline telephone, and also allowing us all to update those we are due to meet about delays to our journeys. These technological developments, however, are a mixed blessing and are open to abuse. Some communications developments now allow us to post up-to-the minute information about where we are and what we are doing to a mass audience and enable others to post information about us on the same scale without our necessarily being aware of it.

The emergence of social media during the second half of the 2000s opened up an online environment that quickly evolved from a new social channel through which to keep in touch with your friends to one in which anyone could engage in mass self-promotion. The second generation web opened up opportunities for greater interaction between human users and technologies and enabled people to become self-publishers and publicists. There was an expansion of online sites that allowed users to make contact with other people and to publish or 'post' information about themselves. Some of these sites also allowed users to post images – both still and moving. Sites such as MySpace and later Facebook were enthusiastically embraced by young people who often disclosed information about themselves with no thought to the consequences.

There are also sites that are operated by independent publishers that attract young people because they deal with topics known to be of interest to them. These sites include fan sites associated with celebrities. Many sites of this type are targeted at girls and are run on behalf of iconic female celebrities who may represent role models for many girls.

One researcher found that celebrity fan web sites were much more likely to contain sexualized images when they represented female celebrities than male celebrities. This was true of both official websites and unofficial sites run by fans themselves. Female musicians were treated in a sexualized way more than other types of female celebrities.[2]

The internet

The internet is a major source of sexual material. As we saw in Chapter 8, the World Wide Web has become the most substantial repository of pornographic material ever known. There is much additional sexual content that is accessible via the internet, as well as that classed as porn. Concerns about the internet in the context of child sexualization overlap with many other media. In part, this is because the other media we have examined already in this book together with the different genres of sexual content that can be found in these media also appear and can be readily accessed online. Most major mass media operators have websites. The content they provide in their traditional offline formats can also be found, often with format modifications, on their websites. The internet is a more open and less regulated communications environment and as such it often presents content that other media would be restricted from publishing. This greater openness is one of the primary reasons why the internet is so popular with children. At the same time, this openness makes the internet a source of concern for parents, teachers and policy-makers, who each have varying degrees of responsibility for the protection of young people.

As we will see in this chapter, pre-teenage and teenage children report exposure to explicit sexual content online. For most of them, this experience happens by accident; but for some it does not. Furthermore, accidental exposure to online sexual content can motivate subsequent searching for it. In terms of how this might affect young people, research with young adults in their late 20s and early 30s has found that when they reflected on the onset of their sex lives, those who had the greatest access to the internet and who made the most use of it between the ages of 12 and 17 also reported the earliest onset of sexual activity such as oral sex and sexual intercourse.[3]

Both pre-teenage and teenage children make extensive use of the internet and most youngsters are skilled at navigating their way around cyberspace. As the popularity of the web has grown, so too has the risk that children will be exposed to sexual content on it. Many children in different parts of the world have reported exposure to online sexual content and their experiences have not always been positive ones.[4]

In the United States, a nationwide survey of adolescents in 1999 found that one in four (25 per cent) young internet users said they had seen explicit sexual content online.[5] Six years later a similar survey found that reported youth exposure to online sexual content had increased dramatically to more than four in ten internet users (42 per cent).[6] In a survey of young people aged between 13 and 18 years in The Netherlands in 2005, a clear majority of males (71 per cent) and a substantial minority of females (40 per cent) reported some exposure to sexual content on the internet.[7] Again in the US, a survey of adolescents aged 13 to 15 years found that one quarter of them said they felt unsafe online and around half of those who were insecure online had experienced unwanted sexual attention from acquaintances or strangers.[8]

Despite the concerns that have been voiced about young people accessing explicit sexual content on the internet, many deliberately seek out such material. In doing so, this online activity is an extension of their developing sex lives in the offline world. Young people recognized the potential of the internet from its early days as an environment in which they could make new social contacts, often for sexual purposes.[9] Sexually explicit material has also been sought out via the internet by young people for their information, entertainment and as a source of sexual arousal. Not only this, but once they had discovered sources of online sexually explicit content, many young users forwarded on the details (and sometimes actual images) to their friends. Much evidence shows that this is an activity involving both genders, but with men engaging in such practices more often than women.[10]

The internet has brought unwanted youth exposure to sexual communications other than by chance exposure to pornographic websites while surfing the web. Although, as we have seen already, some young internet users have reported proactively seeking out sites where they can engage in sex chat and even make sexual connections with other people,[11] others have reported receiving unwanted attention of this kind via email and instant messaging. Such experiences were observed increasingly to take the form of sexual harassment by strangers. One study of a small sample of American university students reported that at least one in ten said they had been repeatedly threatened or harassed via emails or instant messages. Young men and young women were equally likely to have had this experience.[12]

This behaviour was found to have levelled off during the mid-2000s.[13] Two cross-sectional surveys of national samples of American youth aged between 9 and

17 years held in 2000 and 2005 asked respondents about unwanted sexual solicitations, harassment and unwanted exposure to pornography. Specific questions probed young people about whether anyone had asked them to describe what their body looked like, to talk about sex online or to do something sexual. In addition, they were asked if anyone had used the internet to threaten or embarrass them by posting or sending messages about them or by bothering them.

Across these two survey waves there were substantial decreases in sexual solicitation and harassment rates for all age groups of children and teenagers. Reductions of sexual solicitation and harassment experiences when using the internet did not decrease for African-American and Hispanic respondents. Reports of exposure to unwanted pornography online, however, generally increased. Although sexual solicitations as a whole decreased over time for majority white children, there was no change in rates of occurrence of aggressive sexual solicitations. The latter were also frequently linked to offline contact between the senders and recipients of these messages.[14]

In a further analysis of data from the second survey reported above, the same researchers found that 4 per cent of internet-using children and teenagers said they had received a request to send a sexual picture of themselves during the previous year. Such requests were most likely to occur for recipients who had engaged in a close online relationship with the sender, who had engaged in some form of sexual behaviour online previously, and who were in abusive offline sexual relationships. Such requests were also more likely to be sent to girls than to boys and were more commonplace among African-American respondents than among other ethnic groups.[15]

The propensity to respond to unsolicited messages to link to sexually explicit materials online can apparently be mediated by the current relationship status of internet users. American college students aged between 16 and 28 years who were single and seeking a relationship were significantly more likely than other students to follow up unsolicited spam email links to websites containing explicit sexual content. Male and female teenage and young adults in this sample of over 200 students were equally likely to engage in this behaviour. In fact, when a range of other potential predictors of this following-up behaviour were taken into account, including gender, age, race, hours spent using the internet each week, numbers of spam emails received, and self-esteem and perceived stress in their lives, relationship status emerged as the only significant predictor of opening and reading pornography-related spam email.[16]

Even though the apparently constructive uses that young people have identified for online sexually explicit material suggest that they generally have this behaviour under control, there is evidence of potential spin-off effects of repeated exposure to it that raise more alarm. Over time, users of graphic sexual content on the internet grow accustomed to it and develop increasingly positive opinions about it.[17] Male users have reported the importance of using online sexual material as a stimulus for masturbation. Gaining this kind of sexual pleasure from explicit depictions of sex online can enhance their overall enjoyment of seeing this material and might also be linked to developing a dependency on this type of experience.[18]

Although, as we have seen, young people have indicated the importance of the internet in their lives as a channel through which they can seek sexual partners, many restrict themselves to isolated sexual gratification through exposure to online sexual content.[19] Thus, while the internet can be used in a socially constructive fashion to support a young person's social network and enhance their opportunities to make new romantic or sexual attachments in the offline world, it can also become a substitute for real relationships among those who are already socially isolated, providing an easy escape from confronting their social anxieties.[20]

Moving on from evidence that has been obtained from college undergraduates to adolescents at an earlier stage of psychological (and sexual) development, it is known that early and mid-teens use online sexual material for information, entertainment and sexual stimulation. Teenage boys, for instance, may view this material as an aid to masturbation. This behaviour does not necessarily mean that they will become socially withdrawn or sexually warped as a consequence. Indeed, these experiences are often found to be a poor substitute for the real thing. Once they reach a point at which they begin to date other people and become intimate with real sexual partners, pornography may lose its appeal.[21] There are, of course, always exceptions to the rule. Surveys of adolescents have also indicated that there are minorities of young people, often from troubled backgrounds, who develop potentially unhealthy relationships with explicit online sex, develop a dependency on it, and use it to feed compulsive sexual behaviour in the offline world.[22]

Social media and sexual self-promotion

On sites such as Bebo, Facebook and Myspace, users can post biographical information, up-to-date information on developments in their lives, and insights into their thoughts and feelings about all kinds of issues. They can also post pictures of themselves, and in doing so visually expose their personal identities to the world. Although there are built-in mechanisms to enable users to control who gains access to this content, these are not default settings and many forget or deliberately choose not to use them. Even before these social media sites became popular, young internet users used the internet to link socially with others through chat rooms. By 2001, more than seven in ten (71 per cent) of American teenagers aged 15 to 17 years reported taking part in chat rooms.[23]

Self-presentation via social media has become increasingly central to self-definition for many young people in developed countries. Unless you have a Facebook account you may be regarded by your social peers as disconnected. In its seminal format, Facebook was a site developed to enable male Harvard students to comment on the attractiveness of depicted female students. As social media sites have become mainstream, researchers have recorded growing social pressures on girls to present themselves on these sites as sexually active and available. As we will see, some young people try to avoid putting themselves at risk online while others do not.

Research with adolescents who use online chat sites has found significant variances in risk awareness among young internet users. Teenagers who feel greater uncertainty online were less likely to disclose a lot of personal information. When they did disclose personal details, they only did so to sources they knew they could trust. Those chat site users who felt comfortable and safe in this environment tended to disclose more about themselves and were likely to take more risks in terms of what they would say and the range of strangers with whom they would chat.[24]

Further research has indicated that chat rooms provided a space in which adolescents could chat freely and openly about sexual matters. They were forums in which teenagers could air their concerns about their sexuality and also establish their sexual identity as part of a process leading eventually to 'pairing off' with potential romantic and sexual partners.[25]

More than eight out of ten American 8- to 18-year-olds reported visiting social media sites and more than seven in ten (74 per cent) said they had created a personal profile on at least one of these sites. Furthermore, on a typical day, around four in ten (40 per cent) will visit a social network site and spend nearly an hour there.[26]

Although there are lower age limits operated by many social media sites – for example, Facebook users must be at least 13 – these thresholds are not as carefully policed as they might be. Research among young people in the US showed that social media sites are visited even by children younger than 13.[27] These sites provide opportunities for children and teenagers to maintain continual social contact with each other, but also provide sites for self-disclosure and publicity. These sites are very popular among girls and many young female users have been found to present themselves in a sexualized way.[28] Evidence has emerged that some girls use these sites to present themselves as sexually active or available.[29]

Even when teenagers reach the threshold age for membership of the major social media sites such as Facebook, some remain unsatisfied with this and seek out more adult-themed sites for which they must be aged 18.[30]

One study of 24,000 personal profile pictures posted on Myspace found that some women of different ethnicities and social strata used social media to put their bodies on display as sexual objects. The women who did this tended to have slender and shapely body shapes. In general, the posting of explicitly sexualized images was an activity that characterized only a minority of female Myspace users. Many female users, nonetheless, used their sites to place images that displayed their physical selves.[31]

Young women, teenage and pre-teenage girls who engage in such practices are putting themselves at risk. This is all the more serious given the growing popularity of social networking sites among adults who seek out children for sexual contact.[32]

The internet appears to many users to represent a safe haven for communicating freely about any topic and for making new social contacts. It provides openings for talking to others from the safety of one's home and can also afford a degree of anonymity. This can result in a false sense of security that leads users to feel comfortable disclosing personal details of themselves they would perhaps refrain from doing in face-to-face meetings. In the absence of the usual social cues that are present in direct face-to-face communications, the online world also presents us with an opportunity to create a constructed identity that may differ from our real identity. This can work for and against us. Young people may enjoy trying out different identities at a stage in life when their own identity is still under development. This anonymous world in which social presence cues are minimized also means that those with whom children and teenagers communicate online might also not be who they say they are. This environment, therefore, can put young people at risk of being seduced into believing they are making friends with someone their own age when, in fact, they are being groomed by an adult.

There are also examples of adults with no prior track record of sexual deviance joining in these online games and communicating in a sexual way with children.[33] More serious are those internet forums that are developed by adults deliberately seeking sexual contact with children.[34] From the earliest days of the internet becoming publicly available as a communications network, law enforcement agencies voiced concerns about its misappropriation for criminal ends by paedophiles. Four main uses of the internet by paedophiles were distinguished. Paedophiles went online to find and distribute child pornography, to locate and to groom potential victims, and to link up with other paedophiles.[35] Child sex offenders as a marginalized and often isolated group in the offline world were attracted to the online world because it provided them with more and easier opportunities to make contact with each other.[36] In addition, the appeal of the internet to young people also meant that it provided a potentially rich source of targets for these offenders.[37]

At this time there were calls to restrict the access to online pornography on the part of child sex abusers.[38] Not only would these offenders seek out images of children to stimulate their own sexual gratification, some also engaged in grooming young people online and trafficking offensive images to other offenders.[39] In addition, observations of child molesters over time have revealed that regular use of pornography was a further risk factor for high-risk offenders increasing the likelihood that they would offend again in the future even after earlier criminal conviction.[40]

Paedophiles quickly adopted the internet to extend pre-existing offline exchange networks through which child pornography was distributed.[41] Child sex offenders also turned to chat rooms that were openly available to users of all ages for a variety of social networking purposes and pretend to be children or teenagers themselves in order to contact young people and meet them.[42]

In one investigation of this phenomenon, the researcher acted as an active participant in a chat room designed to appeal to gay males and assumed a number of distinct identities as teenage bisexual males.[43] Identity descriptions portrayed these fictional males as athletic, sexually active, financially comfortable and curious. The researcher subsequently engaged in online conversations with other users of this site who contacted him. In all, 1000 contacts were analysed. Around two-thirds of these contacts were seeking personal sexual gratification (called 'cruisers') and around one third were pornographers seeking to collect and distribute sexually explicit materials. A small proportion of these contacts were classified as browsers who were exploring the site expecting to contact real people. Among the cruisers, the claimed ages ranged from 9 to 60 years, although it was assumed that many of the ages given, especially at the younger end of the spectrum, were false. Half of the cruisers sought contact beyond the chat room by regular mail, telephone or even face-to-face meetings.

Paedophiles also established their own 'newsgroups' online to make contact with other offenders as platforms on which to try to justify their behaviour, and to exchange information about potential victims.[44] Newsgroups have been used by paedophiles to link with other offenders and to exchange pornographic files and images. Bulletin Board Systems and Listservs were two other types of online sites used by paedophiles from the early days of the internet to reach out to other offenders, exchange information and locate victims.[45] Although some sites have prohibited illegal content, others have not imposed any restrictions on content at all. By the turn of the century, it was estimated that over 1000 illegal photographs of children per week were being posted online.[46]

Law enforcement agencies have been very active in this field and often orchestrate 'stings' in which they enter internet sites pretending to be sex offenders in order to flush out the real offenders. Once online contact is made with an offender, law enforcement officers encourage face-to-face meetings at which the offender is arrested. One of the most worrying early observations of offenders discovered in this way was that many had no previous recorded history of offending. Some experts have suggested that the internet generates a false sense of security, enticing offenders who believe that the online world is a fantasy rather than reality, and that engaging in online behaviour that would be classed as offensive and even illegal in the offline world does not really count as an offence.[47]

'Sexting' and the sexualization of teens

Social media sites and mobile texting have emerged as sites of sexual provocation, harassment and intimidation. A number of studies have been carried out on this phenomenon with pre-teenage children and teenagers. Growing evidence has emerged that text file sharing is a widespread activity among young people and that it is often used to distribute graphic sexual imagery that they have obtained from online sources or produced themselves. The term 'sexting' has been coined for sending or receiving sexually explicit text messages or images via a mobile phone. While some early indications identified this as a minority behaviour, there is mounting evidence that sexting is becoming more commonplace.[48]

Andy Phippen of the University of Plymouth undertook an online study with young people aged 11 to 18 years about their use of internet and mobile technology. He reported interim findings from a sample of 535 respondents.[49] An overwhelming majority said they used mobile phones to take photographs and to film video sequences (79 per cent) and to distribute these images to other people (78 per cent). Nearly four in ten (39 per cent) claimed to know friends who had sent intimate pictures of a boyfriend or girlfriend in text messages. More than one in four of these young people (27 per cent) claimed this activity occurred regularly or all the time. Although explicit sexual images in texts (or 'sexts') were usually designed to be sent to one specific recipient, many of Phippen's respondents (56 per cent) were aware of instances where the images ended up being more widely distributed. There was further evidence that teenagers were becoming accustomed to this behaviour, with just one in four (27 per cent) saying they believed more help and support around issues of 'sexting' was needed. Even so, three in ten (30 per cent) said they knew of somebody who had been affected by problems associated with this activity.

In the UK, a family support charity called Family Lives has established a project entitled TeenBoundaries which advises teenagers on how to cope with pressures to have sex before they are ready. In one case in London, Family Lives was called in to advise a school in which a 12-year-old girl was filmed on a mobile phone giving a 14-year-old boy oral sex. The film clip was then circulated around the boy's classmates.[50] This phenomenon of 'sexting' in which children film engaging in sexual activity and then send clips to their friends or post them on the internet is growing.

This 'sexting' phenomenon is also linked to premature criminal sexual behaviour such as gang rape. Family Lives dealt with another case in which a 15-year-old girl went to the home of a boy she had a crush on only to find nine older boys waiting there for her. Links between the propensity to send explicit sexual mobile phone messages and high-risk sexuality were confirmed in a large-scale survey of teenagers in the United States. Eric Rice and his colleagues at the School of Social Work, University of Southern California, found that although only a minority (15 per cent) of the young people aged 12 to 18 years whom they questioned admitted to sending a sexually explicit message or photo of themselves; those who did were more likely to be fully sexually active and to engage in unprotected sexual intercourse. These findings do make a proven case for causality, but they also portray a syndrome of high-risk sexual practices among some teens that involves the use of mobile phones.[51]

Despite risks to young people associated with phenomena such as 'sexting', Family Lives' survey revealed that many parents (46 per cent) indicated they had no intention of talking to their children about it before it occurred. Few parents felt they had enough information about this type of behaviour and thus felt ill equipped to deal with it. When it came to children's use of social media sites such as Facebook, many parents felt even more out of touch. When parents accidentally found out what their children were up to on these sites, it often came as a shock to them. As one Family Lives parent commented:

> I just found out on Wednesday that my 11-year-old daughter has been chatting to an older boy (says he is 14) on MSN and from what I can tell she has showed him parts of her body on a web cam and possibly sent him photos of herself. I was extremely shocked to find this out as she has shown no interest in boys/sex/kissing, etc.; but reading through the message history that I have found, she has been discussing sex with him. She has also accessed porn sites.
>
> As soon as I discovered this I have talked to her – she says she does not know why she has done this, that she isn't really interested in boys/sex, etc. I have explained to her all the dangers of what she has done, and also now installed a software package which restricts the length of time she can use the

internet and blocks her accessing inappropriate sites and also tells me what sites she has tried to access ... (p14).[52]

In a front page story in the UK's conservative mid-market newspaper the *Daily Mail*, a research investigation by Channel 4 news reported that boys and girls aged 13 to 16 regularly swap explicit pictures of themselves on their mobile telephones. One girl was quoted as saying: 'I get asked for naked pictures at least two or three times a week.'

In research based on focus group interviews carried out with 220 children aged 13 and 14 years commissioned by Channel 4's *Generation Sex TV* series and the NSPCC (National Society for the Prevention of Cruelty to Children), evidence emerged that children were becoming sexualized earlier. Teenager children reported frequent exposure to pornographic material on the internet, which they used to learn more about sex. The direct and impersonal approach to sex depicted in pornographic videos seemed to have informed teenagers' casual approach to sex.[53]

In a further article on sexting published by *The Sunday Times*, Eleanor Mills reported not only was this behaviour widespread among teenage girls and boys, but that it represented a manifestation of a youth culture in which sex was casually traded between the genders. If a teenage girl found a boy sexually attractive, she would send him a photograph of her breasts while a boy might initiate contact by sending a girl he liked a picture of his genitals. When text messages were sent, instead of being used as an invitation to go on a date, they were often used to make direct approaches for sex. In her interviews with teenagers, Mills reported that familiarity with online pornography was widespread. Porn was used to learn about sexual techniques but also created a set of standards for sexual performance, devoid of emotional commitment, accompanied by expectations especially on the part of boys about what girls would and ought to be willing to do for them. Some teenagers even resorted to producing their own sex videos which were then circulated around their friends and other peers.[54]

This casual and emotionally vacant orientation towards sex could also lead some teenagers to seek out increasingly extreme and graphic forms of pornography, and this might lead some boys into viewing material that combined sex with violence. As we saw in Chapter 8, even quite limited diets of sexual violence were able to product shifts in the sexual attitudes of young men, rendering them more sympathetic towards the use of coercion in sexual relations with women. The direct, interactive engagement of children and adolescents in raw sexual practices that go beyond simply viewing pornography to its production and the incorporation of crude sexual imagery in their electronic interpersonal communications to others has created a climate in which sexual intimidation has become more prevalent.

Cyberbullying

This phenomenon has surfaced with the internet. Bullying is an aggressive behaviour that is repeatedly and intentionally carried out against a victim unable readily to defend himself or herself.[55] Bullying is serious conduct because it can lead to physically and psychologically damaging side-effects for victims.[56] Cyberbullying occurs when bullying behaviour as described above is conducted through actions that occur using electronic forms of communication.[57] It takes the form of verbal harassment online via email, micro-blogging and social media sites, and via mobile phone text messaging. This form of bullying is not yet fully understood but there are signs that it too can cause unwanted psychological side-effects for those on the receiving end.[58]

Evidence has emerged that this phenomenon is widespread among teenagers and perhaps affects most of them at some time or other. Ybarra and Mitchell conducted a series of investigations of cyberbullying in the US. Among 10- to 17-year-olds they found that 12 per cent reported being aggressive to someone online, while much smaller percentages said they had been victims of such bullying (4 per cent) or had been both bullies and bullied (3 per cent).[59] A subsequent study by the same authors reported an increased proportion of American adolescents (9 per cent) who claimed to have been harassed on the internet.[60]

Online bullying can take many different forms in terms of the medium used by bullies to reach their victims. While a number of different forms of text communication exist (e.g. text messages, email, instant messaging, chat rooms), nearly half of cyberbullying incidents that took place at school among one British sample (46 per cent) involved pictures of video clips. Girls were more likely than boys to be victims, but the perpetrators were also as likely to be other girls as they were to be boys.[61] The wider evidence on whether this bullying is mostly carried out by boys or girls has been mixed.[62] Although many cyberbullies had also been bullies in the offline world, there was also some evidence to suggest that the indirect nature of bullying online might appeal more to girls than offline bullying, opening up a risk that girls would engage more in bullying behaviour in this medium.[63]

Although bullying is classified as an aggressive behaviour, cyberbullying can take on a sexual overtone. Again in the US, evidence has emerged from girls who have fallen victim to cyberbullying that this behaviour can include sexually explicit messages.[64] Elsewhere it was reported that around 15 per cent of a sample of American adolescents claimed to have received unwanted sexual advances online. A minority of these occurred more specifically via social network sites.[65]

In the United Kingdom, the sexting trend on mobile phones has been linked to risks of sexual harassment not only between young people but also in the form of grooming by adult offenders. Evidence discussed above indicated that indecent and sexually explicit images of teenage girls and boys often end up being circulated beyond the intended recipient. There are extreme cases where such images are not just circulated around a teenager's school, but also finish up on paedophile chat sites.[66]

Hyper-masculinity

One emergent concern from the increased sexualization of culture has been the indirect impact this might have on the physical and emotional well-being and safety of women in a world where men are conditioned to think of them as sexual objects. Coupled with this distorted sexual orientation is a so-called hyper-masculine ethos that promotes the physical dominance of men over women, especially in sexual settings. Hyper-masculine men are characterized as holding callous sexual attitudes towards women, the belief that to be violent is to be manly and enjoying danger. This extreme machismo leads such men to regard feminine qualities as inferior.

This type of dominant social script shapes the kinds of relationships these men have with women.[67] It is the type of social orientation that might, in turn, lead men to seek out mediated portrayals of women that confirm the dominant social and sexual scripts by which they lead their lives. Young, well-educated men of average age 19 in the US, with personality profiles that reflected female dominance and sexually aggressive propensities, were found in one study to exhibit stronger preferences than other men of their age for sexually violent videos.[68]

We observed earlier that children exposed to explicit sexual material on the internet unwittingly were more likely later on to seek out such material. There is further evidence that the nature of an internet user's personality can influence the type of material they seek out online, having been exposed to it previously by accident. Thus, evidence has emerged that young men in their late teens and early 20s are more likely to seek out explicit sexual material online following accidental exposure to it when they are characterized by having stronger sexual urges and antisocial tendencies. These more strongly sexual and aggressive personality types were more likely than other young men to follow up on unsolicited spam email that linked to websites showing pictures of naked people or people having sex.[69]

Hyper-masculine men may also turn to social networks for men that enable them to mix online with others with their beliefs and values. The mixing of sex with violence in pornography and the more subtle messages of male sexual dominance that permeate other media outputs can produce exaggerated gender role beliefs where sexual relations become a manifestation of male power rather than mutually consenting and satisfying sexual partnerships. The hyper-masculine male demotes romantic sexual relationships and promotes the use of physical power with women to a degree where even the use of assault or rape is deemed acceptable.[70]

The hyper-masculine orientation can be conditioned from an early age. Childhood experiences of gender relationships and of the use of violence in such contexts can often lay down a foundation for its future development as part of a young male's personality.[71] Societies that promote male aggression and dominance as core aspects of maleness tend also to have higher rates of sexual assault.[72]

Brand champions

Advertising and marketing have extended to the digital media from mainstream mass media in new and interesting ways. Whereas traditional advertising is usually clearly signalled in the media as distinct from non-advertising content, in the newer media it is often integrated with non-advertising content or disguised such that children are not instantly aware that they are engaging with material that is designed to influence them as consumers. We have already seen that children can become brand aware from a very early age. Some can name brands from before the age of five.[73] Their understanding of marketing messages continues to develop into their teen years even with advertising forms that are clearly separated from media entertainment or information content.

In the online world, advertising forms have evolved that look unlike any in the mainstream media. Advertising messages and brands are integrated with entertainment content or are embedded in environments that are used primarily for social networking purposes.[74]

Brands have a presence on social media sites such as Facebook. Some brands have created their own social media sites that draw web users in and appear as normal online social networks, but are, in fact, promotional vehicles. Brands have a presence in virtual worlds online and provide open invitations to visitors to engage with brands in competitive or game contexts. Advergames use interactive entertainment formats to attract children and teenagers and use these contexts to bring young consumers into close virtual contact with brands.[75]

Some websites recruit children to become brand champions. In this role they interact with other children in online gaming or interpersonal messaging environments and promote brands. This approach plays on the knowledge that consumers often trust their peers' and especially their friends' opinions and turn to them for clues about the latest fashion trends with which they ought to conform.

Social media environments can be used to present brands in a variety of contexts and to associate brands with attributes, settings and endorsers that have high status with young consumers. This approach also plays on children's fears of being out of touch with brands that are current with their peers. This strategy can be especially effective in relation to clothing fashions.

Regulating exposure to sex

Digital technologies have opened up an enhanced communications environment for children and adolescents unlike anything their older generations had experienced. The internet has created a huge repository of content on diverse themes and subjects that can be readily accessed and searched. It has put a great deal more information and entertainment at our fingertips than was ever available in the online communications era. As the dominant early adopters of these new technologies, young people have developed greater skills in their use than their parents. Having been brought up surrounded by networked-fixed and mobile-computerized devices, the use of virtual environments to obtain information, find entertainment, engage in transactions and communicate with others is second nature to them.

It is understandable that parents and policy-makers express concern about children's use of these technologies. The freedom with which information of any kind can flow around the internet – an aspect of its character that was a founding principle of its existence – in the absence of systems of restriction over users' content exposure, in the context of children's online behaviour, removes parental control in an area of activity that has become such an important part of children's everyday lives.

The evidence that has emerged about the use of digital media to find sexual content or to engage in highly sexualized communications with friends has fuelled calls for tighter controls over what websites should be allowed to publish and over the way in which search engines allow young internet users to access problematic content.

The exposure of children to sexual content did not, however, start with digital media. Teenagers almost invariably display a greater interest in sex as they reach full physical maturity. Even before they reach their teens, children can show curiosity about sex and will, given the opportunity, seek out information about it if they can. Critics might claim that the modern digital media and some content published by the older media, such as television and magazines, have corrupted children and removed the innocence that traditionally characterizes childhood.[76] More reflective observations of childhood and sexuality have revealed that it is difficult to find a period when childhood was shielded from sex and the innocence of children was fully preserved until they grew up.[77]

Despite the evidence that has been reviewed in this book about 'media effects' on children's and teenagers' sexual knowledge, beliefs, attitudes and behaviour, the restrictive methodologies of cause–effect interventionist studies or longitudinal developmental surveys often fail to give young people sufficient opportunity to reflect at length on what sex means to them and where they go to find out about it. Young people also need to be given opportunities to express their attitudes to different kinds of sexual practice, both in terms of the occurrence of sex in their own lives and in relation to the way in which sex is represented in the media or used in marketing.

There is an important caveat that applies to much of this research, especially that used as an evidence base by major government inquiries into childhood sexualization, and that is the need to offer clear and comprehensive definitions of key concepts such as 'sexuality' and 'sexualization' and also to recognize that children are not all equally or invariably innocent, passive recipients of media and marketing messages. Often, they can and do construct their own meanings of these terms and negotiate their own interpretations of sexualization messages in different settings.[78]

Open-ended discussions with pre-teenage and teenage children about sex and the media have revealed that youngsters certainly use any media available to them to find out about sex and often prefer to consult with these sources than ask their parents. Talking about sex with their parents is seen by children themselves as embarrassing to both parties. Indeed, it is so embarrassing that some children would rather pretend to be ignorant about sex and disinterested in it rather than talk to parents about it. Magazines would be frequently nominated as both a useful information source and one that they felt comfortable using. One important factor here is that anonymity of both writer and reader could be preserved. The writer did not know who would read their text and the readers did not have to confront directly the person providing the sex advance. Although television soap operas were seen as relevant sources of sexual scripts, others might be watching with you and this would remove the anonymity that reading articles in magazines could preserve.[79]

What also emerged from interviews with children was their opposition to having their media choices restricted. This position was firmly adopted by those young people in their mid-teens who had reached the age of legal consent to have sex. Nonetheless, there was awareness of age-related content classifications and a willingness to concede that restrictions might be appropriate for younger children in relation to certain types of depictions of sex. Adolescent media consumers are also often aware of arguments about the potential harms of certain types of media content – usually that involving depictions of sex or violence. An ability to be self-regulating or discerning media consumers was articulated even by some pre-teens based on self-professed media literacy.[80]

As the communications environment continues to evolve at an ever faster pace, more of us will become savvier in terms of how to cope with a world in which we can gain access with growing ease to more and more content. Digital literacy, if this is what we should call it, will become more advanced even among older generations of innovation laggards. It will still be the young digital natives, brought up with this ever evolving world of rapidly changing computer technology who will stay ahead of the rest – as it always has been in the past. In most public debates about the sexualization of childhood, children have generally been conceived to be at risk and as potential victims powerless to counter, by themselves, the influences of sexually themed media representations, commercial marketing activities and children-oriented products. Children have agency as well and can negotiate their own interpretations of sexualized messages in their everyday environments.[81]

The debates about potential harms that might be caused by graphic and offensive material that flows across the internet and into our mobile phones echo those held three, four and more decades ago about early novels, silent and then sound motion pictures, horror comics and then television. The difference today, with the presence of wireless networked communications systems, is perhaps that offensive material is more accessible to everyone, including the young, than was true in the pre-internet era when more child protection barriers existed. Further, the audiences for mass media and for the more restricted (pornographic) media outputs were simply receivers of content, whereas today they are also senders and re-senders, as well as creators. This scenario requires a different approach to regulation, policing and public protection. Worldwide communications systems have grown so massive that centralized protection is more difficult than it was for the old print and broadcast media. Nevertheless, advances in technology mean that not only can more content be put out there – it can also be blocked if there is a will.

At the start of this book, we noted that sex and sexual socialization are part of human character, and through a process of natural physical and psychological development interest in sex will emerge across childhood. Another biological factor that has contributed to this process is the earlier onset of sexual maturity among children in some communities. This has been observed, in particular, among girls, who have also tended to be the primary point of focus in debates about childhood sexualization effects. Girls in the US, for example, have been found to begin menstruating and to develop breast buds at earlier ages.

One hundred years ago, the average age of the menarche (first menstruation) was over 14, while today it is a little over 12. The average for first appearance of breast buds was observed to be around ten for white American girls and around nine years for black American girls.[82] Girls who display earlier onset of sexual maturation also tend to become sexually active earlier.[83]

Although there is no evidence that the age of sexual maturity is directly influenced by levels of exposure to commercialized sexual themes, there is evidence that girls who have displayed earlier sexual maturity then show greater interest in sexualized merchandise and media content.[84] The resonance of commercial and socially endorsed sexual themes for children with earlier sexual maturity makes both parental and regulatory sensitivity to the potential effects of sexualized messages aimed at children even more important.

Further concerns have been raised about the overriding emphasis placed on the socialization of girls in the debates about childhood sexualization, while boys have been treated as if they are less at risk. Yet, children and teenagers of both genders enjoy complex relationships with commercial markets and commodities designed for their age groups and also with content they receive through the mass media. The messages about identity or aspiration or social conduct that sexually themed materials are believed to communicate by their critics can often be interpreted quite differently by young people. Boys are confronted with experiences in which they must negotiate sexually themed messages both about the opposite gender and their own gender, and about relationships of different kinds that might exist between genders.[85] If adverse effects can arise from sexualized content or commodities, policy makers and regulators cannot restrict their codes, or parents and teachers their advice about sexual issues exclusively to one gender. Rather, it is important to acknowledge the heterogeneity of the child population, the variances that can be found not only across age bands but also among same-age children in their psychological development and social and cultural circumstances.

Ultimately, computerized communications systems can still be switched off. Despite the use of concepts such as 'clouds' in computer-speak, these are not fluffy ephemeral phenomena beyond anyone's grasp and control. They are electronically driven machines housed in giant warehouses that can be shut down. The main complicating factor here is that back-up systems mean there is usually more than one 'off switch', and these are distributed around the globe. This means that trans-global agreements about controls over the content that flows through information and communications networks must be reached between national governments and pan-national corporations. The main stumbling blocks that remain are ones that have always hampered such international agreements: ideological differences regarding freedom of speech versus censorship and tensions between commercial imperatives and the public interest. Time will tell whether these hurdles can be mounted to bring about optimal settlements that serve everyone's interests. The future health of our children could depend on this.

Notes

1 Ofcom (2012) *Communications Market Report 2012*, http://www.stakeholders.ofcom. org.uk/binaries/research/cmr/cmr12/CMR_UK_2012, accessed 4 January 2013.

2 Lambiase, J. (2003) 'Sex – online and in internet advertising', in T. Reichert and J. Lambiase (Eds.) *Sex in Advertising: Perspectives on the Erotic Appeal*, pp247–269. Mahwah, NJ: Erlbaum.

3 Kraus, S. W. and Russell, B. (2008) 'Early sexual experiences: The role of internet access and sexually explicit material', *Cyberpsychology & Behavior*, 11(2), 162–168.

4 Valkenburg, P. M. and Soeters, K. E. (2001) 'Children's positive and negative experience with the internet: An exploratory survey', *Communication Research*, 28(5), 652–675; Soeters, K. E. and van Schaik, K. (2006) 'Children's experiences on the internet', *New Library World*, 107(3), 31.

5 Mitchell, K. J., Finkelhor, D. and Wolak, J. (2003) 'The exposure of youth to unwanted sexual material on the internet: A national survey of risk, impact and prevention', *Youth & Society*, 34(3), 330–358.

6 Wolak, J., Mitchell, K. J. and Finkelhor, D. (2007) 'Unwanted and wanted exposure to online pornography in a national sample of young internet users', *Pediatrics*, 119(2), 247–257.

7 Peter, J. and Valkenburg, P. M. (2006) 'Adolescents' exposure to sexually explicit material on the internet', *Communication Research*, 33(2), 178–204.

8 Stahl, C. and Fritz, N. (2002) 'Internet safety: Adolescents' self-report', *Journal of Adolescent Health*, 31(1), 7–10.

9 Boies, S. C. (2002) 'University students' uses of and reactions to online sexual information and entertainment: Links to online and offline sexual behaviour', *Canadian Journal of Human Sexuality*, 11(2), 77–89; Weiser, E. (2000) 'Gender differences in internet use patterns and internet application preferences: A two-sample comparison', *CyberPsychology & Behavior*, 3(2), 167–177.

10 Cooper, A., Scherer, C., Boies, S. C. and Gordon, B. (1999) 'Online sexual compulsivity: Getting tangled in the net', *Sexual Addiction & Compulsivity*, 6, 79–104; Weiser. E. (2000) *op. cit.*

11 Mitchell, K. J., Finkelhor, D. and Wolak, J. (2003) *op. cit.*

12 Finn, J. (2004) 'A survey of online harassment at a university campus', *Journal of Interpersonal Violence*, 19(4), 468–483.

13 Mitchell, K. J., Wolak, J. and Finkelhor, D. (2007) 'Trends in youth reports of sexual solicitations, harassment and unwanted exposure to pornography on the internet', *Journal of Adolescent Health*, 40(2), 116–126.

14 Mitchell, K. J., Wolak, J. and Finkelhor, D. (2007) *ibid.*

15 Mitchell, K. J., Finkelhor, D. and Wolak, J. (2007) 'Online requests for sexual pictures from youth: Risk factors and incident characteristics', *Journal of Adolescent Health*, 41(2), 196–203.

16 Fogel, J. and Shlivko, S. (2010) 'Singles seeking a relationship and pornography spam email: An understanding of consumer purchasing behaviour and behaviors antecedent to purchasing', *CyberPsychology: Journal of Psychosocial Research on Cyberspace*, 4(2), article 1, http://cyberpsychology.eu/view.php?cisloclanku=2010120301&article=1, accessed 19 December 2012.

17 Byrne, D. and Osland, J. A. (2000) 'Sexual fantasy and erotica/pornography: Internal and external imagery', in L. T. Szuchman and F. Muscarella (Eds.) *Psychological Perspectives on Human Sexuality*, pp283–305. New York, NY: John Wiley & Sons; Goodson, P., McCormick, D. and Evans, A. (2000) 'Sex and the internet: A survey instrument to assess college students' behaviour and attitudes', *CyberPsychology & Behavior* 39(2), 129–149.

18 Boies, S. C. (2002) *op. cit*; Cooper, A. et al. (1999) *op. cit.*

19 Cooper, A., Mansson, S. A., Daneback, K., Tikkanen, R. and Ross, M. W. (2003) 'Predicting the future of internet sex: Online sexual activities in Sweden', *Sexual and Relationship Therapy*, 18(3), 277–291.

20 Boies, S. C., Cooper, A. and Osborne, C. (2004) 'Variations in internet related problems and psychosocial functioning in online sexual activities: Implications for social and sexual development of young adults', *CyberPsychology & Behavior*, 7(2), 207–230.

21 Longo, R. E., Brown, S. M. and Orcutt, D. P. (2002) 'Effects of internet sexuality on children and adolescents', in A. Cooper (Ed.) *Sex and the Internet: A Guidebook for Clinicians*, pp87–105. New York, NY: Brunner-Rutledge.

22 See Boies, S. C., Knudson, G. and Young, J. (2004) 'The internet, sex and youths: implications for sexual development', *Sexual Addiction & Compulsivity*, 11, 343–363.

23 Henry J Kaiser Family Foundation (2002) *Teens Online*, http://www.kff.org, accessed 18 December 2012.

24 McCarty, C., Prawitz, A. D., Derscheid, L. E. and Montgomery, B. (2011) 'Perceived safety and teen risk taking in online chat sites', *Cyberpsychology, Behaviour and Social Networking*, 14(3), 169–174.

25 Subrahmanyan, K., Greenfield, P. M. and Tynes, B. (22004) 'Constructing sexuality and identity in an online ten chat room', *Applied Developmental Psychology*, 25, 651–666.

26 Henry J Kaiser Family Foundation (2010) *Generation M2: Media in the Lives of 8- to 18-Year Olds*, http://www.kff.org, accessed 18 December 2012.

27 Henry J Kaiser Family Foundation (2010) *ibid.*

28 Kornblum, W. and Smith, C. (2005) *Sociology in a Changing World*. Belmont, CA: Thomsen/Wadsworth.

29 Ringrose, J. (2010) 'Sluts, whores, fat slags and Playboy bunnies: Teen girls' negotiations of "sexy" on social networking sites and at school', in C. L. Jackson, C. Paechter and E. Renold (Eds.) *Girls and Education 3–16: Continuing Concerns, New Agendas*, Basingstoke, UK: Open University Press.

30 Environics Research group (2001) *Young Canadians in a Wired World: The Students' View*. Ottawa, Ontario: Media Awareness network and the Government of Canada.

31 Hall, P. C., West, J. H. and McIntyre, E. (2012) 'Female self-sexualization in MySpace. com personal profile photographs', *Sexuality & Culture*, 16(1), 1–16.

32 Boyd, D. (2008) 'Why youth love social network sites: The role of networked publics', cited in D. Buckingham (Ed.) *Teenage Social Life, Youth Identity and Digital Media*. Cambridge, MA: MIT Press; Slater, A. and Tiggeman, M. (2002) 'A test of objectification theory in adolescent girls', *Sex Roles*, 46, 343–349.

33 Jaffe, M. E. and Sharma, K.K. (2001) 'Cybersex with minors: Forensic implications', *Journal of Forensic Science*, 46(6), 1397–1402.

34 Durkin, K. F. (1997) 'Misuse of the internet by paedophiles: Implications for law enforcement and probation practice', *Federal Probation*, 61, 14–18; Lamb, M. (1998) 'Cybersex: Research notes on the characteristics of visitors to online chat rooms', *Deviant Behaviour Interdisciplinary Journal*, 19, 121–135.

35 Durkin, K. F. (1997) *ibid.*

36 Taylor, M., Quayle, E. and Holland, G. (2001) 'Child pornography, the internet and offending', *ISUMA: The Canadian Journal of Policy Research*, 2, 94–100.

37 Granic, L. and Lamey, A. V. (2000) 'The self-organisation of the internet and changing modes of thought', *New Ideas in Psychology*, 18, 93–107.

38 Davis, L., McShane, M. and Williams, F. P. (1995) 'Controlling computer access to pornography: Special conditions for sex offenders', *Federal Probation*, 59(2), 43–48.

39 Kantrowitz, B., King, P. and Rosenberg, D. (1994) 'Child abuse in cyberspace', *Newsweek*, 14 April, 40; Marshall, S. (1995) 'On-line child pornography busted', *USA Today*, 14 September, A1.

40 Kingston, D. A., Federoff, P., Firestone, P., Curry, S. and Bradford, J. M. (2008) 'Pornography use and sexual aggression: The impact of frequency and type of pornography use on recidivism among sexual offenders', *Aggressive Behavior*, 34(4), 341–351.

41 Carter, D. L. (1995) 'Computer crime categories: How technocriminals operate', *FBI Law Enforcement Bulletin*, July, 21–26.

42 Swisher, K. (1995) 'On-line child pornography charged as 12 are arrested', *Washington Post*, 14 September, A1, A13.

43 Lamb, M. (1998) *op.cit.*

44 Durkin, K. F. and Bryant, C. D. (1995) 'Log on to sex: Some notes on the carnal computer and erotic cyberspace as an emerging research frontier', *Deviant Behaviour*, 16(3), 179–200.

45 Quayle, E. and Taylor, M. (2002) 'Paedophiles, pornography and the internet: Assessment issues', *British Journal of Social Work*, 32, 863–875.

46 Taylor, M., Holland, G. and Quayle, E. (2001) 'Typology of paedophile picture collections', *The Police Journal*, 74(2), 97–107.

47 Jaffe, M. E. and Sharma, K. K. (2001) *op. cit.*

48 Lenhart, A. (2009) 'Teens and sexting: How and why minor teens are sending sexually suggestive nude or nearly nude images via text messaging', www.pewinterent.org/~/media/Files/Reports/2009/PIP_Teens_and_Sexting, accessed 13 March 2013; Mitchell, K. J., Finkelhor, D., Jones, L. M. and Wolak, J. (2012) 'Prevalence and characteristics of youth sexting: A national study', *Pediatrics*, 129(1), 13–20; Ferguson, C. J. (2011) 'Sexting behaviours among young Hispanic women: incidence and association with other high-risk sexual behaviours', *Psychiatry Quarterly*, 83(3), 239–243.

49 Phippen, A. (2009) 'Sharing personal images and videos among young people', December, Exeter, Devon: South West Grid for Learning, http://www.wwgl.org.uk.

50 Griffiths, S. (2012) 'Dangers of the "sexting" generation', *Sunday Times*, 27 May, 20.

51 Rice, E., Rhoades, H., Winetrobe, H., Sanchez, M., Montoya, J., Plant, A. and Kordic, T. (2012) 'Sexually explicit cell phone messaging associated with sexual risk among adolescents', *Pediatrics*, 130(4), 667–673.

52 Family Lives (2012) *All of Our Concern: Hypermasculinity in a Commercialised and Sexualized World*, June. London, UK: Family Lives and Teen Boundaries.

53 Martin, D. (2012) 'Sex texts: The new epidemic', *Daily Mail*, 11 December, 1, 4; Thomas, L. and Harding, E. (2012) 'At last, censors crack down on sexually violent films that corrupt teenage boys' minds', *Daily Mail*, 11 December, 4.

54 Mills, E. (2012) 'Sexting poisons teen romance', *The Sunday Times*, News Review, 16 December, 4.

55 Olweus, D. (1993) *Bullying at School: What We Know and What We Can Do*. Oxford, UK: Blackwell.

56 Hinduja, S. and Patchin, J. W. (2007) 'Offline consequences of online victimization: School violence and delinquency', *Journal of School Violence*, 6(3), 89–111; Juvonen, J., Nihsina, A. and Graham, S. (2000) 'Peer harassment, psychological adjustment, and school functioning in early adolescence', *Journal of Educational Psychology*, 92, 349–359.

57 Smith, P. K. Mahdavi, J., Carvalho, M., Fisher, S., Russell, S. and Tippett, N. (2007) 'Cyberbullying; its nature and impact in secondary school pupils', *Child Psychology and Psychiatry*, 49(4), 376–385.

58 Li, O. (2006) 'Cyberbullying in schools: A research of gender differences', *School Psychology International*, 27(2), 157; Noret, N. and Rivers, I. (2006) 'The prevalence of bullying by text message or email: Results of a four year study', in Poster presented at the British Psychological Society Annual Conference, Cardiff City Hall, vol 31.

59 Ybarra, M. L. and Mitchell, K. J. (2004) 'Online aggressor/targets, aggressors and targets: A comparison of associated youth characteristics', *Journal of Child Psychology and Psychiatry*, 45, 1308–1316.

60 Ybarra, M. L., Mitchell, K. J., Wolak, J. and Finkelhor, D. (2006) 'Examining characteristics and associated distress related to internet harassment: Findings from the second youth internet safety survey', *Pediatrics*, 118, 1169–1177.

61 Smith, P. K. Mahdavi, J., Carvalho, M., Fisher, S., Russell, S. and Tippett, N. (2007) *op. cit.*

62 Olweus, D. (1993) *op. cit*; Raskauskas, J. and Stolz, A. D. (2007) 'Involvement in traditional and electronic bullying among adolescents', *Developmental Psychology*, 43, 564–575.

63 Raskauskas, J. and Stolz, A. D. (2007) *op. cit.*

64 Berson, I. R., Berson, M. J. and Ferron, J. M. (2002) 'Emerging risks of violence in the digital age: Lessons for educators from an online study of adolescent girls in the United States', *Journal of School Violence*, 1(2), 51–71.

65 Ybarra, M. and Mitchell, K. (2008) 'How risky are social networking sites? A comparison of places online where youth sexual solicitation and harassment occurs', *Pediatrics*, 121, 350–357.

66 Hilton, Z. (2011) 'The risks of online sexualized images of young people', *Premature Sexualization: Understanding the Risks*, March, National Society for the Prevention of Cruelty to Children, p9, http://www.nspcc.org.uk, accessed 13 December 2012.

67 Mosher, D. L. and Tomkins, S. S. (1988) 'Scripting the macho man: Hypermasculine socialization and enculturation', *Journal of Sex Research*, 25(1), 60–84.

68 Bogaert, A. F. (2001) 'Personality, individual differences, and preferences for the sexual media', *Archives of Sexual Behavior*, 30(1), 29–53.

69 Shim, J. W., Lee, S. and Paul, B. (2007) 'Who responds to unsolicited sexually explicit materials on the internet? The role of individual differences', *CyberPsychology & Behavior*, 10(1), 71–79.

70 Peters, J., Nason, C. and Turner, W. (2007) 'Development and testing of a new version of the hypermasculinity index', *Social Work Research*, 31(3), 171–182.

71 Flood, M. (2011) 'Involving men in efforts to end violence against women', *Men and Masculinities*, 14(3), 358–377.

72 Murnen, S., Wright, C. and Kaluzny, G. (2002) 'If "boys will be boys" then girls will be victims? A meta-analytic review of the research that relates masculine ideology to sexual aggression', *Sex Roles*, 46, 11/12, 359–375.

73 Lindstrom, M. (2003) *BRANDchild: Remarkable Insights in the Minds of Today's Global Kids and Their Relationships with Brands*. London, UK: Kogan Page.

74 Palmer, S. (2006) *Toxic Childhood*. London, UK: Orion.

75 Mayo, E. and Nairn, A. (2009) *Consumer Kids: How Big Business is Grooming Our Children for Profit*. London, UK: Constable.

76 Hitchens, P. (2002) 'The failure of sex education', in E. Lee (Ed.) *Teenage Sex: What Should Schools Teach Children*, pp49–61. London, UK: Hodder and Stoughton.

77 Cunningham, H. (1995) *Children and Childhood in Western Society since 1500*. London, UK: Longman; Hendrick, H. (1997) *Children, Childhood and English Society, 1880–1990*. Cambridge, UK: Cambridge University Press.

78 Clark, J. (2013) 'Passive, heterosexual and female: Constructing appropriate childhoods in the "Sexualization of Childhood" debate', *Sociological Research Online*, 18(2), 13, www.socresonline.org.uk/18/2/13, accessed 29 October 2013.

79 Buckingham D. and Bragg, S. (2005) 'Opting into (and out of) childhood: Young people, sex and the media', in J. Overtrup (Ed.) *Studies in Modern Childhood, Agency and Culture*. London, UK: Sage.

80 Buckingham, D. (1996) *Moving Images: Understanding Children's Emotional Responses to TV*. Manchester, UK: Manchester University Press; Buckingham, D. and Bragg, S. (2005) *ibid.*

81 Coy, M. and Garner, M. (2012) 'Definitions, discourses and dilemmas: Policy and academic engagement with the sexualization of popular culture', *Gender and Education*, 24(3), 285–301; Kehily, M. J. (2012) 'Contextualising the sexualization of girls debate: Innocence, experience and young female sexuality', *Gender and Education*, 24(3), 255–268; Ringrose, J. and Renold, E. (2012) 'Slut shaming, girl power and sexualisation: thinking through the politics of the international slutwalks with teen girls', *Gender and Education*, 24(3), 333–343.

82 Herman-Giddens, M. E. (2007) 'The decline in the age of menarche in the United States: Should we be concerned?', *Journal of Adolescent Health*, 40, 201–203; Herman-Giddens, M. E. (2006) 'Recent data on pubertal milestones in United States children: The secular trend towards earlier development', *International Journal of Andrology*, 29, 241–246; Kaplowiz, P. (2006) 'Pubertal development in girls: Secular trends', *Current Opinion on Obstetrics and Gynaecology*, 18, 487–491.

83 Deardroff, J., Gonzalez, N. A., Christopher, F. S., Roosa, M. W. and Millsap, R. E. (2005) 'Early puberty and adolescent pregnancy: The influence of alcohol use',

Pediatrics, 116, 1451–1456; Golub, M. S., Collman, G. W., Foster, P. M., Kimmel, C. A., Rajpert-De Meyts, E., Reiter, E. O., Sharpe, R. M., Skakkebaek, N. E. and Toppari, J. (2008) 'Public health implications of altered pubertal timing', *Pediatrics*, 121, supplement 3, S218 –S230.

84 Brown, J. D., Halpern, C. T. and L'Engle, K. L. (2005) 'Mass media as a sexual super peer for early maturing girls', *Journal of Adolescent Health*, 26, 420–427; Linn, S. (2005) *Consuming Kids: Protecting Our Children from the Onslaught of Marketing and Advertising*. New York, NY: Anchor Books.

85 Clark, J. (2013) *op.cit.*

INDEX